ORIGINS OF AMERICAN HEALTH INSURANCE

JOHN E. MURRAY

Origins of American Health Insurance

A History of Industrial Sickness Funds

YALE UNIVERSITY PRESS NEW HAVEN & LONDON

Set in Scala type by Binghamton Valley Composition.
Printed in the United States of America.

Library of Congress Cataloging-in-Publication Data

Murray, John E., 1959–
Origins of American health insurance : a history of industrial sickness funds / John E. Murray.
p. cm. — (Yale series in economic and financial history)
Includes bibliographical references and index.
ISBN 978-0-300-12091-2 (cloth : alk. paper)

1. Insurance, Health—United States—History. 2. Sick leave—United States—History. 3. Absenteeism (Labor)—United States. I. Title.
HG9396.M87 2007
368.38'200973—dc22 2007015555

A catalogue record for this book is available from the British Library.

The paper in this book meets the guidelines for permanence and durability of the Committee on Production Guidelines for Book Longevity of the Council on Library Resources.

10 9 8 7 6 5 4 3 2 1

For Lynn

My conception of the first duty of history: to insure that merit shall not lack its record.

—TACITUS *Annals*

CONTENTS

PREFACE

THIS BOOK examines the rise and fall of a little-understood financial institution: the industrial sickness fund. Such funds, organized by workers through their employer or union, provided the rudiments of health insurance, principally consisting of paid sick leave, to a large minority of the industrial workforce of the late nineteenth and early twentieth centuries. Sickness funds grew steadily in membership at a time of much public debate about increasing the role of state governments in health insurance provision. This book is not a study of the political reasons why the United States lacks a universal, government-directed health insurance system. Rather, it proposes that one reason why such a system did not develop from Progressive-Era efforts was that these funds were reasonably well run and served a large share of the labor force that wanted insurance. In order to make this case, I show how these funds worked and how they managed difficult incentive conflicts that inhere in the insurance contract. The way the funds operated influenced worker behavior in two important ways: how they saved against future misfortune and how they absented themselves from work when ill. Although Progressives and later historians criticized the shortcomings of sickness funds, the historical record indicates that they discharged their obligations competently. These funds declined not because of financial failure and not because of the Depression but because of the rise of a technologically superior competitor: actuarially sound group health insurance.

The findings I present have political implications. If the sickness funds were essentially capable operations, if many workers freely chose to join them (or freely chose not to join), and if they persisted for a time despite the growing technological superiority of group health insurance, then perhaps Progressive proposals to replace them with government insurance were misguided. If the existing network of sickness fund insurers had achieved a modest level of success, as this book argues, then public support for additional government interventions may have been quite limited—contrary to one standard historical narrative. This explanation for the failure of Progressive reform has, to my knowledge, not been made before.

A note on method: inferential statistics guided by simple economic theory provide a useful way to understand certain historical questions examined in this book, especially in Part II. The data for the statistical exercises came from a variety of government publications of the late nineteenth and early twentieth centuries, as described in Appendix A. I also recognize that contemporary writings and later historical analysis provide essential context for understanding these statistical inferences. Scholarly journals in the field of actuarial science provided a largely untapped source concerning the development of group health insurance. My hope is that the reader who is unfamiliar with regression techniques will still be able to follow the book's argument without reference to the regression tables, because I discuss those results in the text.

Interaction with three scholars began my interest in health insurance history. Cal Winegarden proposed that we study the effects of European sickness insurance on mortality rates. Joel Mokyr asked me to review Jim Riley's excellent *Sick, Not Dead* for the *Journal of Economic History*. A few years later at a Carnegie Mellon University seminar, David Hounshell asked, to what extent could the findings concerning the European case inform the history of American insurance? My inquiries into that question resulted in this book.

Many other scholars helped in its preparation. I thank those who offered comments on or assistance with early drafts of particular chapters: Ran Abramitzky, George Alter, Jörg Baten, Joyce Burnette, Ben Chabot,

Lee Craig, Paul Dutton, Herb Emery, Joe Ferrie, Price Fishback, Mike Haines, Bernard Harris, Ruth Herndon, Sheila Johansson, Hirsch Kasper, Ken Kuttner, Kate Lynch, Deirdre McCloskey, Allan Mitchell, Don Parsons, Jim Riley, Elyce Rotella, the late Gary Saxonhouse, Rick Steckel, Bill Sundstrom, Melissa Thomasson, John Treble, Werner Troesken, Lynn Wellage, Warren Whatley, Eugene White, and several anonymous referees. Not all of these people would agree with my interpretations. Their cordial and constructive disagreements made the book stronger. Howard Bodenhorn, co-editor of the Yale University Press series on financial and economic history, really made this book happen. For many years now Rick Steckel has encouraged my work, and I can finally thank him in a book.

For patient advice on writing and economics, I thank Wally Koral, Jim Downie, John Hussong, Jim Cahill, David Segal, Hirsch Kasper, Ed Merkes, Claudio Gonzalez-Vega, Ed Ray, Ben Baack, and Lars Sandberg.

Scholars at Carnegie Mellon University, Indiana University, the University of Michigan, Oberlin College, Stanford University, and the Washington Area Economic History Seminar allowed me to present preliminary results in productive and engaging seminars. Participants in the University of Michigan economic history workshop—Ben Chabot, Andrew Coleman, Maggie Levenstein, Mindy Miller, Gary Saxonhouse, and Warren Whatley—deserve special thanks for enduring presentations of several chapters. Those who attended presentations at the North American Labor History Conference at Wayne State University, the Cliometrics Conference, Social Science History Association conferences, the Economic History Association meetings, and the Cliometric Society sessions at the American Economic Association meetings provided constructive comments. Librarians at the University of Toledo and the University of Michigan and archivists at the Scharchburg Archives, Kettering University, especially David White, were unfailingly helpful. The Earhart Foundation provided a grant that enabled me to give my full attention to this manuscript for one summer, for which I thank them.

It was a pleasure to work with Yale University Press. Comments by the press's readers were invaluable, and Mike O'Malley's enthusiasm and guidance were a great help. I appreciated all the work of the production editors and staff: Margaret Otzel, Jane Zanichkowsky, Steve Colca, and Alex Larson.

Parts of Chapter 3 appeared in "Social Insurance Claims as Morbidity Estimates: Sickness or Absence," *Social History of Medicine* 16 (2003): 225–245. Reprinted with permission of Oxford University Press.

My Toledo colleagues kindly helped out in a pinch. While revising the manuscript, I suffered a painful injury that required surgery. I appreciated the spirit of mutual assistance with which Mike Dowd, Kevin Egan, Kris Keith, and John Petlow made sure my teaching and advising work got done.

My family deserves a special note of gratitude. I so wish my late parents, Jack and Sarah Murray, had lived to see this book. They taught me a great deal about the importance of history, and they made great sacrifices for my education. My wife Lynn's patience, kindness, and generosity enabled me to work on the book for long periods at a stretch. Our daughters, Rose and Sarah, will see that Daddy really was writing his book on his computer while they were writing their books on their computer, although, inexplicably, this one could not be about animals.

ORIGINS OF AMERICAN HEALTH INSURANCE

PART ONE SICKNESS FUNDS IN THE PROGRESSIVE ERA

CHAPTER ONE

Industrial Sickness Funds

> A government could take the place of some of the greatest American associations, and within the Union several particular states already have attempted it. But what political power would ever be in a state to suffice for the innumerable multitude of small undertakings that American citizens execute every day with the aid of an association?
>
> —TOCQUEVILLE, *Democracy in America*

IN THE YEARS before paid sick leave and group health insurance became common, what happened to a worker who became sick and unable to work? The potential for financial as well as physical distress was considerable. Take, for example, the D. family, who lived in the Kensington section of Philadelphia in the spring of 1918.[1] The family, consisting of mother, father, and four children, was described by a visitor as "comfortably off." The father earned $18 per week as a fireman, to which the oldest child added $6 from his job in a textile mill. After contracting erysipelas (a bacterial infection), Mr. D. spent three months hospitalized and unable to work. Although Mr. D.'s co-workers took up a collection to aid him, within two months the family had spent its savings and sought help from charities. The case of the D. family illustrates three sources that families in distress due to illness could call on: their savings, the generosity of co-workers, and organized charity. Those were not the only possibilities.

George Himes worked for the W. F. Stewart Co. of Flint, Michigan, a supplier of car bodies and parts to local auto manufacturers. In 1901 Stewart and other local firms, some of which were later to form General Motors, established the Flint Vehicle Factories Mutual Benefit Association, to which Himes—and many other Flint manufacturing workers—belonged. After falling ill with appendicitis in the spring of 1912, Himes was unable to work, and so the benefit association paid him six dollars each week. Single, twenty-six years of age, and with no family to support, Himes still owed rent to the landlady of his boarding house. Unfortunately for him, medical complications ensued, and he remained incapacitated beyond the maximum thirteen-week period for which the benefit association would provide sick pay. Fortunately, there was a backup. At that point, his case fell under the purview of a longer-term insurance program sponsored by the Manufacturers' Association of Flint, which paid him sick benefits for another two months. This situation might have continued for as long as two years, except that by the end of July Himes had recovered sufficiently to return to work. He informed the Manufacturers' Association that "he was very thankful for the help" they had provided and so the association ceased making payments.[2]

Which example was more representative of Progressive-Era workers in ill health? Although the D. family may not have been typical of all working-class families, their story was a classic example of anecdotes provided by Progressive reformers who debated one of the great issues of the day: government-organized income and medical insurance for workers. If most working-class families lived on the edge of disaster, they might have been eager for the government to insure a portion of their income when they fell ill. But if many workers, like George Himes, had either obtained income security from a private sickness insurance provider or had considered doing so and decided against it, there might actually have been little popular support for compulsory government insurance.[3]

Progressives worked hard to emphasize the deep inadequacies of the chaotic network of insurance arrangements for the working class. A few prudent (or credulous) workers might be able to join sickness benefit funds, according to the Progressive literature, but whether the funds would act as safety nets was in doubt. Reformers argued that the one entity that could be relied on to provide that safety net was government. Thus did their efforts to create sickness insurance at the state level gain urgency in the years 1915 to 1920. In the end, Progressives were unable to generate much political support in any state in which they campaigned, and in the process they created the first of many failures to broaden American health insurance coverage via governmental action. On reflection they attributed these failures to the incompetence of workers' sickness funds, underhanded political efforts of employers and insurers, and the general backwardness of the working class. Many historians who have examined these institutions in this period have concurred with this assessment.

This book calls that assessment into question. It proposes that the sickness insurance funds that workers and their employers organized were stable and capable institutions. Workers such as George Himes, who prudently insured themselves against the financial consequences of illness, were more common than Progressives supposed. Although such prudence may have characterized only a minority of workers, this book also argues that many workers who did not insure themselves also acted from prudence. Young workers recognized the high cost of insurance relative to their good health, and older workers knew the importance of saving in advance of declining health. Industrial sickness funds provided the service that workers most desired—paid sick leave—and skimped on provision of medical care that at best was ineffective and at worst was a cover for coercing sick workers to return to their posts prematurely. It was the success, not the incompetence, of the sickness funds that led to the failure of Progressive reform efforts.

Sickness funds provided insurance. Insurance is a contract in which the insured pays the insurer a small amount of money (the premium) in exchange for a promise to be paid a larger amount of money (the benefit) if a particular event occurs. The ability of sickness funds to fulfill their end of such contracts has been criticized in the literature, and that has led to misinterpretation by many, but by no means all, historians who have struggled with the question of America's lack of government health insurance. Industrial sickness funds faced deep problems that inhere in all insurance contracts and managed them carefully. They were widespread geographically and growing in numbers and membership (see Chapter 4). They provided benefits that workers wanted and by and large did not offer benefits that workers were less interested in (see Chapter 5). Their sensitivity to the demand for their services followed directly from the characteristic that a few Progressives identified as worth emulating: their small size and personal knowledge of members by fund managers.

Sickness funds were sufficiently competent and fair in their delivery of financial and, to a lesser extent, medical assistance that they continued to perform their duties until well into the 1940s. Their existence alone indicates the need to revise a standard view of the history of workplace-provided health insurance, which begins around World War II with tax breaks for Blue Cross–type insurance. Their end as important components of the national health insurance network was not due to the Great Depression. Rather, advances in actuarial methods that developed after 1930 enabled group health insurers to offer a better value from that time onward. The sickness funds that thwarted Progressive insurance reform proposals were actually very capable financial institutions. This book tells their story.[4]

The institution this book examines is the industrial sickness fund, which provided its members with a form of health insurance well suited to the conditions of late nineteenth- and early twentieth-century America. This is a synthesized term that does not generally appear in the literature of the Progressive Era.[5] There were two kinds of industrial sickness funds. Those that were operated under the auspices of a particular company for (and often by) its employees were called establishment funds. The other type was operated by labor unions for their members. These two types of funds are the focus of this book because they formed the basis of the American system of associating health insurance benefits with the workplace. Because of such institutions Americans began to connect health insurance with their employer.

The term *health insurance* is not an anachronism but a formulation that became common currency in the Progressive Era. An older term, *sickness insurance,* referred to the same sort of contract. To Progressives who were sensitive to the impressions their reform proposals made on the masses, *sickness insurance* sounded too similar to the German *Krankenversicherung* to be politically viable during the Great War. As the term used in the 1911 National Insurance Act in the United Kingdom, *health insurance* sounded more reassuringly British, and so that is how reformers christened their proposals.[6] Both phrases referred to a contract in which workers paid regular premiums to the sickness fund in exchange for the fund's promise of a cash payment when the worker fell ill. The benefit payment was contingent on a determination by a physician or fund committee that the worker was unable to work owing to ill health. The terms *sickness insurance* and *health insurance* are used interchangeably in this book.

Employment-based sickness insurance enjoyed two cost advantages over other kinds of turn-of-the-century health insurance. First, costs of collecting premiums were low, thanks to automatic deduction from pay packets or use of co-workers as collectors on payday. Industrial sickness insurance policies, sold as adjuncts to industrial life (or burial) insurance, were more expensive owing to the high cost of sending premium collectors door to door. Second, employment-based sickness insurance attracted a more heterogeneous clientele than did individual health policies sold by insurance companies. Pooling members by workplace reduced the ability of workers who were in ill health to buy insurance directly in large numbers because they first needed to gain employment at an establishment or join a union with a sickness fund.[7]

Men were the predominant beneficiaries of sickness fund membership. Some funds included a substantial share of female members, but very few funds offered benefits to wives or children of members. These exclusions may strike the present-day observer as unfair or sexist, but they were consistent with the goal of most funds. When a member was unable to work and thus earn any income, the fund stepped in and provided a small share of that income. The intention was hardly to leave the worker and his family whole after a severe financial shock, which was far too grand an aim to be feasible, given the simplicity of fund management techniques. The intention was to keep the worker's family out of the poorhouse, no more and no less.[8] By that limited standard, industrial sickness funds succeeded.

The funds' operations were not complicated.[9] First, a worker applied to his fund for admission. By the early twentieth century, relatively few funds imposed restrictions on prospective members that followed from prejudices of the day, such as racial bars. Many imposed prudential restrictions, hoping to keep away workers who were too old via age limits, to exclude those who were already sick by required medical examinations, and to discourage those who believed they might become sick by waiting periods of several weeks between hiring and admission. The goal in each case was consistent with the principle of insurance: to protect the insured from the shock of an unexpected adverse event. These restrictions were intended to exclude those who had already experienced the adverse event of ill health or who expected to experience sickness in the near future.

Once admitted, a worker paid an initiation fee and dues, or premiums, every pay period. Early in the twentieth century the entrance fee averaged a dollar or so and dues typically cost five dollars per year, or about a dime per week. Given weekly earnings of about ten dollars for manufacturing workers in 1909, a typical premium cost a worker about one percent of his pay.[10] When the worker fell ill, he notified his fund, which typically sent out a visiting committee to assess his ability to work. These men usually took their duties seriously, and they bore an important burden on behalf of their fund. It must not have been easy to balance their charge to cheer up an isolated co-worker while giving him the third degree to determine how sick he really was. If the committee agreed with the claimant that he could not work, he received benefits, and if not, he had to return to work in order to receive any income.[11]

Rather than require members who may have been friends of the claimant to make these judgments, some funds assigned that duty to a physician. After examining the claimant the doctor made a diagnosis, and if applicable prescribed a course of therapy. Some funds required that workers be examined by a physician chosen and paid by the fund or that the personal physician's decision be approved by a fund-employed physician. If a doctor diagnosed venereal disease, an illness that predated admission to the fund, or an injury due to fighting or drunkenness, most funds denied the claim. To keep claimants from making things worse, many funds required them to stay close to home (and, in particular, to avoid saloons) while receiving benefits. A mutual association in Camden, New Jersey, issued typical, if detailed, behavioral restrictions: "A sick member drawing benefits is not permitted to leave his house in rainy or unpleasant weather, or after 8 o'clock in the evening, except upon the written advice of his physician or the consent of at least two members of the relief committee." Some historians interpret such conditions as Victorian moral hypersensitivity, but to the extent that these conditions were avoidable or chronic, such denial represented prudence or recognition of the insurance principle. Such conditions were well-known.[12]

Further prudence appeared in sickness funds' unwillingness to underwrite brief, transient conditions. Before issuing benefits, funds typically imposed a one-week waiting period, which began when they were notified of the worker's condition or after they received confirmation from the visiting committee or physician. If the claim was approved, the worker received sick pay of about five dollars per week, which represented about half the worker's usual pay. It was not enough to justify extended absences but was enough to enable the worker's family to survive, the modest goal of the typical sickness fund.

Some funds offered additional benefits such as death or unemployment benefits. The latter were more common among funds administered by national unions rather than locals. Unemployment benefits offered a perplexing incentive for unemployed union members to represent themselves as ill in order to increase their benefit payments. The death benefit was typically a modest $100 or so and often less. Around 1907 more than three-fourths of local union benefit funds paid a death benefit, as did more than nine-tenths of establishment funds. The death benefit was a critical part of the whole benefit package offered by funds. Insurance for burial costs was a highly competitive market, with industrial life insurance available to many workers, and the number of employers offering group life as a fringe benefit was growing steadily. Well-informed observers at that time and since have attributed much of the failure of Progressive efforts to their insistence on including a death benefit in their reform proposals.[13]

Many types of businesses and unions sponsored sickness funds, which were organized in a variety of ways. Local and national unions operated sickness funds, and so did many railroads and manufacturers. Early in the twentieth century, particular funds for hospital expenses resembled later Blue Cross plans, and a small number of establishment funds offered pension or long-term disability benefits. Certain independent benefit societies emerged in particular industries or were organized by workers of particular ethnicities. The sickness funds that enrolled the largest number of members were operated by fraternal societies. Because fraternal sickness funds offered the great advantage of continuity in membership when a worker changed jobs, they had an important similarity to labor union funds. Members of fraternal sickness funds are discussed later in the book, but fraternal funds themselves will not be discussed in any detail. Unlike industrial sickness funds, they have been the subject of careful scholarly study recently and do not demand another examination.[14]

Progressive reformers and historians in the present have attributed the failure of the Progressive health insurance agenda in no small part to the presence of industrial sickness funds. At the same time they have criticized the alleged incompetence of these funds. Too few, too small, and too unstable, they still managed to thwart what had seemed to be the inevitable creation of a universal, government health insurance program. But perhaps their strengths appealed to sufficiently many workers to weaken Progressive health insurance efforts. Given the availability of familiar and reliable sickness funds, many workers may have found government insurance unnecessary. The context of industrial sickness funds in the Progressive Era requires a short excursus into the economics of insurance, and, here and in the next chapter, a review of the claims made by Progressives, their opponents, and historians.[15]

A standard insurance contract produces several complications. First, chronologically speaking, the insured pays the premium before the event occurs, which allows for strategic behavior by the insurer. That is, with the premium in pocket, the insurer can refuse to pay the benefit. The insured may have only expensive legal remedies that would enable him to seek to recover the benefit and so may let that denial stand. According to Progressives, claim denials occurred far too often.[16] Second, it was not always possible to define precisely the event against which the worker was insured. In the case of sickness, disposition of cases that might have seemed obvious at first glance could ultimately have depended on whether the illness began before the claimant had joined the fund, whether it stemmed from a workplace accident (and thus was covered by workmen's compensation, if available), or whether the claim had been properly certified by a physician. Third, the insured sometimes acted with some information that was unavailable to the insurer, a condition known as asymmetric information. Two further difficulties, moral hazard and adverse selection, followed from asymmetric information. Attempts to mitigate these problems resulted in principal-agent conflicts. Finally, pooling health risks by workplace can theoretically keep workers immobilized in an inferior job in order to remain insured. Such concerns were abroad in the Progressive Era as well.

In order to obligate the insurer to fulfill its promise, the insured must pay a premium. Proponents and opponents of government health insurance disagreed about who really paid premiums in the early twentieth century. Compelling all workers to pay some percentage of their wages (Progressives guessed as little as two percent, and their opponents warned of premiums as high as five percent) for sickness insurance would have had the same effect as any tax. If labor was as mobile as economic historians of the period have estimated, then that tax burden would probably have fallen more on the employers rather than the workers. The distribution of the burden is open to interpretation, but it is certain that employers and workers would have paid for social insurance.[17]

We can therefore be skeptical about claims made at the time. Progressives advertised government health insurance as costless. John Lapp, editor of *Modern Medicine,* argued that because health insurance was a moral imperative, its cost should not even be discussed. Because the state would collect premiums and pay out benefits, he wrote, on balance government insurance "does not cost money, it distributes cost already in existence, and it does it without doing harm." This common argument omitted administrative costs of this redistribution, not to mention responses to incentives created by benefit provision. A corollary was that state insurance would operate more cheaply since it did not need to budget for profits. The Progressives' opponents raised the threat of a substantial loss in pay for the taxed workers. Both sides ignored or exaggerated the ways in which the process would work out in contemporary labor markets.[18]

Among informational asymmetries, consider first moral hazard. This term refers to an incentive created by insurance benefits to reduce efforts to prevent the covered event. Thus it describes changes in the injured workers' *behavior* that were induced by the insurance itself. The phrase *moral hazard* is not intended to connote immorality on the part of the insured; it is, as the economist Harold Demsetz observed, "a relevant cost of producing insurance." In the past the dominance of the sick pay benefit made extra time off work the primary moral hazard of sickness insurance. The issue of potential malingering generated much contention. Concern about moral hazard was widespread, and even Progressives acknowledged that sickness funds were able to manage it reasonably well thanks to the peer pressure associated with visiting committees. Progressives also claimed that government insurance would not be subject to moral hazard thanks to the virtue of American workers. Although both the Progressives and their opponents leveled claims and counterclaims about moral hazard, only the funds that actually operated, and not a hypothetical government system, left any evidence about how they managed the problem. Chapter 8 evaluates evidence of moral hazard in industrial sickness funds.[19]

Adverse selection also formed part of the Progressive argument for government insurance to supersede sickness funds. *Adverse selection* refers to the greater attractiveness of insurance to those who are more likely to make a claim. Thus it refers to worker *characteristics* that differed according to their status as insured or uninsured. Adverse selection in health insurance appears when people who are more likely to become ill and make a claim are also more likely to obtain (or try to obtain) insurance. One observable factor that increased the probability of filing a claim was the worker's occupation. When the Chicago, Burlington, and Quincy Railroad offered membership in its Relief Department to employees, those in more hazardous jobs were alleged to have been more likely to join than others.[20] Another relevant and identifiable characteristic of a potential member was his age, because older workers tended to make more claims than younger workers. Managers of sickness funds understood the importance of age in claim frequency and responded by trying to exclude older workers. Progressive proposals aimed to cover older as well as prime-age workers.

Progressive reformers claimed that adverse selection was theoretically a threat to existing voluntary funds. Howell Cheney, a government insurance supporter whose silk firm was well known for its generous health insurance benefits, observed that "under any voluntary plan there is an inevitably higher probability of securing a poorer average risk." Among historians of health insurance, Jacob Hacker and Jason Kaufman have separately asserted that adverse selection undermined fraternal insurers in particular but presented no evidence to support this point. Careful historical investigations have failed to find any evidence that selection problems really threatened the stability of sickness funds. George Emery and Herbert Emery have found no evidence for such problems in fraternal funds, and they concluded that they were generally financially sound. Daniel Gottlieb tested for adverse selection among workers who joined sickness funds relative to those who chose not to join and also found no evidence for selection. Although Progressives were correct to claim that compulsory government insurance would not be subject to adverse selection, thanks to trial periods and medical examinations it may not have been much of a problem for voluntary sickness funds.[21]

To mitigate the problems of moral hazard and adverse selection, sickness funds imposed a variety of tests such as waiting periods for applicants and claimants and the certification by a physician of a member's claim. If the physician was paid by the claimant directly (or indirectly with an indemnity from the insurance fund), his perspective was bound to differ from that of a physician who worked for the fund on salary or for capitation payments. This was a classic principal-agent conflict. One contemporary textbook described it as "a very difficult problem; the doctor has no personal relation with nor interest in the insurance company, but the claimant (his patient) is one of the community in which the doctor earns his income, and human nature asserting itself, the doctor resolves all doubts in favor of his patient, and prepares his certificate accordingly." Under a government insurance system, some method of monitoring those personal physicians might help discourage overly generous benefit payments. Opponents raised the lurid specter of government insurance officials' conducting "espionage" on ordinary doctors and their patients and complained that Progressive proposals to limit physician autonomy had assumed that these old family friends were untrustworthy from the start. Similar dissatisfaction among German physicians in 1903–1904 led to a series of strikes. Reports of these events did not go unnoticed by Americans opposed to government insurance at home.[22]

The association of sickness insurance and the workplace was in part simply a historical artifact. The first benefit societies were organized by trade unions through workplaces, and the first group health insurance policies were bought by large firms for their employees. By the late nineteenth century providing such insurance through the employer or union had become a long-standing custom in some industries and regions. Another advantage of workplace-based insurance was little appreciated at the time but is clearer now: it mitigated adverse selection. Because most people chose employers for reasons other than access to insurance, a given firm's employees contained a mixture of high and low risks, enhancing the sickness fund's stability. This came at a cost, though. If the insurer had specified that benefits would be granted only for conditions that developed after the insurance was in force, then workers who suffered from chronic conditions may only have been able to move at the cost of losing their insurance. This resulting inability to change jobs because of a preexisting condition is sometimes called "job-lock."[23]

In the early twentieth century, fraternal and labor union sickness funds offered their members coverage that was portable from job to job, but establishment funds generally did not. Progressives and labor union officials who favored government insurance criticized company-operated sickness funds because they locked workers into their current jobs. As described in Chapter 7, however, the supply of labor in turn-of-the-century America was extremely fluid, and there is no evidence that many workers at that time suffered from job-lock. In addition, a few clever sickness funds solved the problem on their own. The Flint Vehicle Factories Mutual Benefit Association was distinguished by the portability of its benefits among member firms in Flint. By 1908 ten firms had joined, including Buick Motor Co., and membership in the benefit association numbered around two thousand. About 70 percent of member firm employees joined the benefit association. The Flint association showed that with some cooperation among industrialists and workers, job-lock need not have been a consequence of providing sickness benefits. The level of cooperation needed must not have been insurmountable. The American Association for Labor Legislation, the most important advocate of government insurance, claimed that the Flint association was unique, but at least one similar benefit association emerged in another town with a prominent industry: the Carriage Makers' Mutual Relief Association of Watertown, New York.[24]

Progressive activists who worked to create government-sponsored health insurance in the various states promoted their proposals in contemporary publications. Their opponents did the same, and many times they addressed each other's claims regarding particular points—whether moral hazard and adverse selection were actual problems, why and how seriously workers needed health insurance, and the consequences for states that adopted such programs. In order to illustrate the place of industrial sickness funds in Progressive-Era America, Chapter 2 examines those claims in light of the most reliable data available from the historical record.

CHAPTER TWO

Political Economy of Progressive-Era Sickness Insurance

In order to understand [the Progressives] sympathetically, then, it is important to think of them as not stupid or incapable men who fumbled a simple task, but as men of reasonable and often indeed of penetrating intelligence whose fate it was to attempt, with great zeal and resourcefulness, a task of immense complexity and almost hopeless difficulties.

—RICHARD HOFSTADTER, *The Age of Reform*

REFORMERS who sought to establish government sickness insurance for industrial workers were part of a larger movement whose members hoped to reform much of the American economy and society. *Progressive* is a convenient shorthand term for the advocates of state health insurance, not least because the Progressive Party platform, on which Theodore Roosevelt ran in 1912, promised "protection of home life against the hazards of sickness, irregular employment and old age through the adoption of a system of social insurance adapted to American use." A huge number of reform movements of various sizes in some sense carried the Progressive banner. The era may be best known for its successes: antitrust legislation at the federal level, rationalized service provision at the municipal level, and a variety of efforts at the state level. Some of the better-known federal reforms, for example, the Pure Food and Drug Act of 1906, were preceded by similar legislation enacted by states.[1]

A reform effort that was closely related to health insurance concerned accident insurance, or as it came to be known, workmen's compensation. Prior to state intervention, workers who were injured on the job had only limited venues in which to seek redress. Privately provided accident insurance was rare. Because the law placed a considerable burden of proof on the injured worker to show that he was entitled to compensation, injury-related litigation typically ended in victory for the defendant. When the plaintiff won, awards were usually small. Price Fishback and Shawn Kantor have demonstrated how the development of workmen's compensation proceeded only when all parties—workers, employers, and insurers—realized that state compensation yielded benefits for each that outweighed the costs of the new system. Conversion to state compensation took place quickly: beginning in 1911, forty-one states adopted some form of workmen's compensation in only nine years. The speed with which it happened, the willingness of all parties to accede to state intervention, and the institutional similarities to sickness insurance made reformers optimistic. A prominent New York physician, S. S. Goldwater, proposed that workman's compensation was "just the beginning of a great movement that will result in the establishment here of sickness insurance of the kind already in existence abroad." Rupert Blue, the president of the American Medical Association, predicted, "Health insurance is the next great step in social legislation."[2]

The group that worked hardest to convince state legislators that health insurance was necessary was the American Association for Labor Legislation (AALL). Founded in 1906, the AALL consisted primarily of university professors and other activists. It, too, had good reason to expect that its efforts would eventually pay off in the establishment of state-level health insurance for workers. The association's first project concerned a problem in occupational health. Many workers in the match industry became ill with a gruesomely disfiguring disease called phosphorus necrosis, commonly known as "phossy jaw." Despite the availability of a fairly good substitute for phosphorus, match manufacturers protested against the prospect of government intervention until it appeared that compliance with a variety of state regulations would be much more costly than complying with a single federal regulation. Under pressure from the AALL, in 1912 the federal government began to tax phosphorus matches, and the firm that had held the patent on the substitute, Diamond Match, surrendered it. The problem of phossy jaw began to decline, and the AALL learned a lesson in how to manage a successful health-related reform campaign.[3]

The AALL turned to health insurance in 1912, forming a committee to investigate various social insurance programs. Given the "amazing success," as they saw it, of workmen's compensation, it seemed the appropriate time to push social insurance further into the workplace and beyond. Unemployment insurance seemed too new and too difficult, and old-age pension insurance seemed less pressing. By comparison, recalled one AALL leader ruefully decades later, "health insurance was simple." Their opponents seemed to accept the inevitable, and before 1917 they were not inclined to waste energy fighting the rise of government health insurance. A confident AALL pitched its efforts behind the slogan, "Health insurance—the next step in social progress."[4]

The AALL's plan was to forge a "standard bill" that would stipulate the characteristics of a basic health insurance program. States could vary the details to fit their particular interests. The standard bill required coverage for all industrial workers who earned less than $100 per month at a time when the average manufacturing worker earned a little more than half that amount. Thus a large share of the industrial working class was to be covered. Premiums were to be split by the worker (40 percent), the employer (40 percent), and the state (20 percent). The amount of the premium in dollar terms was to be experience-rated; this provision was intended to provide an incentive for the company to eliminate health hazards. Sick workers would receive two-thirds of their regular pay after a relatively brief four-day waiting period. Such cash sickness benefits, albeit lower ones, were familiar to many workers. What differed was a provision that was central to the AALL's campaign: free medical, surgical, and nursing care for the worker and his family, including pregnancy and childbirth coverage. Remarkably, in later versions of the standard bill the AALL proposed to allow free choice of physician. If the worker was hospitalized, his sickness benefit would be reduced to one-third of his usual pay. The bill included a $50 death benefit. The proposal excluded government workers, domestics, and seasonal agricultural workers, in part to limit administrative costs and in part because the AALL thought that very poorly paid workers were better off receiving charity. An AALL official described it as the best of the German and British systems, but observers tended to recognize a stronger similarity to the German dependence on existing local funds as opposed to the British inclusion of nationwide friendly societies and for-profit commercial insurers alike.[5]

Expecting that opponents would aim to sidetrack consideration of such bills by appointing investigatory committees, the association marshaled arguments to present to such committees. Between 1915 and

1921 eleven state commissions investigated sickness and insurance conditions, producing in the process several reports full of statistical detail. The Massachusetts, New Jersey, and New York legislatures considered the standard bill almost immediately, and twelve more considered such bills in 1917. It appeared that the next step in social welfare policy was going forward as Progressives had anticipated.[6]

But what had seemed inevitable ultimately failed to materialize. Of the eleven commissions formed, only six recommended state intervention in health insurance markets. When California held a referendum on health insurance in 1918, it lost by 358,324 votes to 133,858. In 1919 the New York Senate passed a version of the standard bill, only to see it bottled up in the Assembly. A contemporary survey conducted in Utica, New York, indicated that a mere 1 percent of thirteen thousand factory workers favored the insurance bill that the legislature was about to reject. The New York Senate vote was the only legislative victory reformers ever achieved. At every opportunity voters and legislators spurned government health insurance. Why a movement that was so successful in workmen's compensation and industrial safety failed so consistently with health insurance has puzzled observers ever since.[7]

In order to understand the failure of Progressives to persuade legislatures, commissions, and voters of the wisdom of their plans, it helps to see how these plans appeared in the public debates of the day. In this discourse Progressives (primarily the AALL) and their opponents delivered arguments that were sometimes accurate and cogent, sometimes exaggerated, and sometimes simply wrong. Many historical writers in more recent years have implicitly sided with the Progressives and explicitly demonized their opponents. According to recent accounts, the AALL was "an organization of reform-minded social scientists and philanthropists that persistently campaigned for European-style social policies," and AALL members "were unusually well-educated men and women committed not only to providing better social services to needy Americans but also to researching the causes and consequences of various policy options in depth." According to one historian, the job of an opposition group, the Insurance Economics Society (IES), was to " 'educate' " (scare quotes included) physicians by presenting "distorted" accounts of European social insurance. Other historians have dismissed the opponents' arguments as propaganda, Red-baiting, and smears, but they show little recognition of how closely at least some of their most important arguments hewed to the most accurate data available at that time. The opponents of state insurance at least sometimes had more logical and well-informed arguments than they have been given credit for. The historical record shows that both the AALL and the IES occasionally trimmed their sails to maximize their arguments' persuasive power. Each offered accurate and truthful arguments as well. Qualitative differences in the two sides' rhetoric were smaller than historians have supposed.[8]

Intellectual opponents of state insurance included intelligent and well-informed actuaries, economists, and state commission members. Until now historians have not taken arguments by opponents of government insurance seriously. That may have been because, ironically, it was the losers—and their later supporters—who wrote the histories. One of the earliest retrospectives was *Quest for Security,* by I. M. Rubinow, a prominent advocate for government insurance. His followers included Jason Kaufman, who, regarding the demise of the Progressive and other insurance campaigns, wrote, "The commercial insurance lobby is one obvious villain here (assuming that you, like me, agree that some kind of guaranteed health insurance for all Americans would have been a desirable policy outcome)." Other historians included policy recommendations for expansion of government insurance or left academia to work to advance government insurance proposals. The level of passion and partisanship has aided the creation of rich but incomplete political histories.[9]

Such biases may have blinded historians to relatively simple explanations of the phenomena they studied. Starr, for example, mentioned that ethnic, union, and fraternal benefit societies as well as commercial insurance existed in the early twentieth century, but he omitted mention of establishment funds. "The idea of providing health insurance against the risk of medical expenses," wrote Quadagno about the Progressive Era, "was largely unknown at that time. No government programs existed, and commercial health insurance companies had not yet ventured into the business of insuring health." According to Jacob Hacker, industrial sickness funds served only "isolated pockets of American workers," which may have been just as well because the insurance they offered was "scarce, inadequate, and uncertain." In fact, before 1920 there were thousands of insurance funds that capably covered millions of American workers. If this book can persuade the reader of the shrewdness, prudence, and agency of workers and their sickness funds, it will provide a much better understanding of Progressive reform failures. Workers and employers had created an alternative network of capable and even preferred insurance providers.[10]

Each side could at times acknowledge the accuracy of the other's points. Progressives recognized the capabilities of private sickness funds, which they hoped to supersede. Their opponents did not intend to keep government completely out of health insurance markets. As their arguments showed certain parallels, so, too, did the lives of each side's most prominent representatives.

The most prominent leader of AALL efforts to enlarge government provision of health insurance was the polymath Isaac Max Rubinow (1875–1936). Born in Russia, Rubinow came to the United States at age eighteen and eventually received a B.A., a M.D., and a Ph.D., all from Columbia University. He practiced medicine among New York's poor for five years. Later he served as president of the Casualty Actuarial Society and tirelessly published books and articles in favor of expanding health insurance coverage through government mandates. A biographer described his book *Social Insurance* as "an immediate classic . . . the most impressive statistical and theoretical rationale" for social insurance up to that time. To Ronald Numbers he was "without question the best-informed person on health insurance in the United States." Rubinow, at times a skeptic regarding sickness funds' capabilities, also acknowledged that fund managers' access to information regarding validity of claims was critical and that local sickness funds could do this better than large government agencies. Looking back from the perspective of the early 1930s, he observed that many Americans were familiar with health insurance through their local sickness funds and could see that the government alternative would have been much more expensive than they had been led to believe.[11]

Among the best known of the AALL's opponents was Frederick Ludwig Hoffman (1865–1946). Hoffman was born in Oldenburg, in what is now Germany, and came to the United States at age nineteen. His life's work, conducted primarily on behalf of the Prudential Insurance Company, concerned nearly every possible aspect of insurance-related statistics. His early works about tuberculosis among workers in the "dusty trades" were landmarks in industrial safety and health, and via his lifelong work on cancer statistics he became a founder of the American Cancer Society. According to Numbers, he had earned "a reputation for unimpeachable scholarship." His work on the health of African Americans sparked controversy in his day and ours; he documented sharp differentials in health by race, but attempts to explain those differences in racist terms blemished his reputation. His work on health insurance can be debated on its merits. He initially wrote for the AALL that the "innumerable failures" of benefit societies had been a "disastrous experience" that indicated the need for a professional, actuarial approach to the problem of health insurance. After he broke with the AALL, his *Facts and Fallacies of Compulsory Health Insurance* served as the "Bible of the opposition." Hoffman celebrated sickness funds for providing "truly enormous benefits" to workers. At the same time, he recognized that these fund-operated insurance plans were not so different from policies sold by commercial insurers, and as such needed to be brought under the regulatory oversight of state insurance commissioners. Hoffman believed that for commercial insurers and benefit societies alike, informational asymmetries obstructed the invisible hand.[12]

A few of the most intensely disputed points provide insight into the character of the debates and the quality of the arguments on both sides. Four basic considerations offer good examples of the ways each side made its case: capabilities of sickness funds, consequences of near-universal coverage, how much government insurance would cost, and the importance of medical care. These issues were intertwined, so that, for example, enrollment of nearly all wage workers might yield economies of scale that would reduce costs. Specific strands, though, appear clearly in articles and speeches by Hoffman, Rubinow, and their respective allies and can be considered in their turn.

Regarding the competence of existing sickness insurance funds, Progressives were, oddly, of two minds. To show that sickness funds needed to be replaced, they emphasized their shortcomings, and to show that their own plans were reasonable, they emphasized their similarities to those same funds. Royal Meeker, the Commissioner of Labor Statistics, characterized the existing network of voluntary health insurance funds as "chaos," but at the same time he acknowledged that a group of workers who wanted the benefits of social insurance could simply establish a voluntary fund for themselves. According to Rubinow, "the conditions of mutual insurance are unsatisfactory; the institutions insecure because built by inexperienced hands, the benefits small, and the burden of membership heavy." Because sickness funds lacked secure actuarial foundations, he argued, their instability threatened the workers who had trusted in them. At the same time, their persistence illustrated "the power of mutual aid." As the California Social Insurance Commission observed, "The 'mutual benefit' nature of the societies undoubtedly tends to counteract the tendency to malinger. Persons who might be unscrupulous in dealing with a commercial company are apt to be more careful when dealing with an organization whose financial condition is a matter of direct concern to themselves." Just so, Rubinow noted that workers who insured themselves cooperatively wanted to help manage their sickness funds, and they would act to protect the fund's wealth from fraudulent claims by less scrupulous colleagues. Miles Dawson, an actuary who served as an AALL officer, recommended that "local funds, local trade funds, and establishment funds," precisely because of their participatory nature, could be trusted to form the basis of a state-managed health insurance system. Thus, paradoxically, the existing sickness funds would be the ideal building blocks for government insurance mandates, as in Germany.[13]

Regarding the capabilities of sickness funds, their opponents were single-minded. "Truly enormous progress," Hoffman claimed, "has been made by voluntary agencies serving social insurance purposes." Progressives, he continued, had missed this development because they had failed "to inquire thoroughly into the extent and operation of such funds or methods of social protection developed by wage-earners in their own way and at their own cost." They had missed the increasing number of such funds and the improving quality of their operations, as workers learned to manage sickness fund finances. Because Progressives were unaware of these achievements, warned Hoffman, their analyses were "unworthy of public confidence." Industrial sickness funds could form the backbone of a larger network of health insurers, according to this view, but without government intervention.[14]

The goal of Progressive reformers was not to create a universal health insurance program, as Alan Derickson notes. They aimed, rather, to make the risk pool as large as politically possible. Among perceived limits were uncertainty about the constitutionality of national insurance and the high costs of collecting premiums from workers who did not earn wages and thus were not given pay packets that could be dunned every week or two. Fresh in the minds of Progressives was the widespread success of state-level workmen's compensation activism. The record of experience plus legal, political, and economic limitations combined to indicate that the best they could hope for was statewide (not national) insurance for wage workers (not everybody). Thus, domestic workers, who formed nearly five percent of the American labor force in 1910, were excluded, as were agricultural laborers, who accounted for another 7.6 percent. Beatrix Hoffman observed that each of these exclusions meant that a large share of the labor force that was female or black would be left uncovered. Under the AALL's proposals, members of the labor force who were not particularly well paid would face the costs of illness outside of the compulsory insurance system.[15]

Even if the AALL's standard bill fell short of universality, Progressives claimed that the increase in the size of the risk pool would yield considerable benefits. Miles Dawson noted that compulsion would solve the problem of adverse selection (a term he used) and in the process eliminate the need for financial reserves. If the state compelled large numbers of workers to obtain coverage, then poor and good risks would balance each other out. In particular, over time funds would keep steady shares of younger and older workers. As long as that was so, funds would have no need to carry a reserve as a form of self-reinsurance in case of epidemics or bad luck. The well-known economist Irving Fisher added that cost reductions achieved by enlarging the risk pool via compulsion resembled those enjoyed by newly developed group insurance policies but on a larger scale.[16]

Opponents argued that the actuarial advantages of compulsion came at too high a cost. Their primary argument was that forcing workers into insurance was an affront to traditional American values of individualism. Samuel Gompers charged that compulsion was a patronizing criticism of workers, who were seen by Progressives as incompetent to make their own decisions about such things. (Rubinow's later condemnation of workers who lacked his enthusiasm for state insurance as "materialistic, crude, and infantile" suggested that Gompers understood some of the Progressives' motivations.) Compulsion infringed on their liberty, even their "virility." Gompers also noted that the arbitrarily chosen income requirements effectively furthered class division, splitting the working class into "those eligible for benefits and those considered capable to care for themselves." Hoffman claimed that the independent voluntary societies were growing apace and that if the principle behind compulsion was the goal of insuring more workers, then in time those workers would be insured, if they so desired.[17]

In retrospect, some of these claims were straightforward, and others were more slippery. To the extent that health insurance was good, then to a degree the more widespread the coverage, the better. But only to a degree. As Chapter 7 shows, not all of those who were uninsured wanted to be insured. Some older workers had saved against the possibility of illness, and some younger workers expected, reasonably, to be sufficiently healthy that they would not claim benefits. The latter phenomenon stupefied Progressives. Rubinow complained that "one could notice a differentiation into group interests, the young and healthy and unmarried rebelling against the imposition of a burden to be carried by them for the protection of the older and sickly." But the young were simply recognizing their self-interest and acting on it.[18]

Progressives made theoretical arguments that did not stand up well when viewed against the actual operations of these funds. As noted, adverse selection was not much of a problem at the time—at least, no quantitative evidence has emerged in the economic literature that indicates that it was. The question of carrying a prudential reserve fund also seems moot. The background for Progressives may have been not prudence but the Armstrong Committee investigations in New York State (1905–1906), which uncovered mismanagement and embezzlement of life insurance reserves. Progressives were undoubtedly pleased to remind the public that private insurers had defrauded reserve funds. Small-scale insurers such as industrial sickness funds might find reserves less than useful. They might appear to members as an inert pool of wealth that would do just as well in their own pockets. The question of reserve size was an ongoing source of friction for many funds, because some members wanted to maintain a reserve as an act of prudence, and others wanted to take their chances without one. Because many sickness funds failed to keep a reserve anyway, the issue was not the problem that Progressives proposed it was.[19]

In general, historians have been sympathetic to Progressive arguments. As Dawson claimed about near-universal coverage, Jennifer Klein asserted that "by perpetually fragmenting risks (through experience rating or employer self-insurance), rather than pooling them, [private health insurance] utterly subverts the social purpose and the economic efficiency of insurance." This suggests an otherworldly absence of inefficiencies in very large government bureaucracies, and it ignores the value of reducing the correlation between health and employment—and thus adverse selection—through pooling by employer. The lack of choice entailed in compulsory insurance lent credence to Frederick Hoffman's criticism that it was really just a tax cum poor relief by another name.[20]

Regarding pooling by state, historians have recognized the power behind an argument made by Arthur Twining Hadley, a Yale University economist, in 1897. Any division of states into two camps, those with and without insurance, would disadvantage those with the insurance because its creation and management involve ongoing costs that must be borne by those states—but not by those without insurance. David Moss stressed this issue of "degenerative competition" as a significant part of the opponents' case, as, indeed, it remains to this day when neighboring states' tax policies differ from one another.[21]

If Progressives' opponents hammered home the dangers of taking on costs that neighboring states declined, the forces behind state insurance argued that those costs would ultimately be lower than the cost of private insurance available to wage workers at the time. Progressives claimed that administrative expenses absorbed 6 or 7 percent of fund income in Germany and projected a similar outcome in the United States as well. The president of the United States Casualty Company, Edson Lott, argued that after accounting for the cost of collecting premiums and government inefficiencies, administrative expenses would be closer to 30 or 40 percent. Royal Meeker retorted that the premium rates found in "true social insurance" could be 50 percent higher than private insurance owing to government incompetence and extravagance and still make state insurance a better deal for workers than "profiteering" private insurance.[22]

The reference to insurance profiteers suggests how Progressives aimed to make their case that government insurance would be less costly than the sickness insurance that was on offer. They compared their own plan to the most expensive insurance available. Most so-called industrial insurance policies were taken out on lives of workers who intended that the benefit would pay their burial expenses. Industrial insurance was distinguished from other policies by the means of paying premiums. Every week or so throughout American cities, an army of collection agents fanned out through working-class districts to collect the premium owed by each insured worker. This was slow and costly work that made insurance expensive in terms of loss ratios (the ratio of the dollar value of benefits paid to premiums collected; the loss was to the insurer). In Illinois and California, between 1913 and 1917, industrial health and accident firms reported loss ratios of about 45 percent. Progressives were appalled, but only a minority of workers with health insurance were covered by industrial policies. In Illinois and Ohio, about one-fifth of covered workers had obtained their health insurance through commercial insurers, some through group health policies and others through industrial health policies (the exact division was not reported).[23]

The amount of money that workers, employers, and taxpayers in general would pay in a scheme of government health insurance was open to speculation, and both sides did not hesitate to speculate. Rubinow estimated that paying the total cost of state insurance would require about 3 percent of wages, and the Massachusetts Special Commission on Social Insurance offered a range from 2.5 to 4.5 percent. Hoffman raised the specter of a 5 percent tax for insurance. In fact, no one knew how much it would cost because spending on benefits was open-ended, which made the level of premium charges also uncertain. The AALL may have been at its most persuasive when it emphasized the quality of benefits in detail without clearly describing how to pay for them. But the number of workers, voters, and legislators who wanted to provide a blank check for benefits that were of questionable efficacy was unclear.[24]

The most prominent benefit that was not widely available otherwise was coverage of medical, hospital, and surgical costs for workers and for their families. Family coverage was rare indeed among sickness funds. To Progressives, the lack of medical care made many workers and their families suffer twice, once with the illness itself and once more with the lingering symptoms that medical care could have alleviated. But as noted below, more funds offered medical benefits than Progressives recognized. About one-half of the workers covered by establishment funds were eligible for medical benefits. More important, it is not at all clear that the medicine of the early twentieth century had much to offer a sick worker (surgery was another matter). Yet AALL leaders spoke out about the marvelous power of modern medicine, promoting its ability to prevent sickness by somewhat mysterious and never-quite-specified methods. The report of the Health Insurance Commission of Pennsylvania estimated that "fully one-half of existing sickness could be eliminated if proper preventive measures were taken." Irving Fisher was so firmly convinced that "in the case of human morbidity the degree of preventability is enormous" that he believed "[t]he great virtue of health insurance . . . will lie in prevention of illness." The California Social Insurance Commission expected that as long as employers were forced to pay some of their employees' premiums, the reduction in rates they would enjoy as they removed unspecified causes of sickness from the workplace would provide a powerful incentive for employers to clean up their plants.[25]

That physicians really had such abilities, except in the most indirect manner, seems unlikely now. Some historians have proposed that physicians played an important role in convincing housewives of the importance of cleanliness, especially in the kitchen, and thus reduced the incidence of food-borne disease. Evidence presented below indicates that orders for rest might have led to more certain recoveries. But other than the diphtheria antitoxin, physicians had little in the way of vaccines or treatments that gave them any preventive or curative abilities in the modern sense. Progressives' opponents were happy to point out that powerlessness whenever possible.[26]

There is little evidence to suggest that the expected beneficiaries of access to modern medicine, the insured workers, were very interested in obtaining medical care, as Chapter 5 shows. These findings are consistent with Daniel Fox's claim that the perception of medical progress drove policy developments after the Great War. This suggested a relative lack of interest in medicine in the prior age, when expectations for medical efficacy were low. Rubinow had to concede that workers' interest in medical treatment was "half-hearted" at best and that their main concern was with sick pay. Hoffman, again, was quick to touch this nerve.

According to statistical analysis presented below, he was fundamentally correct when he wrote, "To the insured workman the money benefit is the primary purpose of compulsory health insurance, while medical assistance and disease prevention are of quite secondary importance." If the Progressives were offering the working class access to the most up-to-date medical treatment, and the workers were not interested, it could only mean that, as Rubinow noted years later, American workers would not go where they were led by the experts.[27]

The AALL obfuscated the question of how to organize these services, and in part this was intentional. Most proposed versions of the standard bill promised workers and their families their choice of physician. But early drafts, including the first bill submitted to the New York legislature, did not address the question, because the AALL had hoped to settle the matter after the bill had become law. Rubinow's argument that free choice was unnecessary may have led some to question the AALL's commitment to the principle. The method of paying those physicians was also left to be decided afterward. The Connecticut and New York bills called for (1) free choice from a panel of physicians, (2) "reasonable" free choice of salaried physicians employed by the insurer, (3) other salaried physicians employed by the insurer, or (4) combination of the above. This left an important question unanswered. Based on their prior experience, firms, unions, and their sick funds knew that diagnoses depended on whether the physician was paid by the patient or the insurer and whether he was paid by the visit, by capitation, or on salary. The reticence of the AALL gave its opponents all the ammunition they needed to sap the support for the plan, especially among physicians.[28]

The uncertainty generated by the range of organizational possibilities made physicians anxious and could not have inspired much support among workers. Reformers seemed nearly clueless about the consequences. Alexander Lambert, a physician and AALL official, noted that paying physicians by the visit could be troublesome because "with an unknown morbidity there is always an unknown expense facing the fund." Considering the confusion created by the AALL's proposals, the Massachusetts Special Commission on Social Insurance concluded, "No entirely satisfactory solution of these problems has been offered." William Gale Curtis of the Insurance Economics Society correctly observed that "no definite plan of compensating panel physicians has even been suggested" and that such issues had led to "strikes, wrangles, and bitter strife between physicians and carriers abroad."[29]

Despite shortcomings in the AALL's proposals, they were taken seriously at the time, and given the success of workmen's compensation and various industrial safety movements, it remains something of a puzzle why state-level efforts at health insurance failed so consistently. Many present-day explanations of the failure of Progressive policy proposals begin by assuming that the policies, in general, would obviously have been good for the body politic, and so their repeated failures can only be explained by a malfunction of the political system. Hence, to explain why Progressive proposals failed at the hands of legislators, bureaucrats, or voters is to ask how the political process was subverted and by whom. Four sets of actors have been proposed: physicians, union officials, businessmen, and commercial insurers.[30]

Where physicians would stand regarding this issue was not clear at first. Before the establishment of the British system in 1911, physicians seemed uninterested in government insurance in general. Afterwards, the *Journal of the American Medical Association* reported that government funding promised to eliminate low-paying charity work and provide a more regular income that might grow to become higher than it had been previously. Some hoped that the general quality of health care would increase as well, leading to initial support for government insurance. The AALL made the future of physician incomes and autonomy as unclear as possible, however, and physicians' real incomes seem to have fallen as the political debate proceeded. As the AALL's proposals made their way through the political process, the specter of capitation payments, or payments based on the number of patients in a practice rather than fee-for-service compensation, began to sour a number of physicians on the idea of expanded insurance. Proposals that initially promised to reduce uncertainty about the level and sources of physician income appeared to increase that uncertainty. Although the AALL had hoped that physicians would sign on first and then bargain over their working conditions, by 1920 the American Medical Association voted officially to state its opposition to government health insurance. A sociologist concluded that from this time to the 1960s, physicians were the loudest opponents of government insurance.[31]

Union support shifted over time as well, but in the opposite direction. After initial opposition, labor came to strongly support government health insurance during the New Deal. In the earlier period labor's most prominent leader, Samuel Gompers, framed the debate in terms of higher wages and government insurance as substitutes for one another. Workers could have one or the other, but not both, and it was clear to Gompers that wage increases trumped all. The "living wage" that unions obtained for their members purchased "sanitary homes, conditions of living that are conducive to good health, adequate clothing, nourishing food and other things that are essential to the maintenance of good health." On the other hand the AALL was, in Gompers's famous phrase, a bunch of barnacles attached to the labor movement, retarding progress and impossible to detach. Gompers and other labor leaders also recognized the need for health insurance for workers and sought to provide such insurance through union-operated funds. Some national unions and many locals offered sick pay benefits to members. Leaders of those unions believed that insurance benefits, particularly during slack economic times, bound workers to the union more closely and improved the esprit de corps necessary for effective union activity. Government insurance promised simultaneously to reduce workers' take-home pay and to replace an important source of worker loyalty toward unions.[32]

The beginnings of labor's shift toward favoring government health insurance were present in the Progressive period. Some unions, such as the United Mine Workers and the International Ladies' Garment Workers' Union, represented workers who were at elevated risk of occupationally contracted diseases, especially those of the respiratory system. They created their own insurance programs and medical systems to care for sick members. Their arguments in favor of compulsory government insurance noted that the sum total of union funds protected relatively few workers, and in more normative terms stated that a rich society could afford to provide medical care to all and therefore should do so. Although the first round in the Progressive Era went to the leaders of organized labor who fought government insurance, forces in favor of such insurance ultimately brought the whole of the labor movement to their side during the New Deal. In the Progressive period they did not prevail, but they did make labor a less unified political force.[33]

The third prominent group that opposed government insurance was businessmen. In the AALL's basic proposal, employers were to pay two-fifths of the premium, and workers and taxpayers would pay the rest. A sliding scale reduced premium payments by workers who earned low wages, with the difference to be made up by employers. Many businesses affected by insurance legislation could expect an increase in their costs of unknown magnitude. Unions feared that compulsory insurance premiums would reduce wages, but even if labor markets allowed a substantial cut in wages, some of the cost would remain for employers to pay. In addition, many large and well-known firms had invested in extensive fringe benefits, a program known as "welfare capitalism." These firms saw group benefits, which included health insurance, as a way to increase employee loyalty, just as unions saw them as a way to keep members in the fold. And, like unions, businesses did not see the interposition of government insurers between them and their employees as a good thing.[34]

And so business organized to defeat proposals to institute government insurance. In New York, the National Civic Federation and affiliated organizations published attacks on European social insurance programs. Their estimates of worker illness rates, in one historian's account, low-balled actual sickness and injury rates, overestimated the costs of business's share of contributions, and exaggerated the potential for covered workers to feign illness so as to draw benefits. The prospect that only some states would enact insurance laws, leading to degenerative competition, caused many business groups to oppose any state-level legislation. Like labor, management saw reformers as "chair warmers" (a step up from "barnacles," perhaps) who got in the way of those doing the real work. Unlike labor, business was unified in its opposition to government insurance. The AALL, lulled by its successes with state workmen's compensation, was shocked by the depth of opposition among businessmen.[35] Business proved to be an effective political force, not least in its ability to form anti-insurance coalitions with physicians and, most of all, with commercial insurers.

Insurance companies would seem to have had the greatest incentive to fight the encroachment of government insurance provision. Opposition was divided neatly by the line of insurance. Life insurers objected to the burial benefit of $50, or about one month's pay. Casualty insurers objected to the health insurance provisions but did so more from fear that they might be cut out of future business than that the government would remove a profit-making operation in the present. In the Progressive Era group health was little more than an experiment. A large share of what was known about rates of sickness came from the 1915–1917 efforts by the Metropolitan Life Insurance Company to conduct surveys about sickness in several cities. Such records could have led Metropolitan Life to leverage its expertise in life insurance to market similar insurance in case of ill health—but only if the government did not get there first. And so Metropolitan Life became a vigorous opponent of the AALL's proposals, aided by the Insurance Economics Society. Together they publicized unfavorable data about European social insurance and projected that similar fates awaited any such system in America.[36]

Opposition among commercial insurers to government intervention developed slowly over time. The actuarial mathematics behind life insurance had been understood for centuries, but health insurance was a different matter. Defining *death* could not have been easier, but defining *sickness* raised all kinds of problems. John F. Dryden, the founder of the Prudential Insurance Company, asserted in 1909 that commercial health insurance would never work because "the assurance of a stipulated sum during sickness can only be safely transacted, and then only in a limited way, by fraternal organizations having a perfect knowledge of and complete supervision over the individual members." What had been diffidence must have become hope for future profit, for the Prudential later charged Frederick Hoffman with investigating European social insurance and organizing the fight against similar proposals at home. Still, the commercial insurers could only have been looking to the future, because group health insurance in those days was a hard sell. When the Equitable tried to market insurance for temporary disability in 1911 and again in 1917, it found few takers. Group health was also a consistent money loser. By the late 1920s it was not clear that health insurance could be sold for a profit under any circumstances as insurers pondered Dryden's statement about the need to keep a close watch on policy-holders. The great motivation for the insurance companies to attack the AALL's proposals was the desire to protect their share of the life insurance market. Inclusion of the death benefit in the standard bill, noted Rubinow, signed the death warrant for the Progressives' efforts.[37]

Perhaps it would have taken a miracle to get any legislation past the gauntlet of labor unions, manufacturers, insurers, and physicians. One might guess that, besides those groups, the constituency for government insurance would be limited to a few good-government reformers and some college professors. According to some historians who have studied the question of Progressive failure, though, supporters of government insurance were much more numerous. In the view of Colin Gordon, "reformers always commanded a clear and substantial majority of public support." Therefore, the best available explanation for the consistent defeat of government health insurance in the Progressive era was "the debilitating material disadvantage faced by reformers," who were "overwhelmed by the willingness and ability of health interests to outspend them in legislative hearings, electoral campaigns, and public debate."[38]

This explanation proposes, more or less, that physicians, labor unions, employers, and commercial insurers (not to mention fraternal societies and Christian Scientists) subverted the political process in order to prevent workers from obtaining adequate protection from risk. It has proved irresistible for many historians to cast the struggle as one between right and wrong if not good and evil. As Starr resonantly stated, "The dream of reason did not take power into account." The reformers were the idealistic dreamers, but their dreams were based on reason. Their opponents were politically powerful but bereft of reason.[39]

According to these histories, the weaknesses of industrial sickness funds should have led workers to demand state insurance in short order. In 1917 Irving Fisher opined that they "are, and as far as we can see, always will be hopelessly inadequate." Edgar Sydenstricker complained in 1916 that "voluntary insurance in this country . . . will never come up to our expectations." Sydenstricker and another Public Health Service official, B. S. Warren, suggested that workers chose to remain uninsured because, to them, benefits resembled poor relief. That seems unlikely given the large number of covered workers, who hated to take charity, and steady growth in coverage. The AALL complained about the "uniformly unsatisfactory results" of private sickness insurance "as far as the mass of wage earners is concerned." The AALL characterized the entire collection of establishment, union, fraternal, and commercial insurance funds as inherently weak and "incapable of developing properly to meet" workers' needs. In general, one historian concluded, the ineptitude of sickness funds handed Progressive reformers a powerful argument in favor of government intervention in health insurance markets.[40]

Historians have further charged that sickness funds not only were inept but also obstructed progress in the form of government interventions. If sickness funds had only been incompetent, they would have been forgotten, but they were incompetently run and gummed up the political works. Klein assessed insurance providers as "political, inefficient, inflationary, and unreliable from their inception." Quadagno simply omitted them in her history of health policy. Despite their spectacular ineptitude, complained Roy Lubove, their mere presence as private providers of the collective good of income security stood in the way of rationality and progress. Their existence thwarted reformers' efforts to make the government insure all the people.[41]

The rest of this book is dedicated to challenging these historical judgments. My view that sickness funds were capable and important factors in American health insurance before World War II fits into a growing literature that takes a more skeptical view of the capacities of state insurance. It rejects an idealized, absolute view of government-based efforts in favor of comparing them to other government social insurance efforts and to similar private insurance programs, that is, the sickness funds. To compare those extant private efforts to idealized but nonexistent state programs is to engage in what Harold Demsetz described as a "nirvana" strategy, which is weighted heavily against the actual, flawed efforts mired in this vale of tears. The alternative view begins by noting the utter lack of evidence that there was any popular support for government sickness insurance. Daniel Levine expressed this point in the simplest terms: "Americans did not have social insurance before 1935 because Americans did not want social insurance." Jacob Hacker, a supporter of government insurance, acknowledged this lack of interest but then finessed the issue by noting that there was no popular movement for such insurance in Europe, either, and it came to pass there anyway. In this view, then, the problem lay less in a conspiracy of the powerful than it was in the instruments of democracy itself: bicameral legislatures, independent judiciaries, and such Progressive favorites as initiatives and referenda.[42]

One explanation for this lack of popular support must contain a large grain of truth. Circulated in the contemporary literature and revived by Theda Skocpol, it proposed that widespread familiarity with public-sector corruption and ineptitude made many voters, legislators, and insurance experts suspicious of giving states a blank check for health expenses. Given the inherent difficulties of the insurance contract—moral hazard and degenerative competition, for example—governments that could not manage their own accounts, much less their own efforts at, say, pension insurance, could not be expected to manage sickness benefits competently, either. The Health Insurance Commission of the State of Illinois despaired: "With the experience of doctors frequently asked to certify falsely to sickness disability under present insurance contracts, or the union experience of sickness claims being used as a cover for unemployment, what confidence could be had in a politically controlled and managed fund of such proportions with no practical check upon its disbursement annually to nearly 400,000 in the State?" Samuel Gompers criticized state insurance bills under consideration in New York, Massachusetts, and California: "Failure to provide definite standards and regulations leaves the whole issue wide open for political influences as political doctors would constitute just as serious a menace as political lawyers." The administrative requirements for a health insurance program were substantial. To the extent that workers and voters declined to endorse such programs, they may have acted from a lack of trust in government capabilities that was grounded in both prudence and painful experience.[43]

In revising the conventional account of health insurance history, other historians have established the basic functionality of private insurance, consisting primarily of fraternal societies. David Beito documented the breadth of benefits offered by fraternals, including not only sickness insurance but also orphanages for survivors of deceased members. George Emery and Herbert Emery analyzed the financial soundness of Odd Fellows' insurance activities. Robert Whaples and David Buffum considered patterns in holding of life and sickness insurance by workers of all ages, income strata, and ethnic groups. Viewing a later period, Frank Dobbin noted the existence of mutual benefit associations in large numbers by the late 1920s. The possibility that small-scale funds were well known to workers and capably filled much of the demand for insurance has been overlooked in the historical literature. In fact, as this book contends, private health insurance was an important aspect of worker compensation from the late nineteenth century onward and grew in importance throughout the Progressive Era.[44]

Neither the Progressives nor their opponents had airtight arguments. One hypothesis designed to explain the political failure of the AALL suggests that its "rationalist" rhetorical strategy failed to excite its potential allies in the same way that their opponents' appeals to fear succeeded among most workers and their families.[45] But for a rationalist strategy, one based on the facts and not on emotional appeals, to work, the facts had better be in order. It is not clear that on this basis the AALL had a better set of arguments than did their opponents. A good way to see this, and to consider other aspects of both sides' arguments, is to return to the source of most American ideas about social insurance: Europe.

CHAPTER THREE

Progressive Ideals

PRIVATE AND PUBLIC INSURANCE IN EUROPE

> The education of the American public in matters of social insurance has gone so far that it has learned of the existence of compulsory sickness insurance in Germany.
>
> —I. M. RUBINOW, 1913

> We are often referred to the laws on this subject in force in Germany. The experience of the German government compulsory insurance system, however, has not been satisfactory.
>
> —REINHOLD KOCH, 1912

PROGRESSIVE REFORMERS in America looked to Europe for models of social insurance. Such welfare programs took a variety of forms in turn-of-the-century Europe. Some countries forced all workers in a certain income class or industry to obtain insurance, others attempted to persuade workers to insure themselves by subsidizing its cost, and still others were content to leave nearly everything to the marketplace. This chapter considers the structure and workings of these European funds. Thanks to their heterogeneity, the American situation can be placed in some context. American sickness funds can be compared to voluntary European insurance systems, widely thought to have failed the workers under their care, and to compulsory systems, which Progressives used as exemplars.

The chapter has three goals. First, it shows that theoretical problems of insurance, used by both sides to press their arguments, appeared in European systems. Moral hazard, for example, was widespread in compulsory funds, as was adverse selection in voluntary funds. Second, the chapter aims to clarify the validity of claims made in American debates.

Progressive proposals and their opponents' counterarguments can be better understood in light of data published by these systems. For example, both sides argued about whether expansion of insurance coverage would induce a moral hazard. In analyzing these assertions, this chapter provides an instance of Progressive misrepresentation of relatively clear factual information. Third, it lays down the foundation of later comparisons of American and European systems in which the American situation can be seen as a relatively effective third way between compulsory and voluntary systems in Europe.

When the Progressives imagined what their ideal sickness insurance system would look like, they turned to the compulsory systems of Great Britain and Germany. The German program was founded on an existing network of small sickness funds, and Progressives hoped to replicate the superior ability of such small funds to monitor claims. Compulsory sickness insurance made German workers healthier, they argued. Irving Fisher relayed the results of a German study suggesting that "twelve years were added to the worker's life span during thirty years of health insurance," at least some of which were due to that insurance. There was probably some truth behind this claim, although, as opponents observed, it failed to answer the question why American mortality rates had fallen in equal proportions in the same time. According to reformers, prevention was the mechanism through which insurance had powerful effects on health, but what was prevented and how were never quite made clear. Progressives were certain that important lessons could be drawn from European experience to guide the United States to broader health insurance coverage.[1]

From the mid-1880s to the onset of World War I there were essentially four systems of sickness insurance in Europe.[2] France and Belgium, under the sway of classical liberal ideology, opted for a very low level of government intervention in sickness funds. Except for French miners, who were obligated to obtain insurance, membership in sickness funds was voluntary in both countries, and many funds operated without government supervision, although others benefited from franking privileges and the like. In order to balance their budgets, they turned to civic-minded members of the bourgeoisie, who became honorary members by contributing dues but agreeing not to make claims. These payments plus other donations and subsidies accounted for 12 percent of French fund income toward the end of this period.[3]

Sickness insurance in the Scandinavian tradition began in Denmark. In that country membership was also voluntary, but state provision of subsidies to encourage workers to join funds gave the government a greater role than it had in other voluntary programs. Subsidies formed about one-third of fund budgets by 1910. In an unusual measure intended to accommodate a sparse population spread over many islands and peninsulas, Danish funds in rural areas reimbursed members for the cost of transportation to a physician. By 1909 the covered share of the population, 23 percent, was greater than that in Germany, which suggested that voluntary, subsidized insurance could protect a large share of a population.[4]

The system that appealed the most to American Progressives was that in Germany. Forever associated with Bismarck's political efforts to stymie the socialists, the Reichstag passed its first social insurance law in 1883. It made membership in one of a network of sickness funds compulsory for a large class of workers (those earning less than two thousand marks per year) and required employers to contribute to sickness funds as well. By inspecting employer records, cross-checking fund membership lists, and threatening employers of uninsured workers with fines, the state effectively enforced coverage requirements. Austria followed with a somewhat different system, requiring workers in an enumerated list of industries to obtain coverage. In both cases, the network of health insurance funds covered a large share of the working class. Despite the broad extent of coverage, these systems still confronted problems of adverse selection and physician agency.[5]

The fourth system was that of the United Kingdom, which experienced a transition from a heavily subscribed voluntary network to a system of compulsory insurance under the National Insurance Act of 1911. Before passage of the act, as many as two-thirds of workingmen belonged to friendly societies that provided sick pay and medical attention. The act imposed on working people over the age of sixteen who earned less than £160 per year a tax—four pence per week for men and three for women—and required their employers to pay threepence per week per employee and the state to pay twopence. In turn these workers received free medical treatment and ten shillings per week in sick pay for men, reduced to seven shillings sixpence for women.[6]

Although each European system generated common problems that stemmed from information asymmetries, a great divide appeared between compulsory and voluntary systems. The difference was due to the additional adverse selection problems encountered by voluntary schemes. Thus voluntary systems needed to create additional defensive mechanisms to avoid being swamped by those selection problems. All insurance networks faced moral hazards that they recognized and tried to mitigate by means of various policies.

The variation in each system's characteristics was considerable. Table 3.1 illustrates some characteristics of various American and European sickness insurance programs, chosen on the basis of data availability. Comparison of like to like can be made only with some trepidation. There is no perfect way to make the point that the extant American system was similar to those used in Europe, but that is what this table suggests. Certain characteristics of the American network of private insurers resembled those of many European systems. The American Association for Labor Legislation's proposal was more generous than any of them.

As in the United States, insuring the labor force in Europe meant that the overwhelming majority of insured workers in all countries were men. Because it was typical to exclude agricultural laborers from coverage, the population in each country that was assumed to be eligible for insurance consisted of male nonagricultural workers. In most cases, the estimated sick benefit per day was derived from actual sick pay expenditures, and then divided by the number of sick days among insured workers; a similar process was followed for medical benefit spending. In the British case, $0.41 was simply the statutory sickness payment of 10 shillings per week multiplied by the exchange rate of $4.86, divided by six days per work week.

In terms of coverage rates, the United States at its best tended to be in the middle of the spectrum. As shown in Chapter 4, it seems likely that by 1915 or so the American sickness funds covered about eight million workers, or about one-third of the nonagricultural labor force. This was a larger share than in the unsubsidized systems of Belgium and

Table 3.1.

Health insurance systems of early twentieth-century Europe and America

COUNTRY	YEAR	COVERAGE (IN THOUSANDS OF MEN)	NON-AGRICULTURAL LABOR FORCE	SHARE OF WORKERS COVERED	SICK BENEFIT PER DAY (U.S. $)	AVERAGE DAILY WAGE (U.S. $)	WAGE REPLACEMENT RATE	MEDICAL BENEFIT PER DAY (U.S. $)
United States (actual)	1916	8,000	23,482	0.33	$1.39	$2.35	0.59	0.22
United States (AALL proposal)	1916	n/a	23,482				0.67	0.80
Great Britain[a]	1914	9,667	11,442	0.84	0.41	0.95	0.43	n/a
Austria	1907	2,354	4,421	0.53	0.25	0.62	0.40	0.16
Germany	1906	9,400	13,298	0.71	0.29	0.99	0.50[d]	0.35
France[b]	1905	2,270	7,503	0.30	0.25	0.71	0.35	0.25

Belgium[c]	1904	229	1,806	0.13	0.27	0.61	0.44	0.12
Denmark	1907	553	846	0.65	0.20	0.92	0.22	0.33

Sources: For Germany: Kaiserlichen Statistischen Amt, *Statistik der Krankenversicherung der Arbeiter,* vol. 170. *For Belgium:* Joseph Begasse, "Die Arbeiterversicherung in Belgien," vol. 3, no. 12, in Zacher, *Die Arbeiter-Versicherung in Auslande,* 1906, pp. 8–9. *For France:* Zacher, "Die Arbeiter-Versicherung in Frankreich," vol. 2, no. 4, in Zacher, *Die Arbeiter-Versicherung im Auslande,* 1902, pp. 4, 6–7, 9–11. *For Denmark:* Zacher, "Die Arbeiterversicherung in Dänemark," vol. 2, no. 1, in Zacher, *Die Arbeiter-Versicherung im Auslande,* 1903, pp. 8–9. *For Austria:* U.S. Commissioner of Labor, *Twenty-fourth Annual Report,* pp. 270–281. *For the United States:* Ohio Health and Old Age Insurance Commission, *Health* p. 167. Actual 1916 data are from Emmet, "Operation"; "medical benefit per day" refers to average among funds that offer such benefits. Number covered (average of high and low estimates) and share covered are from Chap. 4 of this book. Nonagricultural labor force is from U.S. Bureau of the Census, *Historical Statistics,* ser. D-17, 1920, men only. *For Great Britain:* Harris, *Origins,* pp. 162–163, 224. Daily wage is from Feinstein, "New Estimates," p. 604, estimated annual earnings for 1911 divided by 300.

Nonagricultural labor force: Mitchell, *European Historical Statistics,* pp. 51–62. Years: Austria, 1910; Belgium, 1910; Denmark, 1911; France, 1906; Germany, 1907; Britain, 1911. *Average daily wage* (unweighted average of skilled and unskilled building and engineering wages): Belgium, Denmark, France, Germany, and Britain are from Williamson, "Evolution of Global Labor Markets," p. 184; Austria: U.S. Commissioner of Labor, *Twenty-fourth Annual Report,* p. 85; United States: U.S. Bureau of the Census, *Historical Statistics,* ser. D-724 at 300 work days.

Note: Benefits are shown in \$U.S. at the following exchange rates: \$4.86 = £1; \$1 = 4.2 DM; \$0.406 = 1 Austrian Fl.; \$0.268 = 1 DKr; \$0.193 = 1 Belgian f and 1 French f. *Sick benefit per day:* for Britain, it is equal to the statutory amount of 10 s. per week for men at exchange rate noted above. Elsewhere, it is equal to the total value of sick benefits divided by the number of compensated workdays.

[a]Excludes Ireland.

[b]Adult, free, and miners' funds.

[c]Recognized funds only.

[d]The statutory minimum in Germany was one-half. The estimated replacement rate of 0.29 may reflect high claim rates in relatively low-wage occupations; alternatively, the wage estimate may be too high because it includes well-paid workers who were not in the compulsory scheme.

France, but a smaller share than in countries where membership was subsidized and compulsory. The large difference in nominal wages between the United States and Europe is mostly real and partly due to the fact that the American figure incorporates wartime inflation. American opponents of state insurance seized on the difference in real wages and claimed that it obviated the need for social insurance in the United States, where workers earned far more than did those in Europe. American workers, claimed these writers, earned enough to care for themselves in time of sickness or accident.[7]

Notwithstanding caveats about differences in data quality and aptness of comparisons, it seems clear that sick pay in the United States was higher than that in Europe. In absolute terms, a covered American worker received several times the cash benefit of a typical European worker. But American workers earned more, so the appropriate comparison is one of replacement rates, that is, of sick pay as a share of regular pay. An average covered American worker received three-fifths of his regular pay; a European worker's benefit was one-quarter to one-half of a regular pay packet. Although criticism of the standard five-to-seven-dollar weekly benefit payment was standard fare among Progressive reformers, none of those reformers compared that sick benefit to the much smaller payments received in the European systems that they hoped the United States would emulate.[8]

The value of medical benefits was estimated by dividing total expenditures on physicians, nursing services, hospitals, and equipment by the number of sick days. This yielded an estimate of spending on medical care per day of incapacitation. In this regard Germany clearly led the other nations, spending more than twice what Austria and Belgium spent and half again as much as France or the United States spent.[9] Denmark spent just a little less than Germany, but this figure included transportation expenses as well as more strictly medical expenses. Again, at least among workers in the United States who enjoyed medical benefits, spending on medical care was comparable to the middle range of the European figures.

The AALL's model bill promised to increase health insurance expenditures substantially, beginning with medical care. The Ohio Health and Old Age Insurance Commission estimated that under the Ohio bill medical care for insured workers would cost six to seven dollars per worker per year. The average number of annual days of sick leave per worker at this time was estimated elsewhere to be six to nine.[10] Medical expenses under this plan could cost anywhere from seventy cents to more than a dollar per day, an increase of a factor of four and well above European levels. In addition, the AALL urged that sickness pay be set at two-thirds of wages, which was not much more than the three-fifths pay that American workers already received and much more than most European workers could expect. Combining the value of sick pay and medical benefits indicates that the average covered American worker could expect an increase in benefits of about 50 percent, from $1.61 per sick day to $2.37.

Other aspects of coverage and financing differed across the various systems. Compulsory systems generally aimed to cover workers who earned less than some annual income level. The AALL converted Great Britain's and Germany's coverage thresholds to $768 and $600, respectively, and proposed that American workers who earned up to $1,200 per year be insured. The higher American threshold reflected the greater real wages paid there, so that about the same share of the workforce would be covered in all these countries. Because that maximum was far above the average in all cases, most workers would find themselves in the system.

For the most part, workers funded existing American insurance. The AALL proposed a funding ratio of 1:2:2 for the state, the employer, and the worker, with a sliding scale that would increase the employer's share and decrease the worker's share for low-paid workers. By dividing costs thus, the proposal resembled the British system, in which the ratio was 2:3:4. In Germany, the ratio of funding was 1:2 (employer:employee). Under all three systems, real and hypothetical, reasonably efficient labor markets would adjust nominal wages to reflect these contributions. At first glance the two-fifths to be paid by workers under the AALL proposal may have had an effect like the two-ninths in Britain or the two-thirds in Germany: to make sickness insurance look like more of a bargain than it really was.[11]

Many American reformers argued that by enrolling a large number of workers, compulsory insurance plans could exploit economies of scale and operate more efficiently than small sickness funds. Comparisons of administrative costs across health insurance systems are difficult to make because of varying definitions of those costs. Establishment

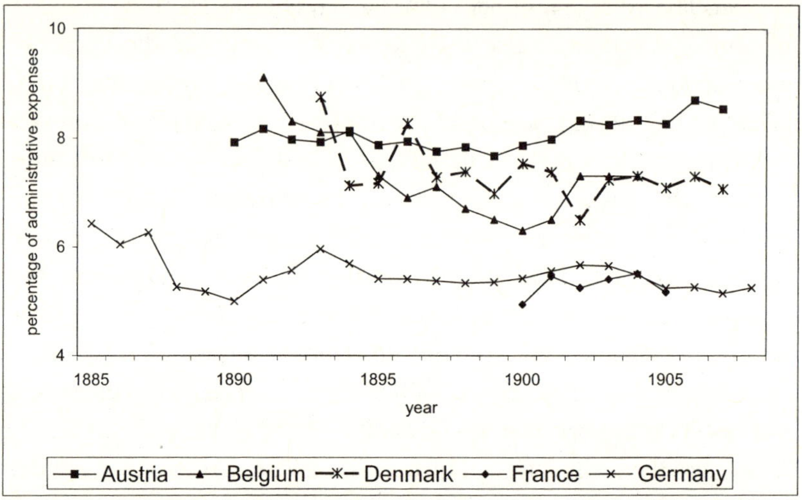

FIGURE 3.1. Administrative expenses as a share of total health insurance expenses. (Data from U.S. Commissioner of Labor, *Twenty-fourth Annual Report*, pp. 279, 486, 617, 781, 1230.)

funds in the United States incurred such costs at a rate of about 11 percent of total expenditures in 1905–1908 and about 16 percent in 1916. The share of total expenditures on management for mutual societies in France was only about 5 percent, and in Germany administrative expenses were even lower, at 3 to 4 percent (figure 3.1). Belgian and Danish funds incurred an intermediate level of administrative expenses, at 6 to 10 percent. Austrian administrative expenses remained about 8 percent of all spending from 1890 to 1907. British administrative expenses ran to about 14 percent of revenues. It is not clear that the American funds spent excessively on administration compared to European funds. In any case, there does not seem to have been a direct relation between compulsory membership and lower administrative expenses. Economies of scale may have helped the German system keep costs down, but that would not explain the low costs of the relatively poorly enrolled French system, nor the higher costs in the compulsory Austrian system as compared to the fragmented Belgian network.[12]

To the extent that American reformers used the German system as a model, the strengths and weaknesses of that system illustrate what the

Progressives expected their proposed program to resemble. But their rhetoric skimmed over and even misrepresented some characteristics that they did not find very congenial to their argument. These characteristics included moral hazard, principal-agent problems, and adverse selection. Compulsion did eliminate adverse selection, as they claimed, or perhaps exacerbated it among surviving voluntary funds. Progressives were only partly willing to admit the existence of the other two problems.

According to widespread anecdotal evidence, medical benefits in voluntary and compulsory funds alike induced moral hazard. In Germany, fund officials reported that insured workers presented with ever more trivial complaints, ones for which they would not have sought help without insurance coverage. A textbook example developed in Denmark, where the initial plan was to pay the entire cost of physician attendance with a government subsidy. Soon demand for such "free" medical care overwhelmed the system, and subsidies for doctor visits rose faster than expected. Spending on physician services, including transportation, increased eightfold from 1893 to 1907, about double the rate of the increase in spending on sick pay during that period. Funds began to require workers to buy "sick tickets" to gain admission to a physician's office for a relatively low price. Raising the price of physician services above zero resolved the problem of excess demand.[13]

American critics of insurance reform efforts claimed that increased absence from work due to sickness in Germany was a sign of moral hazard, or malingering. As soon as workers could avoid work and still receive a large share of their pay packet, they argued, ever more of them would take advantage of those benefits. As proof they referred to the rising number of days missed per worker in Germany. In fact, German workers really were missing ever more sick days on average (see figure 3.2). From 1888 to 1908 the number of compensated workdays that were missed rose from about 5.4 to about 8.5, an increase of more than one-half. To explain this trend, the Progressives' opponents invoked malingering: one German authority, they reported, said that "certain of the insured are no longer as much interested in recovering as quickly as possible." This was due in part, according to Frederick Hoffman, to "dishonesty, deception, and dissimulation" on the part of workers.[14]

According to reformers, their critics ignored or misrepresented evidence concerning the length of typical spells of compensated illness. In

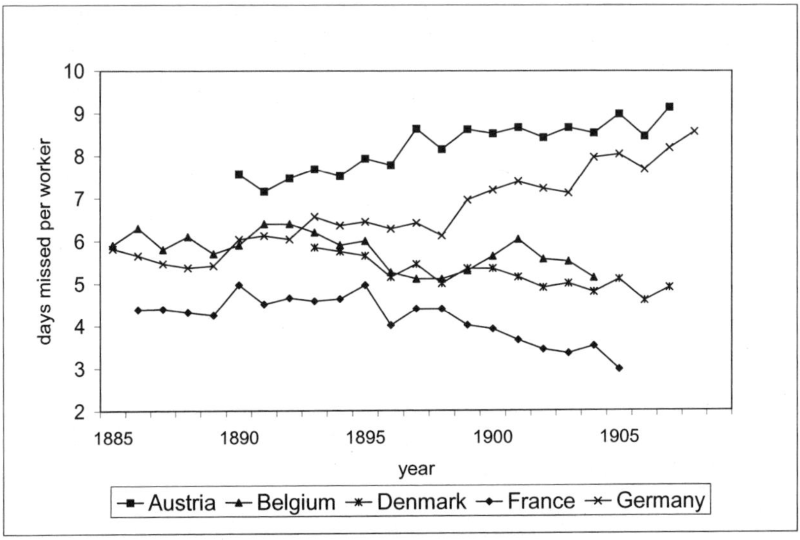

FIGURE 3.2. Trends in compensated absence days (days missed per member year). France included free and adult funds. Belgium included recognized funds only. (For sources see table 3.1.)

this area the Progressive arguments were particularly weak. One writer claimed that "the actual duration of sickness" in Germany had remained constant under national insurance. That does not seem to have been the case, according to the data represented in figure 3.3, which shows the average number of days missed per case by type of compulsory fund. In fact, an increase in duration of illness was evident. Overall, from 1885 to 1904 the average duration increased from 14.1 to 19.7 days, and from 1904 to 1913 it increased by nearly another full day.[15]

The Progressive explanation for this increase had a certain deductive power. The increase in duration, offered I. M. Rubinow, was a statistical artifact that followed from a 1903 German regulation that required all funds to provide benefits for at least twenty-six weeks, an increase from thirteen weeks. The observed increase in duration was due to very long-lasting cases that could now continue in the system for up to an additional three months. Rubinow impatiently criticized opponents who failed to see his point: "That statistical error has been made hundreds of times, [and] has been explained equally frequently." Yet the increased maximum benefit period could not explain much of the increase in the

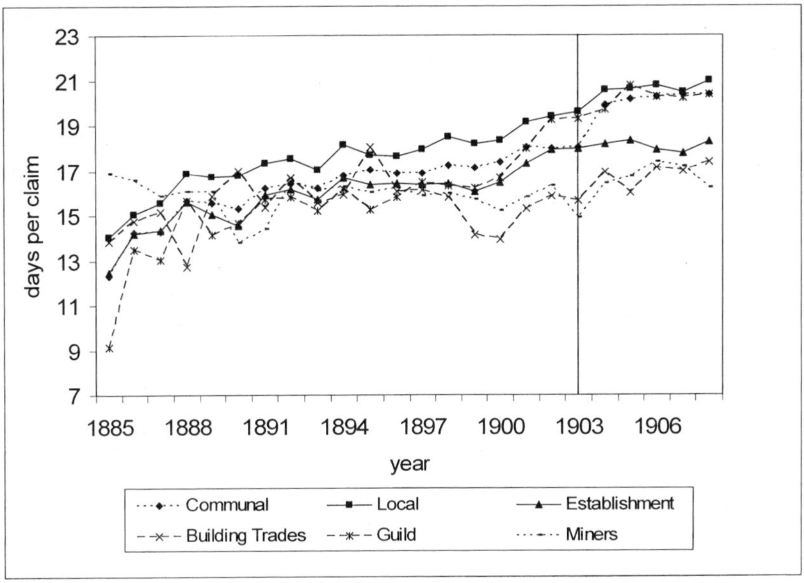

FIGURE 3.3. Average duration of claims in compulsory German funds. The vertical line marks the change in legal minimum number of weeks of benefits from thirteen to twenty-six. (Data from U.S. Commissioner of Labor, *Twenty-fourth Annual Report*, pp. 1244–1245.)

sickness absence time, and this was known, perhaps even by Rubinow, at the time. First, as figure 3.3 shows, the increase in duration long predated the change in the law. Second, actuaries in Leipzig studied this particular question and concluded that an increase in the maximum benefit period from thirteen to twenty-six weeks would, at most, add a couple of days to the claim durations. For example, for a man between the ages of twenty-five and thirty-four, it would increase the average duration of a claim from nineteen days to twenty-one days. The effect of two additional days of absence by workers who made claims would be to add only a fraction to the overall average number of days missed by all workers. Third, from 1885 to 1903, the share of funds that provided more than thirteen weeks' benefits remained small, increasing from 19 percent to 24 percent. The change in the law, then, could account for only a small amount of the overall increase of 3.1 days. As discussed below, a better explanation for the increasing duration of sickness claims in Germany was the moral hazard effect of sick pay.[16]

Requiring physician approval of claims may have reduced moral hazard, but it also added a principal-agent conflict. As in the American case, European physicians made clinical decisions in different ways depending on who their principal was. If it was the worker, he was more likely to be certified as incapacitated; if the fund, the worker was less likely to be so certified. As a result, funds needed fallback policies to counter the agency problem. In France, after passage of the Pension Act of 1910, mutual aid society members who wanted to be examined by their own "treating physician" could do so only after getting approval from a fund-employed "controlling physician."[17] In German funds that offered free choice of physician, fund-employed doctors monitored independent physicians by performing second examinations. The records of such examinations confirm the existence of such principal-agent conflicts.

German funds and their members both enjoyed the right to demand a second opinion from a variety of "confidential medical advisors," either fund-employed physicians or committees composed of physicians' and insurers' representatives. The results suggest that the physician-agent's diagnosis depended on the identity of the principal. Given free choice of nonsalaried physicians, as in most compulsory funds, patients were the principals. The personal physicians who gave the initial diagnoses of incapacitation were their agents. Medical advisors who monitored the primary physicians were agents of the insurers, and the likelihood of claim approval reflected these relationships. Table 3.2 shows the results of such second examinations in three regional fund groups. Whereas initial consultations tended to favor the worker, second examinations favored the fund. Between one-eighth and one-third of workers who had obtained statements from their own physician that they were incapacitated returned to work rather than be examined by a fund doctor. These workers either recovered quickly or lacked confidence in the veracity of their claims, the latter possibility suggesting the moral hazard of absenteeism. German workers, physicians, and their supervisors all understood the implications of agency. Physicians wanted to retain even their most annoying patients, those who presented with dubious symptoms, in order to maintain the capitation fees that accompanied them. Contemporary observers asserted that personal physicians thus gamed the system by approving questionable claims. The fund's medical advi-

Table 3.2.

Results of second opinions in Germany, 1909–1910

FUND GROUP, YEAR	LEIPZIG, 1910		KÖNIGSBERG, 1909		KÖNIGSBERG, 1910		KIEL, 1910	
	N	%	N	%	N	%	N	%
Referrals	8,497		3,179		2,657		1,415	
Returned to work before second exam	1,300	15	544	17	355	13	480	34
Second examinations	5,827		2,635		2,302		935	
Able to return to work immediately	2,739	47	828	31	841	37	346	37
Able to return to work within a week	699	12	545	21	498	22	361	39
Other (e.g., further examination, sent to hospital)	583	10	643	25	436	18	145	16
Unable to work	1,806	31	619	23	527	23	83	9

Source: Gibbon, *Medical Benefit*, pp. 117–118.

Notes: Data for the number who returned to work are given as a share of all referrals; other outcomes are shown as shares of second examinations. In Leipzig, among workers who were not examined a second time were 1,259 who did not appear for the examination and 111 who were excused.

sors then routinely rejected the claims, thereby keeping the fund financially healthy and the attending physician's pay intact, while allowing him to blame the second physician for the rejection.[18]

The point of this example is to note the contemporary understanding of the intricacies of incentive conflicts with regard to physician pay. The AALL seems to have understood only dimly the moral hazard its bill would create (or worsen) and the consequences of their failure to specify how physicians would be organized. An official at the New York Academy of Medicine who was a supporter of the AALL, E. H. Lewinski-Corwin, observed that some American proposals limited the personal physician's authority to grant certificates specifically to prevent "the patronizing of 'easy' physicians observed in Germany." Sensing popular resistance to the surrender of this option, however, the AALL explicitly made free choice of physician part of newer versions of the standard bill. But it also called for a "medical officer" who would examine patients and determine eligibility for sick pay "in the interests of insured patients, physicians, and carriers." This feature removed from the worker's physician the most important authority he possessed and negated much of the attractiveness of free choice of personal physician. Nor did the proposed bill specify how these watchmen would be watched, nor whose interests they would consider first when interests conflicted.[19]

If information problems were pervasive in European social insurance plans, the burdens of adverse selection were unique to voluntary funds. Compulsory funds had to accept all comers and so enrolled risks high and low. Among prospective members of voluntary funds, workers who believed they were likely to make a claim were especially motivated to buy coverage, but for funds to enroll a disproportionate share of high-risk workers was a death sentence. One way to encourage low-risk workers to join would be to reduce their premiums. The French practice was to use a community rate for premiums, that is, to charge one price for all insured workers regardless of risk. Some compulsory funds attempted to charge experience-rated premiums. In Austrian funds the worker's age on joining determined his dues for the duration of his membership, with older entrants paying more. In general, voluntary funds used methods other than community rating to discourage older applicants who were poorer risks. Some simply rejected applicants older than forty because, according to a contemporary advice manual for French fund managers, "the risk of illness is considerably augmented after that age."[20] But such methods were not enough.

The most direct evidence for adverse selection in voluntary funds appeared in German records. Because compulsory and voluntary insurance operated side-by-side in Germany, member age distributions and claim rates in each pool can be compared. Figures 3.4 and 3.5 illustrate male enrollment and absenteeism rates by age group in the best-documented German funds, those operating around Leipzig. Figure 3.4 shows that the age structure of compulsory funds was skewed toward younger members and that of voluntary funds favored older members, indicating adverse selection of older members in voluntary funds. Stronger evidence of selection problems, even after controlling for age, appears in figure 3.5. Within each age group, an average voluntary fund member claimed far more sick days per year than did an average compulsory fund member. Members of voluntary funds who were in their early twenties had extraordinary sickness rates, nearly as high as the rates of those in their sixties. A contemporary German observer explained why in classic adverse selection terms: "Practically all the male population, including the weaker and those who are physically less valuable, are sent to work in the earlier ages; in a few years, however, the weaker persons must give up the occupations in which they are engaged, but *realizing their need for insurance,* continue their membership as voluntary members."[21]

As in the United States, voluntary funds in Europe recognized that disproportionate numbers of applicants were likely to make a claim, but they also knew how to compensate for this disadvantage. The simplest way was to require that applicants be examined by a physician. Whereas compulsory funds did not routinely examine applicants, voluntary funds required medical examinations conducted by physicians whom they employed directly. Danish funds were particularly sensitive to selection problems. They admitted ill applicants into funds as long as they agreed never to make a claim based on current illnesses. Clauses excluding preexisting conditions were typical of American sickness fund regulations as well.[22]

Ultimately, voluntary funds in Europe and in America experienced different fates. European strategies to relieve pressure on finances

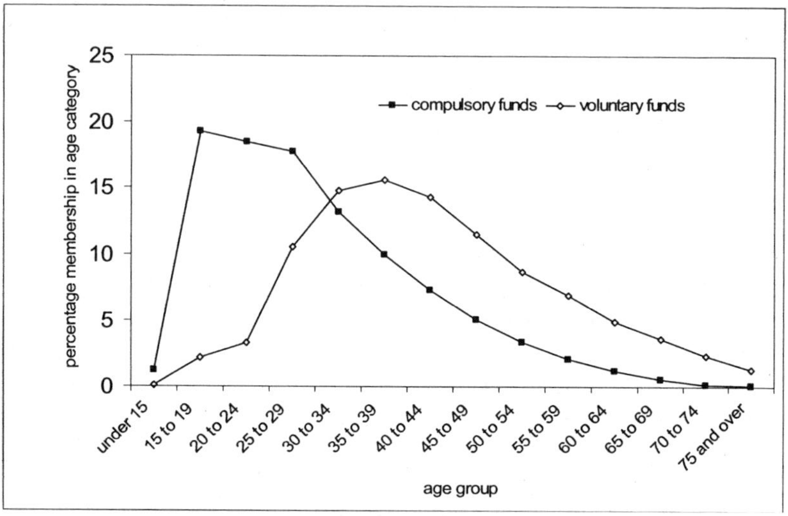

FIGURE 3.4. Age distribution of male members of sickness funds in Leipzig, 1887–1905. N = 952,674 person-years of compulsory members and N = 43,771 person-years of voluntary members. (Data from U.S. Commissioner of Labor, *Twenty-fourth Annual Report*, pp. 1257, 1259.)

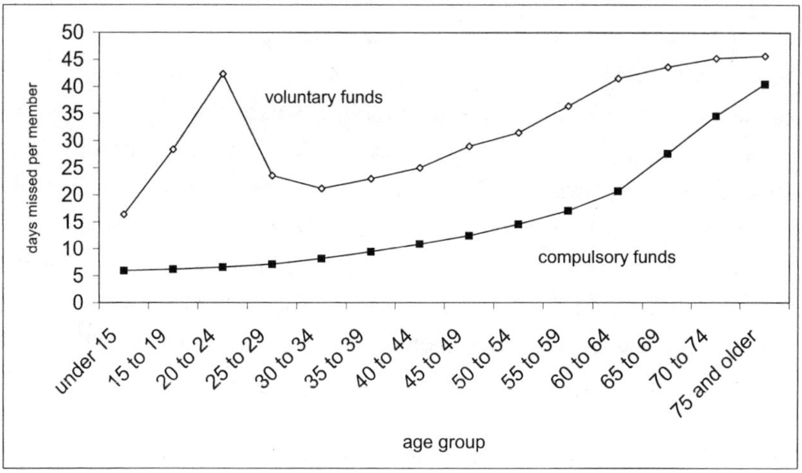

FIGURE 3.5. Sick days by age group, male members of sickness funds in Leipzig, 1887–1905. N = 952,674 person-years of compulsory members and N=43,771 person-years of voluntary members. (Data from U.S. Commissioner of Labor, *Twenty-fourth Annual Report*, pp. 1257, 1263.)

failed, leading to the funds' demise. Belgian funds, desperate to enroll more dues-paying members, offered ever more valuable benefits, which exacerbated their chronic financial problems. Exclusion of the needy and declining interest among the able-bodied represented a serious political problem. During the Great Depression, Belgian funds adopted a policy of rejecting more claims as an explicit survival strategy. Debates about compulsory insurance that had begun in the 1890s continued for half a century until ultimately compulsory coverage became the only way to maintain the Belgian funds' viability.[23]

Similar problems plagued the French system. Funds found themselves in over their heads when they expanded benefits to include pensions and unemployment insurance while their original efforts to provide sickness insurance remained actuarially unsound. Theodore Zeldin summarized the failures of the French societies: "Ignorance of the principles governing insurance was common, methods of administration amateur in the extreme. . . . The most serious omission was that the whole movement was never established on an actuarial basis." French establishment funds became ever more dependent on subsidies from sponsoring firms. Among all French funds, the value of assets per participating member fell by 28 percent from 1898 to 1905. The instability of voluntary insurance was not resolved until after World War II, when compulsory social insurance was imposed.[24]

Because of ongoing financial difficulties, voluntary European funds ordered physicians to limit expenses. Members could have thwarted this strategy by seeking physicians who were willing to bend the rules governing spending, but precisely in order to prevent shopping for physicians who would provide desired diagnoses, these funds typically denied members the ability to choose their own doctor.[25]

The contrast with compulsory German funds was stark. Members were generally allowed to choose a physician from a list of doctors provided by the local medical association. These doctors were not usually on salary but were paid by the procedure. Although German fund physicians were urged to be as economical as possible, constraints on benefits were less binding than in France. Perhaps the clearest difference between the two kinds of funds appeared in the chief complaint lodged against each system's physicians. French physicians were typically criticized for performing too few of their therapeutic duties owing to constraints imposed by the plans. German funds, on the other hand, feared that physicians too readily judged workers to be incapacitated, which resulted in overspending on sick leave and medical benefits. The results of second examinations confirmed German insurers' fears that physicians certified incapacity too readily. The insurers had almost no recourse because the primary sanction imposed on malingering workers was not denial of benefits but bed rest.[26]

Differences in financial health between compulsory and voluntary funds influenced their ability to provide for sick members. Figure 3.2 shows the annual numbers of missed work days per member for which the worker received sick pay. Among the voluntary Belgian, French, and Danish funds the trend was slowly but steadily downward. Financially weak voluntary funds reduced the number of paid days off for sick members. These declines were gradual, but over time they amounted to about a day less per year for the average worker. For comparison, consider the trends in Germany and Austria. In those cases the increase in days missed was considerable. The average Austrian worker missed about two additional days and the average German worker nearly three. There is no evidence to suggest that baseline worker health levels varied much by country.

The increasing availability of sick leave and rising value of benefits played an important role in enabling workers in compulsory insurance funds to absent themselves when sick. Fund finances were critical in determining whether the supply of sick benefits would meet demand. As the French statistician and reformer Jacques Bertillon summarized it: "The fact is that when these societies grant compensation they attach less importance to their regulations than to the state of their till. A rich society gives its help more liberally than a poor one; and this is absolutely the sole cause of the large English societies, which are often very old and generally rich, granting more daily indemnities than the French (for instance), who are obliged to exercise the strictest economy."[27] As for the English, so for the German societies, whose liberality I examine more closely.

The relation between sickness insurance and absenteeism in the German compulsory funds can be estimated statistically and then compared to the corresponding American data. The German funds are especially useful because the American reformers repeatedly claimed that they would serve as models for American reforms. Compulsory funds for all workers other than miners fell into five categories. Local sickness funds *(Ortskrankenkassen)* were funds for workers in particular industries and regions. Establishment funds *(Betriebskrankenkassen)* were sponsored by particular firms. Guild funds *(Innungskrankenkassen)* served members of particular guilds, and builders' funds *(Baukrankenkassen)* typically were created for construction workers who were building a particular project. Communal sickness insurance *(Gemeindekrankenversicherung)* served as a catch-all institution, established by local governments to provide insurance to workers who were required to obtain it but were not covered by any of the other funds.

Table 3.3 shows the results of a series of fixed-effects regressions in which the sickness insurance funds of a particular group in a particular year reported information about claims and benefits. In order to show how sickness insurance claims were related to benefits, the table reports three measures of claims as dependent variables. "Days missed" represents the total number of compensated sick days divided by the number of fund members, or the prevalence of absence due to sickness. "Frequency" (or incidence) reports the number of members who made a successful sickness claim divided by the number of members in the fund, so it is the share of fund members sick enough to make an approved claim. "Duration" is the number of compensated sick days divided by the number of claimants, so it approximates the duration of a typical case. The number of days missed is the product of frequency and duration. It is not necessary that a given independent variable have the same impact on both frequency and duration.[28]

The regression results provide another perspective on the role of medical treatment and the existence of moral hazard. The effect of medical benefits is statistically unambiguous—it led to fewer and generally shorter absences—but how this occurred is less clear. It is possible that medical treatment enabled workers to recover in such short order that they did not miss enough work to qualify for sickness benefits. The efficacy of medical and surgical therapeutics was improving during this period. Physicians may have been able to get their patients back to work sooner by directly improving their health.[29]

At the same time, one negative coefficient, that for medical spend-

Table 3.3.

Sick leave and benefits in compulsory German insurance funds, 1888–1908

DEPENDENT VARIABLE	MEAN	A DAYS MISSED	B FREQUENCY	C DURATION	D DAYS MISSED	E FREQUENCY	F DURATION
Mean value		6.95	0.38	18.19			
		(3.16)	(0.20)	(1.78)			
Intercept		−18.67***	0.49	−19.02***	−26.95***	−6.37	−21.58***
		(3.37)	(3.46)	(2.30)	(3.96)	(3.89)	(2.27)
Log of real sick pay	0.23	0.72***	0.71***	0.21***			
per day	(0.06)	(0.10)	(0.10)	(0.08)			
Share over 50%	0.12				0.74*	1.23***	−0.30
	(0.07)				(0.40)	(0.39)	(0.24)
Log of real medical	0.23	−0.90***	−1.03***	−0.17*	−0.33***	−0.44***	0.04
benefits per day	(0.05)	(0.09)	(0.08)	(0.09)	(0.07)	(0.06)	(0.05)
Log of average	628	0.14***	0.14***	0.04	0.09	0.06	0.04
fund size	(296)	(0.05)	(0.05)	(0.03)	(0.06)	(0.06)	(0.03)
Year	1900	0.001***	−0.0008	0.01***	0.02***	0.003	0.01***
	(6.08)	(0.0002)	(0.002)	(0.001)	(0.002)	(0.002)	(0.001)

Frequency				−0.29***			−0.16***
				(0.07)			(0.06)
Communal fund	0.17	−0.06	−0.16**	0.05	−0.35***	−0.37***	−0.04
		(0.06)	(0.06)	(0.04)	(0.07)	(0.07)	(0.04)
Local fund	0.52	−0.30***	−0.45***	0.03	−0.22**	−0.32***	0.05
		(0.06)	(0.06)	(0.05)	(0.08)	(0.08)	(0.05)
Building fund	0.002	0.31***	0.28***	0.11**	0.38***	0.42***	0.03
		(0.07)	(0.08)	(0.05)	(0.10)	(0.10)	(0.06)
Guild fund	0.02	−0.24***	−0.35***	0.007	−0.26***	−0.36***	0.05
		(0.03)	(0.03)	(0.03)	(0.04)	(0.04)	(0.03)
Adjusted R^2		0.97	0.96	0.93	0.96	0.95	0.93

Sources: U.S. Commissioner of Labor, *Twenty-fourth Annual Report;* Kaiserlichen Statistischen Amt, *Statistik der Krankenversicherung.*

Notes: N = 105. Dependent variables in regressions are logged; mean values are weighted but unlogged for all variables. In columns, frequency = number of claimants divided by the total number of members; duration = number of compensated days divided by the number of claimants. Share 50% or more = proportion of funds that provided sick pay above the legal minimum of 50% of regular pay. Medical benefits includes payments to physicians and for medicines and equipment; excludes hospital charges. Establishment funds omitted. White tests indicated homoskedastic residuals. Regressions weighted by number of fund members. Mean values: standard deviations in parentheses; regression results: standard errors in parentheses.

*significant at the .1 level; **significant at the .05 level; ***significant at the .01 level ing in regression C, may also reflect the ability of employers to get physicians in their employ to end workers' eligibility for benefits sooner rather than later, without regard to the workers' actual health. When American reformers advocated for the German system instead of the British system, they noted that British physicians made clinical decisions separate from the financial state of the insurance carriers, which may have increased British physicians' willingness to certify those workers as too sick to work. The other side of the coin, as reflected in these regression coefficients, may have been that German physicians were more aware of fund finances in certifying workers for compensated absence, even if French physicians were, perhaps, too well aware of financial concerns.[30]

More valuable benefits were associated with greater absenteeism, which provides strong evidence for moral hazard. In these regressions German sickness benefits were measured two ways: the share of all funds that offered more than the legal minimum of half of regular pay and the real value of payments divided by the number of sick days. Coefficients for both variables were positive and significant in all but one case. Sick pay seems to have been particularly influential in increasing the frequency of absence. Both sick pay measures are consistent with moral hazard: as sick benefits became more valuable, workers took more time off, and in particular a larger share of the workforce took time off.

Workers may have benefited from the increasing incidence of compensated absence. Considering duration as a function of frequency indicates that the greater the share of the workforce that made any claims of illness, the shorter those episodes were. That is, funds were underwriting either relatively short-term absences for many of their members or rather longer absences for a few. To some extent this may have represented a shift in absenteeism regimes. Early in this period workers had stoically reported for work while becoming sicker and sicker and then missed many weeks of work after their condition became critical. Later in the period more and shorter absences became common, but that was precisely because workers could afford to take time off to rest when somewhat ill. As a consequence they recovered before becoming gravely ill. In this regard the American opponents of state insurance misled the public when they interpreted rising sickness rates as evidence of declining worker health, when in fact increasing absenteeism was really a sign that ever more workers were able to rest in a timely fashion, and this prevented later declines in their health.[31]

The state of European sickness insurance presented a puzzle to Progressives and their opponents in the United States. The Progressives recognized the breadth of the German system's coverage but did not acknowledge that it, too, suffered from basic problems caused by information asymmetries. Their proposals reflected this denial. Their opponents chose to ignore failures of the completely voluntary schemes used in France and Belgium. Increased absence from work in Germany was due in part to incentives provided by the sickness insurance program, but that did not necessarily mean that workers were sicker—only that they were absent more often, in part for financial reasons. Miles Dawson saw a shift in explanations for this trend away from invoking moral hazard and adverse selection. With approval he noted that more researchers were coming to understand that workers were increasingly obeying their physicians and staying home. In proposing the latter explanation as the better one, he was, in part, correct.[32] But he simply pushed the issue of causation one step back rather than resolving it. What inclined more workers to listen to their doctors and follow these particular orders? Much of the answer must have been the increasing availability of paid sick leave that allowed workers to obey those orders to stay home. That is, ultimately moral hazard explained much of the increase in absenteeism.

By virtue of their voluntary membership and lack of government aid, the American funds most closely resembled the French and Belgian funds. Unlike the British and German systems, the American system was voluntary, and no government subsidies were forthcoming, as they were in Scandinavia. But the difference between the American system and the Gallic ones was that it was sustainable. Whereas the voluntary European networks eventually collapsed and were replaced with compulsory insurance, the voluntary American networks laid the foundation for continual defeat of proposals to create state-sponsored insurance.

One way to address the question why the United States differs from Europe in terms of universal health insurance has been to ask how it came to differ from Great Britain and Germany. It might be more productive to consider the French and Belgian cases and ask why the United

States did not end up with a similar national insurance plan, because before World War I the structural similarities among the three cases were great. Yet the American funds also differed in important ways, for example, by offering benefits that were much higher in value. Additional structural differences included the American focus on sickness insurance, and in the broader picture, the role of nonmembers. Instead of enrolling honorary members (outsiders who joined essentially as an act of charity), American funds promoted worker self-reliance while strategically accepting funds, in-kind payments, and advice from employers.[33] The next three chapters explore the impact of these factors on the funds' success.

PART TWO RISE AND OPERATION

CHAPTER FOUR

The Rise of Sickness Funds

> Existing agencies for health insurance in the United States are impressive because they clearly show that within the comparatively short modern industrial period a large number and a variety of collective efforts have been made by the wage earners themselves to provide against sickness.
>
> —EDGAR SYDENSTRICKER, 1916

AROUND 1907 the three brothers who owned and operated F. C. Huyck and Sons investigated how a sickness fund might work at their company. Huyck and Sons (the three were the sons) employed about 275 workers in Rensselaer, New York, producing papermakers' felts. Through personal connections they were able to hire a well-known consulting actuary from New York City, Miles Dawson, who had designed and established such funds in several other plants. Dawson would later travel to Europe to examine social insurance institutions there on behalf of the Russell Sage Foundation, and still later he became an officer of the American Association for Labor Legislation. The Huyck brothers handed Dawson a roster of employees with their ages, occupations, and tenure at the mill, with instructions that the company was to make all the payments into pension and accident insurance funds and most of the contributions to the health insurance fund.

Dawson drew up a proposal that limited employee payments for health insurance to 1 percent of wages, with additional costs covered by the company. The fund would pay half wages after the third day of sickness, as well as all medical, surgical, and hospital bills. A separate fund for each sex would be managed by a committee composed of one member-worker and two company officials. The Huycks accepted Dawson's plan and offered it to their employees on 1 May 1911 on the condition that 95 percent of the workers signal their intention to join within the next month. As it turned out, 98 percent joined within a week, which was more than enough to inaugurate the Huyck and Sons sickness fund. Although membership remained voluntary, nearly every new employee under forty-five years of age (and who passed what Edmund Huyck described as a "simple" medical examination) joined. The company hired a salaried physician whom workers could visit at work or who would come to them at home. The sickness fund grew with the firm so that by 1917 it covered around four hundred employees, about 40 percent of whom were women, at a cost of 1.6 percent of the payroll. Peer pressure from co-workers kept sick employees from abusing their rights to benefits, according to Edmund Huyck. He concluded that the ability of the fund to improve employee health and attendance made it "worth to our company far more than it has cost us."[1]

The story of the Huyck and Sons fund contains far more detail than is generally known about the genesis of most sickness funds. Its design by one of the most prominent health insurance experts of the day made the fund unusual. But it had many characteristics typical of most sickness funds, and the desire of the firm's owners may not have been very unusual among certain Progressive-Era businessmen. The Huyck brothers may have begun the fund for benevolent reasons, but the conclusion that it was a good idea because it pulled its weight financially was a common hope among businessmen who operated or sponsored such funds.

The Huyck and Sons sickness fund is an illustration of a larger-scale phenomenon of the later nineteenth and early twentieth centuries: the founding and growth of industrial sickness funds. This chapter explores the motivations of companies and workers for establishing such funds and sketches the history of attempts to protect workers from unexpected ill health in the nineteenth century. It then describes the breadth and growth of sickness insurance in the United States. It was far from marginal: the earliest tally of nonfraternal sickness funds, performed in 1890, found 1,259 mutual assistance societies that offered cash or medical benefits or both to their members. The three decades leading up to the Progressive efforts to create state-sponsored insurance were a period of growth and development for the nascent private insurance network.

* * *

Companies that began sickness funds did not do so out of the kindness of their hearts. They did it to make money. At the Chicago, Burlington, and Quincy Railroad, "the justification for the Relief Department," one official wrote in 1895, "must be that it pays. . . . That it does pay directly, we know from the figures." One way in which employers expected benefit associations to pay for themselves was to reduce costly absences and turnover. Thomas I. Read of the New Jersey Zinc Company explained how this worked: "As in the case of accidents, when the man is absent another man must be supplied to take his place, and this increases both the labor turnover and the accident rate; in other words it is a source of considerable loss to the company as well as to the man. Realization of the seriousness of the situation is compelling some employers largely as a business proposition to institute more or less complete medical care for sick employees, and to encourage the formation of establishment funds for the payment of cash sick benefits."[2]

The employer and the employee enjoyed a coincidence of interests in the sense that the employer wanted his workforce to show up for work, and the worker did not want to be so ill as to be unable to work. There were exceptions to these generalizations. The employer was happy for union organizers to stay home, and at least occasionally the worker looked forward to "blessid idleness," as Finley Peter Dunne's fictional Mr. Dooley observed, since "no matther what's th' matther with him, he don't suffer half as much pain as he would in pursoot iv two dollars a day." In most cases an alignment of interests worked to reduce absence due to sickness. The healthier the worker, the fuller his pay packet and the lower the employer's costs. As one executive said, "The worker's health must be attended to, or dollars slip into the 'loss' column."[3]

Some historians have interpreted the offer of fringe benefits such as health insurance as an effort to coerce workers into surrendering their mobility. Benefits were fine per se, according to this view, but by making eligibility contingent on continued employment they froze workers in place and thereby contributed to job-lock. Compensating workers with cash that they could take with them to their next job encouraged turnover, but rights to benefits that were not portable led to a workforce that was less free to quit and move on. Thus insurance translated into a kind of control that management could exercise over workers. These historians have dismissed labor union and fraternal society benefit operations, which offered portable insurance, as financially unstable and thus unreliable.[4]

Workers understood, if grudgingly, that in providing benefits companies expected funds to make money, or at least not to lose any. To workers, sickness insurance that cost their employer more than it earned for them looked like a gift, and workers who wanted to join a sickness fund wanted no part of a charitable operation. Worse than being a charity recipient was the prospect of being known as a charity recipient, and relief obtained with no contribution appeared to be charity. Employees at the New Jersey metal shop of Samuel L. Moore and Sons demanded to pay for hospital services that the firm proposed to provide for free, specifically so they would "not be regarded as charity patients." Where the choice was between medical attention they could not afford and charity care, some workers suffered unattended "because they do not want to become objects of charity," according to a New York hospital manager.[5]

Activists and companies alike were quick to weigh in. "Health insurance, in the real sense of the term," wrote Warren and Sydenstricker, "is not relief or charity." Charles G. DuBois, comptroller of the Bell System, explained, "This plan is not in any sense a charity, and it is not so regarded by employees. . . . The problems involved are not essentially different from other business problems which have to be worked out carefully and thoughtfully, that the advantages of sickness insurance from a business point of view are probably worth the cost." Employers presented sickness insurance as a worthwhile investment for both workers and firm owners.[6]

Workers viewed sickness funds as a great improvement over a simple alternative: passing the hat. To keep the wife or widow and children of a co-worker from entering the poor house on his death or incapacitation, workers sent a paper around their shop, and contributors wrote their name and a dollar amount they deemed appropriate. The amount varied with the injured employee's popularity, his time on the job, the time of year, and other concerns. This practice led in some cases to injured workers' receiving much more than they needed and in others to needy families' suffering doubly from the initial catastrophe and then by the insult of a small collection. Irregular dependence on the charity of the employer could produce equally unfair results. Chicago, Burlington, and Quincy general manager Thomas Potter explained his strategy for relief of injured employees or their survivors: "We make the best settlement we can. It should all depend on how good a man he is whether you allow him anything or not."[7]

The solution to this arbitrariness was to systematize collection of contributions and provision of relief to the sick, the injured, and survivors of the deceased. Replacing discretion with rules created a systematic and thus fairer process, and workers preferred regular collection of dues to surprise solicitations (or surprise assessments). A Colorado employer praised sickness funds because they enabled employees "to get rid of these subscription lists and to take care of these cases without the stigma of charity." The decline of unsystematic sickness, accident, and death benefits was evident. A few of the sickness funds that appeared in the 1890 census described their benefit payments as "at the discretion of the society," but within two decades the practice had virtually disappeared.[8]

The main motivation behind the institution of sickness funds was to protect members in case of sickness—but how often did that occur? This is a much more difficult question than it may first appear, particularly from the perspective of the party insuring against such an event. Payment of life insurance benefits is triggered by a very easily defined event: death of the insured. Payment of sickness insurance benefits would follow sickness, but it cannot be as clearly defined as death. As the California Social Insurance Commission understood, "being or feeling sick is purely a subjective matter which can scarcely be recorded statistically. But being unable to pursue the employment, and especially receiving compensation for such a disability[,] is a definite fact which yields itself to statistical observation." Thus, whereas in reality a worker's state of health fell at a point on a continuum, for insurance purposes *sickness* described one member of a dichotomy between being healthy or insufficiently sick to stay home, on one hand, and being too sick to work, on the other. The division between the two was not a bright line but one that shifted depending on the worker's age, sex, and cultural background, whether he carried sickness insurance, and, if so, how valuable its benefits were and how difficult it was to obtain them. Thus, to measure the ill-defined phenomenon of sickness we have to use a well-defined measure, compensated absence from work, which includes the effects of other factors besides physical health.[9]

The California Social Insurance Commission noted another problem for the study of American rates of absence due to sickness: "It is extremely difficult to establish a reliable sickness rate in advance of some system of health insurance."[10] Because it lacked a central governing agency, the United States had no single source of consistent statistics about membership, claims, or benefits. There was nothing comparable to death registration for cases of morbid illness. That helps explain the absence of sickness funds from much of the historical record. The statistics that are available were produced in hit-or-miss fashion by infrequent federal surveys of funds, one-off state surveys of workers and funds, and private surveys such as the Metropolitan Life sickness surveys of 1915–1917. The disparate record these investigations left nonetheless tells a consistent story of sickness insurance in Progressive-Era America.

Given the lack of systematic evidence, it may not be surprising that Progressives and their opponents did not agree about the magnitude of sickness rates. Estimates of absence due to illness in this period fall into two sorts: those with and those without supporting data. Each type reported on the same phenomenon: a day of work missed by a worker due to illness. Estimates with data indicated that, on average, a worker took about six sick days per year. Table 4.1 records the results of several contemporary surveys of workers and funds, all but one of which reported a range of absenteeism from 4.3 to 7.4 days per worker. These figures were consistent with absenteeism data from state labor bureau surveys of the late nineteenth century, as can be seen in Chapter 7. These figures indicate that, as a share of a work year that contained about three hundred days, about 2 percent of that time was lost due to illness, which, surprisingly, is about the same rate as found in present-day data.[11]

The one source that yielded a substantially higher absence rate made its mark in the Progressive literature. In *Final Report of the Commission on Industrial Relations,* B. S. Warren of the Public Health Service concluded that the average absence rate for more than thirty million American wage earners was nine days—but without evidence that would explain how the figure was derived. A later government statistician, Ernest Bradford, refused to include it in his 1922 compilation of causes

Table 4.1.
Estimated rates of absence owing to sickness

YEAR(S)	NUMBER OF WORKERS	SAMPLE	SICK DAYS PER WORKER YEAR
1901[a]	25,440	National sample of working families	5.2
1904–1914[b]	84,359–140,426	New York state union members	4.4
1908–1914[b]	66,968–183,202	Massachusetts union members	4.6
1912–1916[c]	185,018	Workman's Sick and Death Benefit Fund	6.6
1913[d]	170,000	Iron and steel workers	9
1915[e]	34,490	Rochester, New York	5.9
1915[e]	3,491	Trenton, New Jersey	6.1
1916[e]	66,007	State of North Carolina	7.1
1916[e]	97,259	Boston, Massachusetts	5.6
1917[e]	24,043	Chelsea district, New York City	4.3
1917[e]	374,301	Pennsylvania and West Virginia cities	5.7
1917[e]	34,267	Kansas City, Missouri	7.4
1917[d]	n/a	Dallas survey	6.8
1917[d]	302,584	California Social Insurance Commission	6.0
1917[f]	12,019	Philadelphia survey	5.7
1919–1921[d]	6,700	Rubber workers in Massachusetts	6.6

Note: All samples are nationwide unless specified otherwise.

[a]From U.S. Commissioner of Labor, *Eighteenth Annual Report*, p. 45.

[b]From Warren and Sydenstricker, "Statistics of Disability," p. 993.

[c]From Emmet, "Disability," p. 25.

[d]From Bradford, "Industrial Unemployment," p. 32.

[e]From Metropolitan Life surveys of policy holders, "nearly all . . . of the wage-earning group," reprinted in State of Illinois, *Report*, p. 5, with days estimated by multiplying the percentage who were sick on a given day by 309 workdays.

[f]From Health Insurance Commission of Pennsylvania, *Report*, p. 53.

of industrial unemployment "on account of inability to judge of the character of the supporting data." Nonetheless, to Progressives who advocated for government insurance to address high rates of worker sickness, nine days it was, and occasionally higher. The abundant data that support the claim of fewer rather than more days lost to sickness suggest that the smaller number was closer to the truth. The larger number may have been inflated by enthusiasm for the Progressive cause.[12]

Apart from the quantity of sickness, Progressives and their opponents could not agree on the meaning of qualitative changes in measurements of it. We know now that the composition of causes of death shifted dramatically during the late nineteenth and early twentieth centuries away from infectious disease (for example, typhoid fever) and toward chronic conditions (for example, congestive heart failure). Other studies have indicated that differences in cause of death and cause of absence due to sickness could differ considerably, so it is important to examine causes of illness specifically where such scarce data can be found. Table 4.2 illustrates this epidemiologic transition in terms of causes of illness in 1880 and again in 1921. Combining tuberculosis with more general infectious disease shows a decline in such infectious disease, and a slight increase in chronic illness, similar to well-known patterns in cause-of-death data, appeared. To Progressives, the rise in chronic illness such as congestive heart failure was an avoidable tragedy that government insurance could help prevent. Their opponents countered that no evidence existed to show that the medical care that insurance coverage enabled workers to obtain had any effect on such diseases. Medicine did, however, have some limited powers in regard to heart conditions—the use of amyl nitrate and nitroglycerin to control angina symptoms developed in this period. Many chronic conditions that were becoming more common were excluded from coverage by many sickness funds, and such exclusions boded poorly for future well-being. As many fund charters stood, should medicine ever develop effective therapies for circulatory disease, heart disease, and cancer, members would not receive benefits for their treatment. This suggests that sickness funds would need to develop medical coverage in the not-too-distant future.[13]

The first attempts to protect American working men and their families from the consequences of unexpected illness dated from the late eigh-

Table 4.2.
Relative shares of causes of sickness among men

CAUSE OF SICKNESS	1880 U.S. CENSUS (% OF TOTAL)	1921 PUBLIC HEALTH SERVICE SURVEY OF SICKNESS FUNDS (% OF TOTAL)
Infectious diseases	10.9	2.9
Tuberculosis	8.8	2.1
Other respiratory problem	8.2	35.4
Injury or accident	12.7	8.9
Neurological or cognitive problem	11.6	5.4
Sensory or motor problem	8.1	0.0
Chronic or other problem	39.7	45.4

Sources: Elman and Myers, "Age and Sex Differentials" (for 1880); Brundage, "Sickness" (for 1921).
Note: The Census Bureau asked about sickness on the day of the census. The Public Health Service asked about claims of sickness that lasted eight days or longer in the previous quarter and excluded on-the-job injury. The Public Health Service sample size was 66,084.

teenth century. Skilled craftsmen organized mutual assistance societies whose members pledged to aid stricken members in various ways. In Philadelphia in 1796, the Mutual Assistant (sic) Society of Hair Dressers, Surgeon Barbers, Etc. promised to attend customers of sick colleagues. The Carpenters' Company offered to complete the contracts signed by members who became ill, as did the Stone Cutters' Company. A century later, unions representing these very trades were still among the leaders in providing sickness benefits to members. By early in the nineteenth century many such associations had shifted their benefit provisions from in-kind offers of substitute labor to small cash payments. At about this time they also assumed new roles in dispute resolution and efforts to increase wages and earnings.[14]

The first public effort to provide health insurance (and not poor relief) in the United States attempted to manage a particular problem: that of sick itinerant workers. Poor relief in America had been modeled on the English precedent, which required a potential recipient to have established residency (a "settlement") in the town or parish to which he had applied for relief. The federal government recognized that American merchant sailors spent most of their working lives far from their hometowns and that the ports where they landed had little incentive to care for such strangers when they were ill. In 1798, federal customs collectors began to tax arriving American ships twenty cents per sailor to pay for construction and maintenance of marine hospitals. Tax revenues paid for the building of the first marine hospital in Norfolk, Virginia, in 1800, and within a few years new hospitals opened in Charlestown, Massachusetts, and Charleston, South Carolina. Where hospitals were not available the Marine Hospital Service (which continued as the Public Health Service in the twentieth century) arranged for care of ill seamen, paying hospitals or boarding houses three dollars per week.[15]

The Granite Cutters' Union created the first formal union sickness benefit fund in 1877. Membership was voluntary, and the union soon dissolved the fund. It is possible that the granite cutters faced problems with adverse selection that they could not resolve. Whether the Granite Cutters' Union drew in a disproportionate number of the sick and failed to attract the younger and healthier members, as economic theory would suggest, cannot be determined, but given that they set their maximum age for new members at a relatively high fifty-five years, it is a possibility. By 1887 five national unions operated benefit systems: the Cigar Makers, the Iron Moulders, the Granite Cutters, the Carpenters and Joiners, and the German-American Typographia. More detail about these and other union sickness benefit funds appears in Chapter 6.[16]

Commercial health insurance was first offered in the United States in 1847 by the Health Insurance Company of Philadelphia, which was soon joined by firms in Massachusetts and New Jersey. These policies were sold to individuals. The Health Insurance Company estimated the necessary premiums by age, with each group of older policy holders charged more than younger groups were charged for a fixed indemnity of four dollars per week. Like the Granite Cutters' sick fund, each commercial insurer that offered health insurance failed after its beginning. In this case, too, later observers speculated, the culprit was adverse selection. The primitive actuarial information used by these firms had implicitly underestimated claims by older workers and so charged them too little, and they similarly had overpriced policies for younger people. Their policies proved much more popular among older people, and this led to insolvency. This market lay dormant until the 1890s, when some life insurers offered a rider stating that the company would pay cash benefits if a policy holder suffered from one of a short list of "zymotic" (that is, infectious) diseases. Aware of the experimental nature of this insurance, issuing firms attempted to protect themselves with a clause that authorized them to cancel the policy at any time and for any reason.[17]

Group accident and health insurance began in 1891, and two decades later more than one hundred firms in the United States made it their principal or only business. These were still relatively small operations; the first important group contract was sold by the Equitable to Montgomery Ward in 1912. As with individual health insurance, group health and accident insurance appeared without the necessary actuarial technology in place to estimate premiums and benefits properly. To simplify the process, insurers charged the round sum of one dollar per month (much more than a typical industrial sickness fund charged) and guessed at a range of feasible benefits. If the insurer promised benefits that were too generous for available premium income, then the firm strained to deny claims or invoked the cancellation clause. This provoked several state legislatures to consider mandating standardized group health contracts. When the AALL began its efforts to create state health insurance, the idea of group health was still "in its infancy," according to one observer. Whether it could be made profitable was a question that would take several decades to answer, as described in Chapter 10.[18]

The exact date when the first American company founded a sickness fund for its employees cannot be established. By the time the federal Commissioner of Labor surveyed such funds in 1908, the oldest funds dated from the Civil War era. The first was founded in 1863 at a piano factory, and two others had begun in 1865, one at a silversmith's shop and the other at a watchmaker's shop. If the initial establishment funds, like the initial labor union funds, served highly skilled craftsmen, then funds that began after the war such as those at a cotton textile mill

(1869), an iron or steel mill (1870), and a pottery factory (1872) focused on the broader masses of unskilled workers. Larger plants tended to sponsor sickness funds; the average employment in these six establishments (as of 1907) was 1,476 workers. About half of the funds in the sample had been founded in the previous ten years, suggesting that although the survey missed older funds that had dissolved in earlier years, the number of funds early in the twentieth century was growing fairly rapidly.[19]

Estimating the rate of growth in fund numbers or membership is not really feasible. To do so would require comparable statistics of membership at two points in time, and no complete national census of all sickness funds was ever undertaken. The 1890 Census attempted to count all "independent benefit societies," that is, noncommercial and nonfraternal insurance societies that offered sickness and death benefits. Many of these funds, especially those founded before 1870, were organized for men of particular ethnicities, religions, or crafts. Still, plenty of establishment funds were begun in the 1880s, and overall the kinds of societies that fell under this rubric varied tremendously. In Ohio alone there were funds sponsored by manufacturers in small towns (Encaustic Tile Makers' Mutual Aid Company, in Zanesville) and large (Milburn Wagon Company Employees' Mutual Aid Association, in Toledo), by tradesmen (Wheelmakers' Aid and Benefit Association, in Dayton), and by neighborhood residents in a large city (East End Mutual Aid Association, in Cincinnati). Many funds were established and run by ethnic societies.[20] Unfortunately, many of the reported data (numbers of members, for example) did not distinguish between payment of death benefits and sickness benefits, so all that can be extracted now is the number of societies by state. That is valuable information nonetheless, particularly because the Census inquired about the insurance funds years before the height of the Progressive-Era reform attempts.

The census information helps fill large gaps in our understanding of industrial sickness funds regarding location and benefits offered. To show how geographically widespread sickness funds were as early as 1890, figure 4.1 illustrates the numbers of nonfraternal sickness funds by state. The highest numbers were in the most heavily industrialized states of the Northeast and Midwest. But other states such as California,

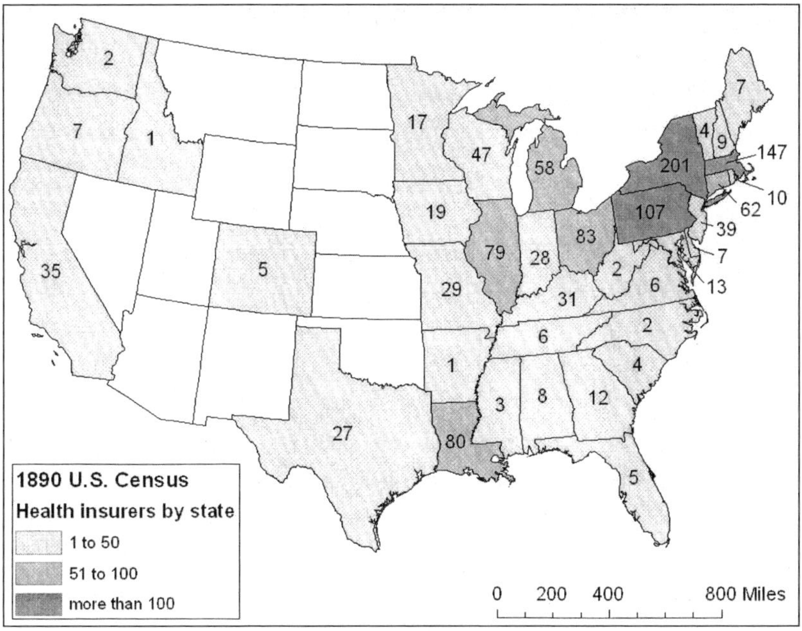

FIGURE 4.1. Independent (nonfraternal) sickness benefit societies appearing in the 1890 Census. (Data from U.S. Department of the Interior, *Report on Insurance*. Map by Timothy Ault, Department of Geography, University of Toledo.)

Kentucky, Missouri, and Texas also hosted large numbers of such societies. The number of Louisiana funds is notable. David Beito suggested several reasons for the popularity of sickness funds there, including Creole leadership in founding and managing funds, support from local Catholic churches, old and ongoing European influences, and fear of frequent yellow fever epidemics.[21]

Progressives often claimed that an important shortcoming of sickness funds was that so few paid for medical services. As early as 1890, about 18 percent of sickness funds offered cash medical benefits or in-kind nursing assistance. Some funds provided a visitor to help the sick member around the house, others sent caretakers to spend the night with the invalid, and still others paid expenses for medicines and equipment. In the South, about half of funds in the band of states from Georgia to Texas offered medical benefits, in contrast to only six percent of funds elsewhere. In fact, the South as a whole, led by Louisiana, accounted for as many funds that provided medical benefits as did the

Northeast and the Midwest combined. It was not the case that the southern funds were of obviously lower quality; an average claim in the South Central states paid $9.34, whereas the average in the North Atlantic states paid $10.71, or nearly two weeks' worth of benefits in both cases. Unfortunately, the Census Bureau did not report numbers of members when it aggregated data for publication, so the numbers of workers and the share who had insurance cannot be determined.[22]

An additional way to understand the breadth of service performed by sickness funds is to consider the variety of industries in which firms sponsored establishment funds. Table 4.3 shows several of the industries that reported on their sickness funds in the 1908 federal survey. Critics of the funds charged that few existed in industries other than railroads and metalworking or in a few "model" employers such as International Harvester. This table suggests that sickness funds served tens of thousands of workers in other manufacturing industries such as ceramics and service industries such as department stores. The "other" category contains a cornucopia of industries such as automobile, firearm, and textile manufacturing, which accounted for a large number of funds and covered workers. Excluding the highly developed railroad benefit programs, and depending on definitions of metal and transportation industries, it is not clear that there were many more covered workers in the model industries than elsewhere. The establishment fund was a widespread phenomenon.[23]

Labor union funds served many union members also. Apart from the leadership of the American Federation of Labor, few believed that labor union sickness funds served their members well. By 1917, though, the California Social Insurance Commission had found that 41 percent of union members there obtained sickness insurance coverage through their union. Lubove detested union funds in particular, describing them as "defective by rational economic criteria" and guided by neither "actuarial controls nor sound management." And yet, a wide range of tradesmen had organized their unions so as to provide sickness benefits. Table 4.4 shows the different types of unions that offered sickness benefits as of a federal survey of funds conducted in 1908. The unions listed in this table were locals, but some national unions operated sickness funds. According to the 1908 survey, nineteen nationals with 4,625 local branches provided sickness benefits. As three-fourths of a century earlier, these

Table 4.3.
Types and numbers of companies with establishment sickness funds and membership, 1908

INDUSTRY	NUMBER OF PLANTS	NUMBER OF MEMBERS
Agricultural implements	8	7,948
Brass goods	7	2,277
Brewed beverages	6	718
Bridges	4	597
Carriages and wagons	3	816
Cereals and flour	4	794
Chemicals	5	3,874
Coal	29	60,821
Cotton goods and related product	9	1,526
Electrical apparatus, and so on	6	7,339
Express company	6	2,724
Furniture	7	1,081
Iron and steel	20	30,365
Leather and leather belting	6	737
Locomotive and railroad	18	24,510
Machinery, tools, machine shops	24	12,511
Mining (zinc, copper, iron ore)	7	7,992
Newspaper	12	1,490
Paint and varnish	4	901
Paper and pulp	11	3,616
Pottery (sanitary and china)	16	1,074
Printing and lithography	15	1,937
Rubber	6	1,231
Shipbuilding	7	5,109
Shoemaking	8	1,449
Store, department	22	29,862
Street railway	25	31,671
Wire	7	1,952
Railroad	31	262,747
Other	125	77,785

Source: U.S. Commission of Labor, *Twenty-third Annual Report.*

nationals included unions for barbers, carpenters and joiners, cigar makers, and granite cutters. The variety of crafts may be surprising, given the criticism of establishment funds for concentration in only a few industries. The large number of railroad union funds, combined with the great extent of benefit funds operated by the railroads themselves, made coverage of railroad workers truly extensive.[24] Overall, the variety of trades represented is notable.

Starting in the late 1870s, several state labor bureaus conducted surveys of individual workers. These surveys seem to have been managed carefully and are among the earliest detailed individual-level surveys. Given the relatively primitive state of data processing technology, many of these agencies opted not to publish summaries of their findings in statistical tables, which would have taken considerable effort to compile. Instead they published the raw data, consisting of line-by-line responses from each worker, with identifying information omitted. Some of these surveys asked workers whether they belonged to a benefit society and how large a benefit they expected to receive if they were injured or ill. These questions allow for estimation of early insurance coverage rates among workers.[25]

Figure 4.2 shows enrollment rates reported in labor bureau surveys for various years and states. This collection included all digitized surveys that asked about benefit society membership. Each point represents the share of workers who reported belonging to a benefit society, without regard to the society's sponsor (fraternal, establishment, union, or other). The first survey was of 347 Iowa teachers in 1884; the last, conducted in 1896 in Kansas, included 539 male wage workers. The largest consistent samples included nearly 15,000 manufacturing and mining workers in Michigan around 1890. The total number of workers who responded to the society membership question was 21,859, and the number responding in the affirmative was 5,881, or 27 percent.[26]

The Connecticut Bureau of Labor Statistics provided a closer look at enrollment rates in its 1891 survey of sickness funds. The bureau examined records of a variety of benefit societies, aiming to cover "all mutual benefit societies doing business within the State." The coverage seems to have been thorough, consisting as it did of a "town-to-town and shop-to-shop canvas, supplemented with more than usual success by inquiries conducted by mail." The Connecticut report included an intrigu-

Table 4.4.

Types and numbers of local unions offering sickness benefits and their membership, 1908

UNION	LOCALS	MEMBERS	UNION	LOCALS	MEMBERS
Barbers	6	1,062	Clerks	1	152
Bill posters	2	414	Electrical workers	6	1,401
Blacksmiths	1	91	Elevator constructors	1	248
Boilermakers	4	248	Engineers, locomotive	7	592
Bookbinders	6	383	Engineers, marine	3	374
Box makers	2	1,716	Engineers, stationary	7	793
Brewery workmen	2	200	Engineers, steam	2	349
Brick workers	1	115	Federal Labor Union (excavators)	1	5,000
Bricklayers and masons	19	9,727			
Bridge workers	3	2,201	Federal Labor Union (horsenail workers)	1	130
Broom makers	2	128			
Brushmakers	1	238	Federal Labor Union (rockmen)	1	1,088
Car workers	1	197			
Carpenters (Brotherhood)	18	7,852	Federal Labor Union (scalemen)	1	25
Carriage workers	2	212			
Cigarmakers	1	28	Federal Labor Union	3	77

Table 4.4.

Types and numbers of local unions offering sickness benefits and their membership, 1908 (*continued*)

UNION	LOCALS	MEMBERS
Fireman, locomotive	3	636
Flour and cereal mill employees	2	58
Foundry employees	2	433
Freight handlers	1	35
Garment workers (ladies)	2	326
Garment workers (united)	3	212
Glass bottle blowers	1	160
Glass workers, flint	6	720
Glass workers (International Association)	2	118
Hatters	4	540
Hod carriers	3	650
Horseshoers	10	1,200
Hotel employees	21	3,573
Iron	1	52
Lace operatives	2	72
Lathers	1	125
Leather workers (amalgamated)	2	352
Letter carriers	7	2,494
Longshoremen	7	3,179
Machinists	10	5,139
Meat cutters	1	70
Metal polishers	1	229
Metal workers	4	436
Mine workers	16	3,879
Miners (Western Federation)	18	11,116
Musicians	4	641
Painters	11	4,866
Pattern makers	2	1,044
Photo engravers	2	150

Plasterers	4	1,092
Printing pressmen	4	1,534
Railroad telegraphers	3	601
Railroad trainmen	10	3,339
Railway carmen	8	1,575
Railway clerks	3	493
Railway conductors	5	516
Railway employees (street and electric)	3	822
Roofers, composition	1	275
Shipwrights	2	142
Slate and tile roofers	1	195
Spinners	1	70
Stage employees	1	67
Steam fitters	3	464
Stereotypers	1	127
Stove mounters	1	36
Switchmen	6	1,054
Tailors	2	910
Teamsters	3	2,968
Typographers	7	1,816
Wire weavers	1	58
Total	324	95,700

Source: U.S. Commissioner of Labor, *Twenty-third Annual Report.*

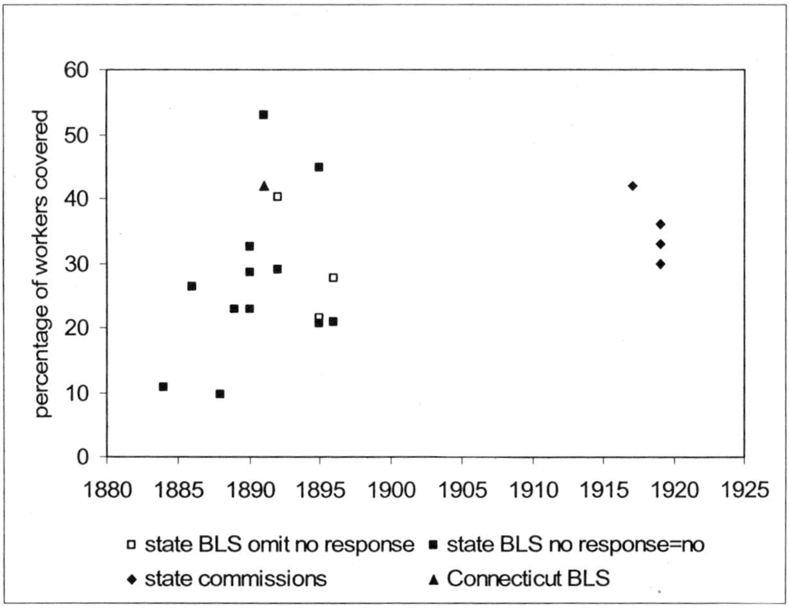

FIGURE 4.2. Percentage of surveyed workers belonging to a benefit society. (Data from State labor bureau surveys in codebooks compiled by Carter et al., www.eh.net/databases/labor. The surveys include Iowa teachers, 1884; Kansas workers, 1884–1887; Michigan stone and clay workers, 1888; Michigan furniture workers, 1889; Michigan agricultural implement workers, 1890; Maine workers, 1890; Missouri workers, 1892; California wage earners, 1892; Wisconsin farmers, 1895; and Kansas wage earners, 1895 and 1896. For the 1891 Connecticut survey see Cummings, "Report" and Lee et al., *Population Redistribution.* For the California, Illinois, and Ohio commissions see table 4.6. For Pennsylvania see Health Insurance Commission of Pennsylvania, *Report,* p. 158.)

ing note that suggested that the 1890 federal census underestimated by far the number of such funds. The state report observed that many fund officials told them that they had had no contact with marshals regarding the 1890 census of insurance, which found sixty-one nonfraternal sickness insurers in the Nutmeg State. Because the state survey found many times that number of funds, it is possible that the federal survey considerably underestimated the number of sickness funds nationwide.[27]

The Connecticut benefit societies were divided into endowment societies, providers of life insurance, societies that offered sick and funeral benefits, and trade union funds. The last two categories, which provided sickness benefits, are of interest for my purposes. The numbers of covered members were impressive. Including branches of larger funds, the number of sick and funeral societies statewide was 791. Among men in nonagricultural occupations, there were 82,219 members of 308 sick and funeral societies and 21 trade union funds. Compared to the 196,500 men in nonagricultural occupations statewide, this suggests that as early as the beginning of the 1890s more than two-fifths (42 percent) of men in Connecticut were covered by sickness funds. In addition, the growth rate of membership was also large. Between 1887 and 1891 the number of members of such societies increased from 46,092 to 79,921, implying an annual rate of growth more than ten percent. One observer proposed that growth in these funds began earlier in the 1880s. Union-sponsored funds grew steadily as well: those in Connecticut had grown about 5.5 percent per year in the late 1880s. In 1880 the number of workers nationwide who belonged to union-sponsored sickness funds—which are examined in more detail in Chapter 6—was less than 6,000, a figure that grew by the end of the century to at least 300,000 and within a few years was close to a half-million.[28]

Growth in enrollments was apparent even to Progressive reformers who believed nonetheless that sickness funds inadequately protected workers. They thought that membership growth indicated that sickness funds provided valuable services; therefore, such services should be provided to all workers; therefore, the failure of the private sector to provide universal insurance indicated the need for the government to do so. As John Lapp put it, "The extent to which voluntary health insurance is now purchased is the best evidence of its probable failure to meet the need for universal insurance."[29] From this perspective, it was impermissible for industrial sickness funds to attain success.

During the 1890s and the early years of the twentieth century, growth in the number of sickness funds across the country proceeded at about the same rate in most regions of the country. Table 4.5 reports the share of sickness funds by region in the 1890 Census and in the 1908 federal survey of funds. Each source reported on nonfraternal sickness funds, but the first attempted to be a census of all such funds and the second was a survey of some sampled funds. In both years, more than three-fourths of sickness funds were found in the most heavily industrialized parts of the country, the Northeast and the Midwest. Other states were home to substantial numbers of funds as well, and the share of funds in the West in particular doubled during those years.

Table 4.5.
Distribution of nonfraternal sickness funds by region, 1890–1908

	1890 CENSUS		1908 COMMISSIONER OF LABOR SURVEY	
REGION	N	%	N	%
North Atlantic	601	47.7	437	44.1
South Atlantic	88	5.6	82	8.3
North Central	371	29.5	331	33.4
South Central	164	13.0	60	6.1
West	52	4.1	81	8.2
Total	1,259	100.0	991	100.0

Sources: U.S. Department of the Interior, *Report on Insurance Business*; U.S. Commissioner of Labor, *Twenty-third Annual Report*. Note that the earlier report was intended to be a complete census of sickness funds, the later report, only a sample from a larger universe.

The figures and tables discussed so far in this chapter should suggest that industrial sickness funds were not marginal operations. They may have been concentrated in particular regions, trades, or industries, but they were found nationwide and as early as 1890 or so covered perhaps a quarter of the industrial labor force. But what was the absolute number of workers covered? And how did such a figure fit into Progressive-Era debates regarding the general lack of coverage by sickness funds? To answer these questions exactly would require far more data than are at hand or likely to be discovered. Reasonably solid numbers, however, begin to appear toward the end of the Progressive period, late in the second decade of the twentieth century.

The several state investigatory commissions produced volumes that are of varying usefulness. Some briefly recapitulated the commission's considerations along with a list of members' votes. But a few conducted their own surveys of workers, insurers, or sickness funds, analyzed the results, and even provided a history of political actions regarding health insurance. The reports of California, Illinois, Ohio, and Pennsylvania are sufficiently rich to be important historical documents in their own right. Summaries of the estimates of the first three regarding insurance coverage appear in table 4.6. These figures include not merely numbers of workers but the sources of their sickness insurance. Illinois, Ohio, and California each found about a half-million workers with some kind of sickness insurance. In California, nearly three-fourths of insured workers were covered by their fraternal society. In Ohio that proportion was closer to two-fifths, with a quarter or so of covered workers enrolled in establishment funds. Union funds and commercial insurance were particularly important in Illinois, covering one-fifth each.

The share of covered workers, according to these refined calculations, was a little higher than the standard one-third reported by historians, who relied on these reports. In order to arrive at the proportions described above, I divided the sum of all the covered workers as reported by the state commissions into the number of workers who were eligible or likely to join such sickness funds or purchase commercial or industrial health insurance. The California and Illinois commissions supplied their own estimates of the relevant labor force; the Ohio figure came from a more recent publication. The proportion of insured workers was indeed one-third in Ohio and slightly greater in Illinois. The California *Report* estimated that one-third of workers were covered; probably the percentage was 10 percentage points or so higher.[30]

The absolute numbers of covered workers, however, were much higher than the estimates of Progressive activists before the state commissions reported their findings. The estimates by Progressives can be retrieved from their writings. In 1913, I. M. Rubinow proposed that the number of covered workers was "perhaps less than two millions in the United States (although trustworthy statistics are lacking)." Rubinow apparently derived his figure by adding the number of covered workers according to the U.S. Commissioner of Labor's 1908 survey—which was based on a sample and did not purport to examine all sickness funds in the country—and data from the *Insurance Year Book*. Referring to this estimate in 1917, Irving Fisher estimated that as a share of the labor force "only about 5 percent of our workmen needing insurance actually have it." Because there were about twenty-five million workers in the nonagricultural labor force in 1917, these two estimates are roughly consistent with each other. The Commissioner of Labor's study was based on a sample, so the possibility of an underestimate must be acknowledged. But how great was the underestimate?[31]

To answer this question would require a census of funds (or a survey

Table 4.6.
Sources of insurance in three states

SOURCE	ILLINOIS	OHIO	CALIFORNIA
Fraternal society	250	200	291
Establishment fund	116	130	50
Union fund	140	85	38
Other sick fund	12	n/a	35
Commercial insurance	140	85	2 (?)
Total	660	500	416
Eligible labor force	1,850	1,500	995
Share insured	36%	33%	42%

Sources: State of Illinois, *Report*, pp. 4, 109–132; Ohio Health and Old Age Insurance Commission, *Health*, pp. 120–121; California Social Insurance Commission, *Report*, pp. 84–107, 228; Lee et al., *Population Redistribution*.

Notes: Illinois figures are taken directly from State of Illinois, *Report*, except for establishment funds, which it estimated at two-thirds of 175,000 workers. Other sick funds reported as "foreign," i.e., ethnic societies for foreign-born residents. The report suggests a range of insured workers from 660,000 to 750,000, but some reductions are needed because of double enrollment (p. 146).

The Ohio figures are adjusted from those in the state report as follows. The Ohio report reported 593,000 "persons" covered by fraternal health insurance. Illinois estimated that 750,000 persons there were covered by some sort of fraternal insurance, including life, which it reduced to 250,000 wage earners covered by health insurance. I used the same proportion to reduce the Ohio figure to 200,000. This may underestimate coverage since the original Ohio figure excluded persons with life insurance. Ohio reported that "at least" 100,000 workers belonged to 150 establishment funds statewide. Illinois estimated that 116,000 workers belonged to 134 funds statewide; thus, on average each fund covered 866 workers. Assuming the same membership levels in Ohio, $866 \times 150 = 130{,}000$. Since Ohio reported the value of benefits from each type of insurance but not the number of covered workers, and 20% of those covered by commercial health insurance were wage earners, the 85,000 reported here represents members/benefits in fraternal funds × benefits paid by commercial insurers × .2.

The California figures originated in a survey of funds that made no claims to completeness and therefore should be considered a lower bound. Coverage by commercial insurers is estimated as 10 percent of 20,000 (p. 88). "Other" includes ethnic benevolent societies in San Francisco and Los Angeles only (14,000; p. 84) and commercial hospital association members (21,000; p. 100).

Labor force measures for the Illinois report (p. 4) estimate the number of wage earners. Those for Ohio, from Lee et al. (p. 617), estimate the number of male nonagricultural workers. Those for the California report (p. 288) estimate the number of wage earners.

with a weighted and stratified sample, a technique that would not be used until the 1935–36 National Health Survey). One can work around this lack of data by making two strong but reasonable assumptions: first, that the average number of members per benefit society was the same nationwide, and second, that the regional distribution of sickness funds, which did not change much between 1890 and 1908, also remained about the same from 1908 to 1917. With these two assumptions the state commission data imply that Rubinow and Fisher underestimated the number of covered workers by a factor of about four.

The sum of covered workers in California, Illinois, and Ohio as shown in table 4.6 was a little less than 1.6 million. The Pennsylvania commission's report did not provide such detailed information, but it did estimate on the basis of a series of regional surveys that "not more than 30 per cent. of the wage earners carry any insurance protection against the sickness risk." The male nonagricultural labor force in Pennsylvania numbered about 2.5 million in 1920. In order to prevent overestimation, suppose that the insured workforce in Pennsylvania then numbered around 25 percent of 2.4 million, which would total 600,000 men. This yields an estimate of the number of insured workers in these four states equal to about 2.2 million. This figure exceeds Rubinow's estimate for all 48 states by ten percentage points or so. Clearly Rubinow and Fisher had underestimated the nationwide number of insured workers, but by how much?[32]

We can rely on proportional estimates based on the 1890 census of insurance and the 1908 survey of funds. Figure 4.1 indicates that 306 of 1,259 sickness funds operated in California, Illinois, Ohio, and Pennsylvania. Table 4.5 suggests that the distribution of sickness funds across regions had changed little between 1890 and 1908. Let us assume that the average number of members per sickness fund was the same in all forty-eight states and that sickness funds in these four states comprised 24 percent (306/1,259) of all funds in the United States. In that case, the four states would have accounted for about one-fourth of covered workers, and so the number of insured workers throughout the United States would have been closer to nine million. This revised estimate is more than four times the size of the Progressives' best estimate. This revised estimate must be more accurate than the one Rubinow proposed, in part because it is based on carefully estimated numbers from particular states that were published after his estimates of 1913.

To view the revised estimates another way, suppose that southern and western funds had tended to be much smaller in membership than those in the four states under consideration, which would lead the present estimate to be biased on the high side. Now set the South and the West aside for a minute. Make a reasonable assumption that sickness funds in New York, New Jersey, New England, and the rest of the Midwest had as many members per fund as did those in the four states above. This is reasonable because sickness funds seem to have been as widespread and as well-established elsewhere in the Northeast and the Midwest as in Illinois, Ohio, and Pennsylvania, or perhaps more so, because the Connecticut survey of 1891 found about thirteen times the number of nonfraternal sickness funds as did the federal census of 1890. In this case, the total number of covered workers in the Northeast, Midwest, and California would still be more than seven million.

With a revised estimate of nine million insured workers in the late Progressive Era, we can revisit one explanation for the failure of government insurance proposals at that time. Paul Starr suggested that one reason for this lack was the dearth of private, voluntary sickness insurance as a precedent for public programs. According to this view, compulsory European insurance grew because the private sickness funds that were already in place provided a basis for growth and had educated the working classes about the value of such insurance. In the United States, this was not the case. But were American workers really so unfamiliar with private sickness insurance?[33]

The private sector insured a larger share of the American population late in the Progressive Era than it had in Germany on the eve of imposition of compulsory insurance. Further, the difference between the United States and England was small. If, as proposed above, there were nine million insured workers in a nonagricultural labor force of 25 million, then nearly two-fifths of the workforce was covered. The national population was about 100 million, so if very few dependents were covered, about one-tenth of the population was insured. Regarding the preparatory effects of prior experience with private health insurance, the share of the insured population in Germany rose from 5 percent in 1880, which was prior to the beginning of compulsion, to 11 percent in

1888, after three years of compulsion. The share in England before 1911 was about 13 percent. The share insured privately by the American network on the eve of its hypothetical shift to government insurance was nearly double that of the German network on the eve of its actual transformation and 2 or 3 or so percentage points less than in England. This difference suggests that prior experience with insurance (or path dependence) cannot explain American exceptionalism in regard to sickness insurance.[34]

This chapter has provided the quantitative evidence that allows me to sketch the rise of industrial sickness funds in the United States. The collection of numbers presented should drive home the point that sickness insurance via benefit societies was a widespread phenomenon in the United States in the late nineteenth century and that it grew throughout the Progressive Era. Progressives estimated that only 5 percent of the industrial labor force was covered, but on investigation the figure turned out to be closer to 30 percent. The sixfold underestimate could not have helped their credibility. Further, if the share of covered workers had only grown from about one-fourth to one-third from 1890 to just before 1920, such growth occurred at a time when the nonagricultural labor force grew from about 13 million in 1890 to about 30 million in 1920—growth that no European labor market had to deal with. Far from insignificant, incompetent, and inert, the network of American sickness funds was a healthy set of financial institutions able to respond to a dynamic labor market unlike any other. Exactly how the individual establishment and labor union funds worked is the subject of Chapters 5 and 6.

CHAPTER FIVE

How Establishment Funds Worked

I do not know how many of you are aware of the fact that there are nearly 700 benefit and relief associations in this country operating to-day more or less successfully, more or less efficiently managed.

—F. W. BOSWELL, Flint Vehicle Factories Benefit Association, to Conference on Social Insurance, 1916

INDUSTRIAL SICKNESS funds operated in a relatively simple fashion, collecting premiums regularly and paying benefits to members with certified illnesses. That brief description masks many critical decisions that funds and their members made when initially structuring the fund. Whether the fund was to secure its income primarily from initiation fees or ongoing dues, how generous benefits should be, whether to offer medical benefits, and whether workers or company management should make daily decisions were all questions that needed to be addressed. If the fund collected too little in revenue relative to expenses, it would dissolve, and if it collected too much, members would protest.

This chapter considers how establishment funds of the early twentieth century addressed these questions. Structural differences such as management makeup and the nature of membership led to different levels of premium and benefit payments. The effects of voluntary membership and employee management suggested what workers wanted in sickness insurance and what they were willing to forgo. One of the most important conclusions is that medical benefits, crucial to the Progressive campaign for government health insurance, were expensive and not in high demand by workers. Workers wanted sick pay benefits and were willing to pay higher premiums for them. They were less interested in paying extra for medical benefits. Overall, the benefits they received cost them only about half of what the more extensive German social insurance program charged its workers and employers.

A detailed snapshot of establishment funds appeared in the extensive 1908 survey by the U. S. Commissioner of Labor, from which table 5.1 was derived.[1] Responses from 176 establishment funds described income and benefit characteristics in fiscal year 1906, with 215 responses for 1907 and 70 for 1908. The report published the industry of each fund's sponsoring company and the number of employees but no further identifying characteristics such as company name or location. The survey seems to have been conducted carefully, since the bureau reported having sent special agents to particular firms, unions, and sick fund offices to inquire about the funds. What they found was that the average establishment fund had 730 members in a workplace with 1,652 employees and hence covered about 44 percent of the workforce. The median fund covered a slightly lower share at about 40 percent. Because larger workplaces enrolled a greater share of the workforce, the share of covered employees was closer to 48 percent.

Three characteristics determined the structure of establishment funds: choice as to membership, income sources, and the source of fund managers. The conventional history of sickness funds misleads by claiming that most funds were compulsory. Some historians have interpreted management offers of fringe benefits as attempts to coerce workers into surrendering their mobility, in part by making eligibility for benefits contingent on continued employment. To maximize the number of workers who were under pressure to stay put, membership in sickness funds was typically required as a condition of employment, according to these accounts.[2]

This picture has little to recommend it in terms of either common sense or empirical testing. Empirically speaking, every survey of sickness funds reported that compulsory funds were few in number. In the 1908 survey only 16 percent of funds were found to be compulsory, a figure that declined to 10 percent a decade later, and in a 1923 survey it remained at about 9 percent. Employers did not typically force workers into joining sickness benefit associations. They had reasons for keeping membership voluntary, including the illegality of compulsion in several states.[3]

Table 5.1.
Mean values of establishment fund characteristics, 1908

VARIABLE	N (FUNDS)	ALL FUNDS			MEAN FOR VOLUNTARY FUNDS ONLY
		MEAN	STANDARD DEVIATION	MEDIAN	
Number of employees	427	1,652	3,130	648	1,567
Number of members	427	730	1,962	202	563
Share of workforce enrolled	427	0.44	0.30	0.40	0.40
Firm-managed	434	0.06			0.02
Jointly managed	434	0.19			0.14
Employee-managed	434	0.74			0.84
Employer contributes to income	434	0.29			0.07
Firm derives income from entertainments	434	0.25			0.05
Firm has interest or dividend income	434	0.53			0.03
Voluntary	434	0.84			1.00
Age of fund (years)	429	12.15	8.44	9.00	12.34

Minimum dues ($/year)	413	4.55	2.72	3.60	4.71
Maximum dues ($/year)	413	5.81	3.55	5.20	5.86
Entrance fee charged	434	0.66			0.77
Minimum entrance fee ($, if charged)	285	1.00	0.91	1.00	1.43
Maximum entrance fee ($, if charged)	285	1.39	1.81	1.00	1.02
Extraordinary assessment permitted	429	0.47			0.51
Probationary membership period (weeks)	429	6.15	8.09	4.00	6.94
Waiting period after illness begins (days)	434	6.02	3.20	7.00	6.43
Maximum duration of benefit payment (weeks)	427	16.03	11.01	13.00	15.10
Minimum benefit payment ($/week)	400	4.64	1.87	5.00	4.78
Maximum benefit payment ($/week)	400	5.80	2.42	5.00	5.87
Medical benefit available	434	0.20			0.14

Source: U.S. Commissioner of Labor, *Twenty-third Annual Report.*

Employers were aware that compulsory membership muted adverse selection problems. An Indiana businessman described a textbook example of a death spiral due to adverse selection at his firm. When sickness fund membership was voluntary it attracted "the older and less healthy employees . . . while the younger and active element would have nothing to do with it." Because dues did not suffice to service claims, "extra assessments had to be made, and the organization in general got into a very bad state." Some firms with ostensibly voluntary funds pressured workers to join, but these seem to have been relatively few. On the other hand, even if employers wanted to immobilize workers with health insurance, they also knew that workers would recognize that strategy and react to it. A Chicago businessman reported that employees would question the company's "ulterior motives" for providing compulsory benefits. A New York state automaker reported that workers at his plant saw compulsory insurance as robbery. Workers forced into a fund could try to get all their contributions back willy-nilly by making fraudulent claims or malingering.[4]

Many employers hoped that sickness insurance funds would reduce turnover and increase productivity. A decline in turnover, to the extent that it reflected workers' choosing to remain at a job that offered better compensation, was not necessarily bad for either party. Lower turnover was a sign that workers were satisfied with their job conditions, but turn-of-the-century American workers were extremely mobile. Employers who wanted workers to build up job-specific human capital had a strong incentive to do what they could to keep them on the job by providing more attractive levels and kinds of compensation, including sickness insurance.[5]

Whether fund managers consisted of workers, owners, or both suggests how and in whose interests the fund made business decisions. Employees managed three-fourths of funds. Because these tended to be smaller funds, they accounted for only 37 percent of enrolled workers. A minority (only 6 percent) of large funds were operated by firms, and these funds accounted for one-fifth of workers. In between were the one-fifth of funds that were jointly managed by workers and firm owners and administrators, which enrolled two-fifths of covered workers. Voluntary and compulsory firms were managed all three ways, so that, as Progressives complained, "in some cases employees have no share in the management of the funds and in not a few such instances membership is nevertheless compulsory." The 1908 survey found that about 7 percent of all funds (including some that did not offer temporary disability benefits) were managed exclusively by the company, and within the category of company-managed funds, a little more than half had compulsory membership. Whether 4 percent of funds constituted "not a few" is hard to say. It was equally common for compulsory funds to be managed entirely by workers; other contemporary observers found this to be the truly odd arrangement. Firms that maintained some degree of management control over sickness funds generally preferred to limit their role to giving advice and letting workers run day-to-day operations. If the firm had too big a hand in directing the sickness fund, workers would question whether it was really operated for their benefit. Assigning as much responsibility to workers as they could handle, according to firm officials, led to successful fund operation.[6]

Closely associated with management duties was the critical issue of a fund's income sources. Progressives railed against "the evil of permitting sick-benefit funds to be controlled by employers, while supported wholly or in part by employees."[7] But this was an unusual arrangement. Only about 6 percent of funds that offered sickness benefits were operated by the establishment with no worker input in decision making. Because establishment-operated funds tended to be large, they accounted for 21 percent of all covered workers. The share of the fund's income that came from employees tended to be unrelated to the identity of the fund managers. For employee-managed funds the employees provided 85 percent of income; for company-managed funds the figure was 84 percent, and for jointly managed funds it was 82 percent.

Reformers proposed that sickness insurance premiums that were actuarially fair (equal to the value of benefits multiplied by the probability of a claim) would be too expensive for most workers. Such was the case with fraternal and union funds, they argued, which explained why those funds offered competitive sick pay but almost never offered medical benefits. Inclusion of the latter would have priced membership beyond the average worker's budget. As a result, wrote I. M. Rubinow, "with very few exceptions the entire burden of the cost of sick-insurance falls upon the shoulders of the wage-workers, which is neither ethically just nor socially expedient."[8]

Actually, funds drew on a variety of income sources. Only about a quarter (27 percent) of funds relied completely on members' contributions. Twenty-nine percent of funds accepted payments from the firm, a proportion that grew to 34 percent by 1917. In fact, in 1908 more than one-half of workers belonged to funds that were underwritten in part by their employer. This support took several forms, including a fixed payment per fund member, more commonly a direct subsidy as a share of fund income, and less commonly an annual lump sum payment. Some firms agreed to pay the fund's administrative expenses and others promised to make good any deficit. Employee-operated funds occasionally rejected direct subsidy offers by the company, but in these cases they often accepted in-kind donations of printing or clerical time.[9]

Some enterprising sickness funds collected revenue from social and recreational activities. The one-fourth of all funds that did so in 1908 engaged in a variety of these "entertainments." The industry whose funds relied most heavily on income from social activities was, perhaps not surprisingly, brewing. In that industry funds reported that 23 percent of income came from entertainments. The overall contribution of such sources to fund income was relatively small at 2 percent, but these activities may have been more important than their dollar value suggests. The financial viability of American sickness funds depended on a delicate balance among incentives, rights, and duties of fund members. An important aspect of many funds was that members knew each other personally and felt invested in the fund as stakeholders. Alan Derickson observed of the Western Miners' Federation funds that their most valued work was sending able-bodied miners out to bring food or coal to bedridden men who lacked a family to take care of them. Margaret Byington described the importance of ethnic benefit societies in integrating the newly arrived with countrymen who had lived in Pennsylvania for a relatively long time. As others have noted, the creation of mutual obligation was part of the story behind fraternal fund rituals, whose aim was to bond members to the society and to each other.[10]

Establishment funds worked in much the same way. If compulsory membership led workers to extract the value of their premium from a fund, then by implication, in the majority of funds with voluntary membership, workers made decisions about finances and claims out of a sense of responsibility toward the fund itself and toward their fellow members. It seems unlikely that the feelings of mutual obligation among members, which even Progressives saw as necessary for efficient fund functioning, would have survived the transition to state-supervised compulsory insurance.

Lacking rituals to bond workers to the fund, establishment funds brought members together to socialize. When researchers for the National Industrial Conference Board (NICB), a pro-business group, recommended to its members that a "picnic or excursion" or a dinner or a dance was good advertising for a voluntary fund or a morale-builder for all funds, they understood that the real advantage for the fund was the increased appreciation of mutual obligation. Dependence on social activities as an income source had disappointing results because their primary effect was intangible. It was important nonetheless. The NICB's interviews with individual members revealed two groups of workers who were satisfied with their membership: those who had drawn benefits in time of need and those who belonged to funds that operated social and recreational activities.[11]

Funds did depend primarily on worker contributions, which constituted about four-fifths of fund income in 1908. The one-fifth (19 percent) that came from firms, entertainments, interest income, and donations can be put in perspective by noting the structure of income sources in Europe. In France honorary fund members and donations made up one-eighth of fund income. In Germany employers contributed one-third and workers two-thirds of premiums. In Denmark the government paid a little less than one-third of fund income. And in Britain, workers paid four-ninths and employers and the state paid the rest. Thus, in the American case income sources other than workers provided a share of income greater than in France but less than in Denmark. It was not the case that workers shouldered the load entirely.

Sickness funds did not accept all comers. Although reformers and historians alike found this objectionable, some membership restrictions made economic sense from the fund's perspective. The denial of membership or of the right of fund members to claim benefits for a chronic condition from which a worker suffered at the time of application—the pre-existing condition clauses that appeared in contemporary European funds as well—was a simple application of the principle of insurance against unforeseen events. The pre-existing condition was not unforeseen but observable to the worker and the insurer alike. Another characteristic that helped predict the likelihood of a claim and was, within limits, easily observable was the worker's age, and some funds would not accept relatively old workers. Still, most funds questioned in the 1908 survey admitted new members with no upper age limit. Of the 177 with such bars in place, the lowest was set at thirty-five years, the highest at seventy, and the median bar (among funds not admitting applicants over a certain age) was fifty.[12]

Women played a small and often overlooked role in sickness funds. Establishment funds were more open to the possibility of admitting women as members than were fraternals. Nine percent of all workers covered by establishment funds in 1908 were women, but women constituted 24 percent of the nonagricultural labor force, so that, to be sure, women were underrepresented in the covered population. Most funds covered by the 1908 survey had no women members, and there were no all-women establishment funds. But about 28 percent of funds had some women members, and twenty-nine establishment funds, most for department store or other retail employees, had more women members than men. Twenty-three of these were employee-managed, so it is reasonable to suppose that in at least some cases women were managing their own sickness funds. It is true that maternity benefits were practically never offered. In fact, one women's fund called the Women Clerks' Benefit Association of Boston (maximum age for new members, sixty years) specifically ruled out benefits for "cases of confinement, or sickness from disease incident to pregnancy before the time of confinement, or within four weeks thereafter." Women joining this fund faced an unusually long probationary period of three months before they could draw benefits, perhaps to screen out newly pregnant clerks who needed help to pay early pregnancy expenses. The point is that women and men who were both fund managers and potential claimants recognized that pregnancy represented an expensive type of claim, and one that could be avoided. Whether maternal benefits constituted enough of an incentive actually to raise fertility rates was hotly debated at the time.[13]

Racial exclusion occurred. Funds that did not explicitly limit membership to whites (or blacks) may well have considered membership applications in light of informal racial bars. There were formal exclusionary rules aimed at blacks (primarily but not exclusively in the South) and Chinese (primarily in the West). Indeed, the 1891 survey of Connecticut sickness funds found that of 308 sickness and funeral benefit societies, 300 admitted whites only, and the other eight admitted blacks only. Three-quarters of these funds admitted men only, and five percent admitted women only. These restrictions, or at least the formal ones, were on the decline. The federal survey of 1908 found that three-fourths of the 461 funds it examined excluded no employees from membership. Women were explicitly excluded by 54 funds and blacks by only 37. By 1923 a survey conducted by the NICB found that only 13 of 382 funds restricted membership to white male employees.[14]

This book aims to show that establishment and union sickness funds were essentially well run: not that they were paragons of efficiency, and not that they covered all workers who were sick and out of money, but that they made reasonably competent decisions, given their objective of protecting a share of workers' pay packets in case of incapacitation due to ill health. Historians and reformers alike have criticized these funds for their lack of actuarial soundness. According to Charles Henderson, "the principal evil in connection with these voluntary local societies is that they are generally organized and administered without the aid of competent actuaries and are utterly without scientific foundations." He conceded that the influence of actuaries in sickness funds was growing, if only gradually. It was not clear how actuarial wisdom might aid sick benefit societies at that time because, Henderson acknowledged, actuaries themselves had "only traditional standards to guide them."[15]

Although nearly every fund's books were regularly audited, it was true that few funds consulted with actuaries. A 1917 survey suggested that only 5 percent of 159 funds involved had ever had an actuarial examination, and only two had contracted with actuarial consultants. But given the primitive state of health insurance actuarial science at the time, the value of an actuarial examination might have been small. When John Dryden of the Prudential wrote that his firm had abandoned sickness insurance because it could not monitor beneficiaries, he was not so much reflecting on the shortcomings of privately provided health insurance as he was acknowledging both the powerful effect of economic incentives and the underdeveloped state of actuarial science. Even when Blue Cross began operation in the late 1920s, there were still no actuarial models to guide its group underwriting decisions.[16]

Historians have overestimated the availability of such models in the early twentieth century. Roy Lubove claimed that English friendly societies used "sophisticated actuarial principles." Because the purpose of such models is to enable the insurer to set premiums and benefits so as to earn greater profits, it is hard to believe that the Prudential and small industrial funds would ignore such technology and persist in doing business with greater uncertainty than necessary. In fact, according to the most knowledgeable student of British friendly society insurance, James Riley, actuaries who advised these funds consistently erred in their estimates. The best alternative, rule-of-thumb guesswork, proved to be adequate to the task at hand; experienced fund officials were generally quite able to price their product prudently. Herbert Emery estimated measures of the implicit degree of risk loading and the probability of ruin for Odd Fellows' sickness fund operations and found that they did not engage in unsound or nonactuarial premium pricing. In fact, fraternal premiums and commercial insurance premiums, relative to risks and benefits, were similar.[17]

Sickness funds tried to limit their liability. They screened out high-risk applicants and limited expenses by providing benefits for a maximum number of weeks. Only 54 funds of the 461 included in the 1908 survey provided permanently disabled claimants with an open-ended pension; those offering temporary disability benefits typically limited their liability. Eighty-five paid for thirteen weeks of disability in a year, 77 paid for twenty-six weeks, and 29 funds paid for an entire year, with many maximum periods falling in between these points. In order to avoid compensating workers for transient conditions, most funds imposed a waiting period of a few days between diagnosis and payment. On average, a worker had to be sick for six days (one work week) before receiving sick pay.[18] Still, the risk of an exceptional number of claims remained.

If criticism of sickness funds really concerned their financial viability in the face of uncertainty, reinsurance offered an alternative. An insurer purchases reinsurance to guard against unexpectedly high costs, and commercial insurers were willing to sell reinsurance policies to benefit associations. In the early 1920s, sickness funds still did not generally consult with actuaries, but many, especially smaller funds, recognized the value of buying reinsurance. Sickness funds could choose to keep a reserve fund, which sometimes generated contention, or reinsure with a commercial insurer. A small benefit association that received contributions from the firm was in a good position to spread its risk by reinsuring while still maintaining relatively high benefits, for example, of two-thirds of a worker's regular pay, because it could supervise claimants with its own visiting committee. In that sense, reinsuring was a middle way between the riskier but independent local sick fund and the direct purchase of group insurance, which made close monitoring of claimants infeasible. In addition, reinsurance allowed a reduction in reserves, fewer membership restrictions, and broader benefits (for example, in cases of venereal disease). To the sick fund, these were advantages of reinsuring, but to the commercial insurer they were moral hazards. In order to make the additional risk to reinsurers worthwhile, they needed to make the risk pool sufficiently large. Thus they required that 75 percent of eligible workers be enrolled in the sick fund, a level that funds often were able to achieve.[19]

Many funds that were unable to make ends meet reverted to an alternative version of passing the hat, known in language of the day as "extraordinary assessments." Funds might collect three kinds of payments from members: initiation fees, regular premiums (usually called "dues"), and assessments, which were of two kinds. Ordinary ones covered normal expenses, and extraordinary ones dealt with financial emergencies. Thus the latter served as a kind of stopgap solution when a fund became desperate for income to meet its obligations. The 1918–1919 influenza epidemic was one such occasion; many funds required members to pitch in with little notice.[20]

Not every fund's charter enabled it to impose extraordinary assessments, and among those that were able, some did not impose these collections and others did so rarely. The share of funds whose charters allowed extraordinary assessments was about 45 percent in 1908 and in 1923. One reason to avoid imposing them was that they were roundly despised by the rank and file, who, after all, had joined the fund to avoid surprise pass-the-hat collections for injured and deceased co-workers and their families. The unappealing randomness of extraordinary assessments was mitigated by charter restrictions that limited assessments to pro rata shares of a fund's deficit or a fixed amount of cash. The need to levy such charges suggested that the fund had not been as careful with members' contributions as it might have been, which served as an incentive for voluntary funds to avoid them. One executive reported that assessments were "dreaded and more than apt to cause dissatisfaction."[21]

It appears that these assessments were not very common. The 1908 survey reported what provisions, if any, fund charters had for extraordinary assessments (whether a quarter, a nickel, a sum determined by trustees, or a pro rata share of some amount) and how many times this clause had been invoked in the previous five years. Slightly less than half of all funds were enabled to make these assessments; table 5.2 reports descriptive variables for these funds. Only 11 percent of them in fact did so. These funds averaged 5.7 assessments, or slightly more than one per year, and five particularly unlucky or profligate funds made 24 extraordinary assessments during that time. It appears that invocation of these assessments was limited to a small number of funds that operated with a thin margin of error. Overall, assessments do not present a picture of widespread instability.[22]

Table 5.2 further reports characteristics of funds that were most likely to lead to making assessments and to greater numbers of assessments. Two regressions were fit to observations of the 196 funds with the authority to levy extraordinary assessments. Potential influences on the decision to levy them, as well as the number of assessments, included the structure of fund management and financing, claim requirements, and available benefits. Among the estimated coefficients, three particular variables stand out. First, consistent with the claims that members intensely disliked these assessments, voluntary funds were significantly less likely to make them. That is, voluntary funds, which had to be more responsive to members' desires than did compulsory funds, in fact conducted their operations in a manner consistent with reports about what workers wanted in a sick fund. Second, funds that received a greater share of income from the sponsoring firm were more likely to make extraordinary assessments. This is consistent with the suggestion that extraordinary assessments were limited to the 5 percent or so of all funds that were in financial trouble and hence accepting

Table 5.2.
Imposition of extraordinary assessments

VARIABLE	MEAN (STANDARD DEVIATION)	LOGIT: FUND HAS IMPOSED ASSESSMENT IN PRECEDING FIVE YEARS	TOBIT: NUMBER OF ASSESSMENTS IN PRECEDING FIVE YEARS
Mean of dependent variable		0.11	0.61
			(2.65)
Intercept		−0.52	−4.69
		(1.28)	(6.70)
Members (thousands)	0.458	0.17	1.05
	(0.777)	(0.37)	(1.83)
Employee-managed	0.84	−0.67	−3.93
		(0.66)	(3.41)
Firm contributions as share of fund income	0.06	5.32***	23.36**
		(1.72)	(9.70)
Voluntary	0.91	−2.24***	−12.38***
		(0.84)	(4.48)
Age of fund	12.56 years	0.02	0.19
	(8.35)	(0.03)	(0.17)

Table 5.2.

Imposition of extraordinary assessments (*continued*)

VARIABLE	MEAN (STANDARD DEVIATION)	LOGIT: FUND HAS IMPOSED ASSESSMENT IN PRECEDING FIVE YEARS	TOBIT: NUMBER OF ASSESSMENTS IN PRECEDING FIVE YEARS
Probationary period	7.08 weeks	0.004	0.04
	(8.34)	(0.03)	(0.15)
Waiting period	6.33 days	0.14	0.53
	(2.78)	(0.10)	(0.50)
Maximum benefit period	14.24 weeks	−0.06	−0.34
	(8.48)	(0.04)	(0.22)
Medical benefits	0.13	−2.55**	−12.22**
		(1.25)	(5.93)
Maximum sick pay/week	\$5.55	−0.13	0.16
	(1.94)	(0.20)	(0.75)
Minimum sick pay/week	\$4.58	0.18	0.51
	(1.83)	(0.19)	(0.84)
N / Pseudo R^2 / −2 Log Likelihood	196	0.19	55.89

Source: U.S. Commissioner of Labor, *Twenty-third Annual Report.*

Notes: Sample limited to those funds permitted to levy extraordinary assessments. Omitted categories include some establishment management, compulsory membership, no medical benefits available. Standard errors in parentheses for regression estimates.

*significantly different from zero at the 0.10 level; **significantly different from zero at the 0.05 level; ***significantly different from zero at the 0.01 level

money from the employer. Finally, funds that provided medical benefits were significantly less likely to impose emergency assessments than were other funds. Provision of medical benefits may have been a key part of efforts to maintain financial solvency, through the ability of the physician whom the fund paid to send claimants back to work as soon as possible.

The question of who wanted medical benefits included and why was misconstrued by Progressives. Fund-provided medical benefits were only for the insured worker and generally only for the duration of the insured illness or injury. Many funds expected sick workers to find their own physician and pay for his services with the standard sick pay benefit. Funds that provided medical benefits paid for physician visits as long as the sick member visited a physician employed or approved by the fund. Covered workers with and without medical benefits needed to see a physician to certify their inability to work; the difference was in who paid for that physician's services. Doctors who conducted "contract" or "lodge practices" for fraternal societies or other sickness funds were controversial figures. They were usually paid on the basis of a capitation contract, that is, an annual fee per fund member of about two dollars that guaranteed the member access to the physician when ill. Contract practice enabled large numbers of working people to gain access to physicians they might not have been able to see otherwise. In Buffalo in 1911 as many as 150,000 people belonged to such practices, and in industrialized districts of Rhode Island about half of the workers were covered by these contracts. Noncontract physicians usually despised lodge practitioners, because annual bidding on contracts reduced physicians' incomes generally.[23]

Sickness funds that provided medical benefits were not common, but medical benefits were not impossible to come by, either. Nearly half (48 percent) of workers included in the 1908 survey were covered by establishment funds that provided medical benefits. In many industries no sickness funds provided medical benefits. But in several industries larger funds did so; in heavy manufacturing (for example, agricultural implements, chemicals, and iron and steel), nearly all workers enjoyed medical benefits, and in other fields such as retailing or shoemaking, nearly half of workers did. It simply was not the case, as some Progressives argued, that sick pay and medical benefits were almost never offered together. The share of funds providing them seems to have been in decline, however. The 1908 survey reported that 20 percent of funds provided some medical benefits, which generally included medical and surgical treatment and medicines for the member while he was incapacitated. In 1917 this figure had fallen to 17 percent of funds, and in 1923 only 12 percent of funds reported providing medical benefits during the worker's disability. The latter figure may underestimate the value of medical benefits because it excludes funds that paid for hospital services.[24]

It is not clear now how efficacious (by our standards) medical therapeutics was at that time. Surgical diagnostics and therapeutics were making great strides forward, just in time to take advantage of the rise of state-mandated workmen's compensation. Rapid improvements in diagnostic techniques such as x-rays and surgical techniques such as Listerian antisepsis were especially helpful in dealing with occupational injuries. Equipment such as trusses for workers who suffered from inguinal hernias reduced suffering and enabled workers to return to their jobs sooner than they had been able to earlier.[25]

Medical therapeutics may have been increasing in efficacy, but was outstripped by advances in surgery. By the late nineteenth century the day of humoral theory had largely passed, and no longer did workers need fear physicians who practiced heroic medicine, with its venisection and violent purgatives and emetics. Many pharmaceutical treatments were harmless, if inefficacious, in this era of therapeutic nihilism. By the early twentieth century some observers believed that medical therapeutics had gained considerable ground. The Harvard University biochemist Lawrence Henderson could propose around 1910 that "a random patient, with a random disease, consulting a doctor chosen at random had, for the first time in the history of mankind, a better than fifty-fifty chance of profiting from the encounter." Still, physicians possessed few disease-specific cures other than the diphtheria antitoxin, which primarily benefited children. Physicians could do little to treat many common infectious diseases. As Edward Shorter observed, "It would be unwise to exaggerate the therapeutic accomplishments of the modern doctor before 1935." Even if Henderson's was an accurate estimate, it was clear that not all parties to the insurance contract understood the meaning of these advances. For them, the real value of any medical benefits lay elsewhere.[26]

In the context of insurance, the physician's role was apparently an indirect one. Insurers, workers, and physicians saw the role of medicine less as curing the patient than as getting him back to work as soon as possible. There was a strong correlation between healing the patient and his returning to work, but in most cases the goal was the latter rather than the former. This goal was made evident in the incentives facing physicians. Typically, a worker whose fund provided medical benefits was seen by a physician who was paid by the fund. In few cases did funds offer to members free choice of physician; if a member saw his own physician he had to pay the bill himself. A physician paid by an establishment sick fund, much like a salaried company doctor, only saw employed fund members who believed they might miss several days of work. The fund, like the company, did not like to see workers absent and living on sickness benefits for very long. The ability of workers to obtain a physician's approval for a claim, according to Public Health Service official Edgar Sydenstricker (no fan of establishment funds), was closely related to the state of the local labor supply. Workers were aware of these relationships and tended to discount the importance of medical benefits.[27]

Another set of regression estimates can help illustrate the ways in which different parties viewed the importance of medical benefits. Table 5.3 shows some of the influences on the probability that a particular fund offered medical benefits. Apart from the tendency of larger funds to provide medical benefits, several relationships stand out, primarily those having to do with fund structure. Funds that were employee-managed and those that were voluntary were significantly less likely to provide medical benefits, holding other characteristics constant. These kinds of funds, which had to appeal to workers to gain and keep members, were less interested in providing medical benefits. According to these results, employee-managed funds were between 10 percent and 13 percent less likely and voluntary funds 13 percent to 25 percent less likely to pay for physician services. Among employers a different picture of the value of medical benefits prevailed: the greater the share of fund income that was provided by the company, the more likely it was that the fund would offer medical benefits, which helps answer the question, cui bono? It

Table 5.3.
Prevalence of medical benefits

VARIABLE	LOGIT: FUND OFFERS MEDICAL BENEFITS	LOGIT: FUND OFFERS MEDICAL BENEFITS	LOGIT: FUND OFFERS MEDICAL BENEFITS
Intercept	−1.19**	−2.65***	−1.90***
	(0.59)	(0.71)	(0.72)
Members (thousands)	0.16**	0.19**	0.16**
	(0.08)	(0.08)	(0.08)
Employee-managed	−0.83**	−0.65*	−0.84**
	(0.36)	(0.39)	(0.36)
Firm contributions as share of fund income	3.68***	5.75***	3.78***
	(0.90)	(1.06)	(0.90)
Voluntary	−0.80*	−1.57***	−0.98**
	(0.44)	(0.48)	(0.45)
Age of fund	−0.006	0.004	−0.002
	(0.02)	(0.02)	(0.02)
Probationary period	0.05**	0.05**	0.04**
	(0.02)	(0.02)	(0.02)

Waiting period	−0.01	0.04	−0.007
	(0.05)	(0.06)	(0.05)
Maximum benefit	0.01	−0.03	0.0006
period	(0.01)	(0.02)	(0.02)
Maximum initiation	−0.24		
fee	(0.21)		
Minimum initiation	0.27		
fee	(0.28)		
Maximum dues		0.21***	
		(0.07)	
Minimum dues		0.14***	
		(0.05)	
Maximum sick			0.08
pay/week			(0.06)
Minimum sick			0.11
pay/week			(0.08)
Pseudo R^2	0.16	0.25	0.17

Source: U.S. Commissioner of Labor, *Twenty-third Annual Report.*

Notes: N=391. Omitted categories include some establishment management, compulsory membership. Standard errors in parenthesis.

*significantly different from zero at the 0.10 level; **significantly different from zero at the 0.05 level; ***significantly different from zero at the 0.01 level

seems that workers and employers were divided concerning the value of medical benefits. Employers liked them; workers did not. In addition, funds with higher levels of required regular dues payments were more likely to provide medical benefits, so one reason that voluntary funds in particular might have declined to offer them was to keep dues payments low.[28]

If workers valued sick pay benefits highly and considered them more important than medical benefits, characteristics of typical funds can tell us whether sick funds were a good deal for workers. If they paid into the funds much more than they received in benefits, then insurance would have been an unfair bet, and funds that paid out more than they received would have dissolved. It appears in round terms that sickness fund membership was quite a good deal for most workers. Table 5.1 reports that after an initiation fee of a dollar (about a half-day's wages), members paid in on average about five dollars per year, or about a dime per week. Since benefits were, roughly, intended to replace about half a worker's wage, a typical sick pay benefit was five dollars per week. Whether that was a lot or a little relative to premium payments depended on how often workers made claims; this is discussed in Chapter 8. As table 8.6 shows, the chance of a turn-of-the-century worker missing any work due to ill health was about one in four, and the typical duration of ill health among those missing any work was about a month, or four and a half weeks of work. Thus, among all workers, the average worker missed about a week of work in a typical year.

The reason to buy insurance was to protect against income loss from illness longer than a week in duration. Few funds paid for the first week of an illness, which acted as a deductible to discourage claims for minor, transient conditions. Workers who made a claim and missed the typical four and a half weeks of work could expect three and a half weeks of sick pay at five dollars a week: a total of $17.50. If one factors in the probability of a claim the expected value of benefits was the product of 0.25 and $17.50, or between four and four and a half dollars. Relative to the five-dollar premium payment, this was a pretty good investment.[29] And so workers seemed to think.

The relative burden of premium payments can be compared to other systems real and hypothetical. Rather than comparing absolute levels of costs and benefits, as in Chapter 3, the following discussion concerns levels relative to average incomes in each system. According to the public health officials B. S. Warren and Edgar Sydenstricker, "The benefits provided in existing plans in the United States, besides being more expensive to the insured than those under European systems, are more limited." For all the reporting by Progressives about the great expense of American health insurance, it was much less costly than European insurance. If an average American worker who earned ten dollars per week paid a dime to his sickness fund, his premium payment was about 1 percent of his wage. This may have seemed expensive to Progressives, but in Britain the average worker earned about a pound per week, so that the health insurance premium there of four pence was nearly 2 percent of wages, and this estimate does not include any drop in the equilibrium wage that would follow from the even greater tax on employers, plus additional taxes to pay for the government's contribution, five pence in total. Many funds in the German system, which enjoyed a generous and legally required subsidy from employers, charged workers more than double what American workers paid. In 1908 the median fund among all German compulsory funds charged between 2 and 3 percent (one-third of which was paid by employers), and one-sixth charged more than 3 percent—much more than the American average.[30]

Progressive proposals for America were considerably more expensive than the insurance that was actually available. John R. Commons and A. J. Altmeyer estimated that according to typical proposals premiums would cost 4 percent of the payroll. Warren and Sydenstricker suggested a program that would cost American workers twenty-five cents per week, plus another twenty cents from the employer and five cents from the government. The worker's direct premium would more than double, and that still did not include indirect charges in the form of higher taxes and lower equilibrium wages. Benefits would be greater, to be sure. Workers would get sick pay of $7 per week, a considerable increase for some covered workers, for a maximum of twenty-six weeks, when the average covered worker was eligible for nearly twenty weeks of sick pay already. Under the AALL proposal a worker who earned a not unreasonable $50 per month would pay out of pocket an eighty-cent monthly premium. That would represent a near doubling of the premium compared to the typical establishment fund. Again, this figure did not include any adjustments in the wage after the employer and the state paid their shares, an additional $1.20 per worker per month. To be sure, sick pay and especially medical benefits in these proposed and actual programs were more generous, but the findings presented in this chapter concerning the demand for medical benefits in the United States should raise doubts about how strongly workers wanted costly medical benefits.[31]

Firms, funds, and workers used a variety of methods to transfer dues payments from worker to fund. Historians have viewed payroll deduction of fund dues as coercive, intrusive, and apparently typical. But within the business community its usefulness was a subject of debate. Payroll deduction was convenient for the firm and the fund and let the fund avoid the appearance of "operat[ing] a collection agency in addition to a mutual relief association," as one metal processing executive put it. On the other hand, automatic deduction meant additional work for the payroll department. Funds that collected dues from workers believed that it brought home to members their responsibility for the fund's well-being. The 1908 survey found that a solid majority of 57 percent of funds collected dues directly from members, and only 43 percent used payroll deduction.[32]

What determined levels of costs and benefits for workers? Table 5.4 provides the results of regressions in which measures of costs and benefits, as well as conditions for claiming those benefits, were regressed on structural characteristics of establishment funds. We might imagine a situation as in the beginning of Chapter 4 in which labor, management, or both initially decided questions such as whether membership would be voluntary and who would manage the fund, and the number of employees would allow for a reasonably good guess at how large the sickness fund would be. On the basis of those decisions, they determined the initiation fees and dues, the benefits, and the eligibility requirements. This table suggests that the most important characteristic influencing these decisions was whether fund membership was voluntary or compulsory. Voluntary funds needed to provide benefits that workers wanted at a cost that those workers found reasonable. The market for sickness insurance exerted a form of discipline on voluntary funds that it could not exert on compulsory funds.[33]

Table 5.4 shows the things that funds thought workers wanted. The answer, expressed in the simplest cost-benefit terms, was that they were

Table 5.4.
Costs and benefits and conditions of fund membership

DEPENDENT VARIABLE	INTERCEPT	MEMBERS (THOUSANDS)	EMPLOYEE-MANAGED	VOLUNTARY	AGE OF FUND	ADJUSTED R^2
			Costs to member			
Minimum dues	3.76***	−0.12*	−0.24	0.94**	0.003	0.19
	(0.51)	(0.07)	(0.34)	(0.44)	(0.02)	
Maximum dues	6.05***	0.06	−1.14**	1.01*	−0.02	0.10
	(0.69)	(0.09)	(0.47)	(0.59)	(0.02)	
Minimum entrance	−0.09	−0.02	0.22**	0.43***	0.02***	0.17
fee	(0.15)	(0.02)	(0.11)	(0.13)	(0.005)	
Maximum entrance	−0.38	−0.05	0.32	0.60**	0.04***	0.12
fee	(0.28)	(0.04)	(0.21)	(0.25)	(0.01)	
			Benefit to member			
Minimum benefit	3.75***	−0.05	0.20	0.80**	−0.003	0.18
payment	(0.38)	(0.05)	(0.24)	(0.32)	(0.01)	

Table 5.4.

Costs and benefits and conditions of fund membership (*continued*)

DEPENDENT VARIABLE	INTERCEPT	MEMBERS (THOUSANDS)	EMPLOYEE-MANAGED	VOLUNTARY	AGE OF FUND	ADJUSTED R^2
Maximum benefit payment	5.66***	0.08	−0.46	1.03**	−0.03**	0.04
	(0.53)	(0.07)	(0.35)	(0.45)	(0.01)	
			Membership and claim conditions			
Probationary period	−4.52*	−1.69**	2.73*	5.45**	0.25***	
	(2.69)	(0.76)	(1.64)	(2.25)	(0.07)	
Waiting period	4.65***	−0.01	0.63	1.54***	−0.01	0.06
	(0.57)	(0.08)	(0.42)	(0.50)	(0.02)	
Maximum benefit period	20.30***	0.26	−2.56*	3.04*	0.08	0.11
	(1.98)	(0.29)	(1.42)	(1.73)	(0.06)	

Note: Each regression included dummy variables for industry. All estimated by ordinary least squares except probationary period estimated by tobit due to large number (42 percent) of zero values (i.e., immediate eligibility for benefits). Standard errors in parentheses.

*significantly different from zero at the 0.10 level; **significantly different from zero at the 0.05 level; ***significantly different from zero at the 0.01 level

willing to pay higher dues and fees in order to receive the promise of higher benefit payments. And the differences were substantial. In the lowest class of membership, voluntary funds charged nearly a dollar more (ninety-four cents) in annual dues in exchange for weekly benefit payments that were eighty cents more than compulsory funds offered (holding other characteristics constant). Similarly, among the highest class of membership in voluntary funds, a dollar more in annual dues led to a dollar more in weekly benefits. In addition, voluntary funds paid those benefits for about three weeks longer that did compulsory funds. Voluntary funds imposed longer waiting periods to join and to receive benefits, but workers tolerated those as long as they received higher levels of sick pay.

A few firms were not above taking unfair advantage of new employees. They might enroll a worker in the sick fund on hiring him and then require him to submit express written refusal of membership to leave it, expecting that he would be so busy with other concerns (not to mention physically exhausted) that he would fail to leave the fund. In industries with especially high turnover rates some funds aimed to shift their income sources away from dues from long-time members and toward the initiation fees paid by new hires who, presumably, would quit before collecting any benefits. These shady practices seem to have been exceptional, however.[34]

In order to maintain a healthy level of membership, voluntary funds had to offer attractive terms. To encourage enrollment some funds paid commissions to current members who recruited new members, and others advertised the benefits that members enjoyed. To the extent that these efforts worked, the NICB wrote in 1923, "one of the best measures of success of a mutual benefit association in which membership is voluntary is the percentage of eligible employees who are members." How many employees might be expected to join a sickness fund, and what fund characteristics were associated with the number enrolled? Andrea Tone observed that workers would participate in employer welfare programs if they believed it benefited them to do so, which was more likely to be the case if they had been consulted so that the benefits would be offered, at least in part, on their terms. At the same time, workers were aware that the company would not provide insurance unless it benefited as well, which simultaneously led to a degree of skepticism regarding the company's motives.[35]

Firms that offered sickness fund membership as a benefit of employment found that varying numbers of employees were interested in joining. In the 1908 survey, about 45 percent of workers at firms with funds actually enrolled in them. Where membership was compulsory, that proportion was 86 percent. Presumably the other 14 percent consisted of white-collar workers, women, older workers, and others barred from membership. Where membership was voluntary about 40 percent of workers joined. Membership rates seem to have grown toward the end of the Progressive Era. In 1914 a Bureau of Labor Statistics survey covered 525 firms with sickness funds employing 1,178,000 workers. Of these, 749,000 belonged to the funds, a 60 percent enrollment rate.[36] At that level, the three-fourths participation rate required to buy reinsurance would have been a feasible goal for many funds, enhancing their stability further.

Determinants of membership rates can be considered using the regressions reported in table 5.5. The four specifications reflected different measures of membership rates: the number of members at the end of the year divided by the number of employees at the same time, the average number of members over the course of the previous year, and whether the regression controlled for industrial categories. The most consistent characteristics of funds with high membership rates were their lower entrance fees, lower regular dues charges, and higher weekly sick pay benefits. Other factors may also have played a role. Smaller firms and funds managed by the company had higher enrollment rates than did funds in larger firms and those with any worker management. Workers appear to have considered monetary costs and benefits to be the most important factors in deciding whether to join a sickness fund. They were more likely to enroll in funds with lower costs and higher benefits.

Medical benefits do not seem to have exerted a particularly strong attraction because they were statistically significant in only one of the four regressions. Workers did not simply avoid funds with medical benefits because they were more expensive. The strength of the present result derives in part from estimating it with regressions, because doing so held constant the effects of all the other influences besides medical benefits.

Table 5.5.

Determinants of share of the workforce choosing to enroll in voluntary sickness fund

VARIABLE	OLS: END-OF-YEAR SHARE OF WORKFORCE ENROLLED	OLS: END-OF-YEAR SHARE OF WORKFORCE ENROLLED	OLS: AVERAGE SHARE OF WORKFORCE ENROLLED	OLS: AVERAGE SHARE OF WORKFORCE ENROLLED
Intercept	0.26***	0.34***	0.26***	0.35***
	(0.08)	(0.09)	(0.08)	(0.09)
Employees (hundreds)	−0.01	−0.01*	−0.01*	−0.01**
	(0.01)	(0.006)	(0.007)	(0.006)
Men in workforce (%)	0.18***	0.16*	0.19***	0.16*
	(0.07)	(0.09)	(0.007)	(0.08)
Establishment-managed	0.16	0.20*	0.18	0.21**
	(0.11)	(0.10)	(0.11)	(0.10)
Age of fund	0.001	0.0008	0.001	0.001
	(0.002)	(0.001)	(0.002)	(0.002)
Trial membership	−0.0003	−0.002	−0.00003	−0.002
	(0.0006)	(0.002)	(0.002)	(0.002)
Waiting period	−0.003	0.0008	−0.003	0.0002
	(0.002)	(0.005)	(0.004)	(0.005)
Maximum benefit period	0.002	0.001	0.002	0.001
	(0.002)	(0.001)	(0.002)	(0.001)

Table 5.5.

Determinants of share of the workforce choosing to enroll in voluntary sickness fund (*continued*)

VARIABLE	OLS: END-OF-YEAR SHARE OF WORKFORCE ENROLLED	OLS: END-OF-YEAR SHARE OF WORKFORCE ENROLLED	OLS: AVERAGE SHARE OF WORKFORCE ENROLLED	OLS: AVERAGE SHARE OF WORKFORCE ENROLLED
Extraordinary assessments allowed	−0.01	−0.01	−0.02	−0.02
	(0.03)	(0.03)	(0.02)	(0.03)
Maximum entrance fee	0.005	0.01	0.004	0.01
	(0.01)	(0.01)	(0.01)	(0.01)
Minimum entrance fee	−0.04*	−0.05**	−0.04*	−0.05**
	(0.02)	(0.02)	(0.02)	(0.02)
Maximum dues per year	0.01	0.01	0.01	0.01
	(0.01)	(0.01)	(0.01)	(0.01)
Minimum dues per year	−0.03**	−0.03***	−0.03***	−0.03***
	(0.01)	(0.01)	(0.01)	(0.01)
Maximum sick pay/week	−0.01	−0.01	−0.01	−0.01
	(0.01)	(0.01)	(0.01)	(0.01)

Minimum sick pay/week	0.02**	0.03**	0.02**	0.03**
	(0.01)	(0.01)	(0.01)	(0.01)
Medical benefits	0.08*	0.06	0.06	0.04
	(0.05)	(0.04)	(0.04)	(0.04)
Industry dummies?	No	Yes	No	Yes
Adjusted R^2	0.05	0.10	0.06	0.10

Source: U.S. Commissioner of Labor, *Twenty-third Annual Report*.

Notes: N = 348. standard errors in parentheses. White tests indicated homoskedastic residuals for regressions without industry dummies; heteroskedastic-consistent standard errors reported for those regressions. Omitted categories include any employee management of fund (exclusively or jointly with the firm), extraordinary assessments not allowed by fund charter, and medical benefits not available.

*significantly different from zero at the 0.10 level; **significantly different from zero at the 0.05 level; ***significantly different from zero at the 0.01 level

Thus, among funds charging the same monetary fees and dues and offering the same sick pay benefit, medical benefits had hardly any effect on enrollment rates. Medical benefits did not seem to matter nearly as much to workers as they did to Progressive reformers, who made their availability a centerpiece of their reform proposals.

Funds that offered medical benefits seem to have operated quite differently from those that did not, even if they enrolled workers at about the same rates. The former were much less likely to impose extraordinary assessments. That maintenance of budget stability suggests that physicians were, in fact, able to send workers back to work quickly, thereby maintaining the fund's financial health.[37] Funds that offered physician services to members needed to pay for them by charging more in dues and fees. Higher dues payments, in turn, reduced membership rates. So the tradeoff with medical benefits might be summarized as follows. Their availability was something the company liked, because funds managed by firms were more likely to offer medical benefits. Those benefits induced sick workers to return to work sooner. Workers themselves paid for this benefit in higher premiums. Most workers seem to have preferred that higher premiums pay for higher sick pay benefits rather than medical benefits. Given workers' experiences, reformers' proposals to expand access to medical care may not have appealed to a large number of working people in the early twentieth century.[38]

A few fund characteristics seem to have been consistently important in determining worker enrollment and fund behavior. Voluntary membership was at the top of the list. Management of the fund by employees was somewhat less important but still mattered. Employee-managed funds were less likely to offer medical benefits but were not consistently different from funds that were partly or entirely managed by the company in regard to extraordinary assessments, membership costs and sick pay benefits, and enrollment rates. Perhaps funds that workers operated on their own were different in some ways that surveys of establishment funds could not address. One such kind of fund was operated by trade unions, and that is the subject of Chapter 6.

CHAPTER SIX

How Labor Union Funds Worked

> Compulsory sickness insurance for workers is based upon the theory that they are unable to look after their own interests and the state must interpose its authority and wisdom and assume the relation of parent or guardian. There is something in the very suggestion of this relationship and this policy that is repugnant to free-born citizens. Because it is at variance with our concepts of voluntary institutions and freedom for individuals, Labor questions its wisdom.
>
> —SAMUEL GOMPERS, 1916

THE PROGRESSIVE coalition that fought unsuccessfully for nationalized health insurance faced formidable opposition. Along with businesses, physicians, and commercial insurers, Samuel Gompers led organized labor in support of voluntary sickness insurance, conducted by and for workers. The role of Gompers and the American Federation of Labor (AFL) more generally in these political battles is well known.[1] What has been much less thoroughly studied is the institution for which Gompers was advocating: labor union sickness funds. By the time of the Progressive battles over state-mandated health insurance, a sizable minority of unionized workers were covered by their unions' sickness funds.

However small the number of covered workers, the effectiveness of labor leaders in ultimately prevailing over compulsory health insurance advocates indicates that the historical importance of these funds was greater than their numbers would suggest. Relative to that importance, historians have given little consideration to these sickness funds, except to criticize them for ineptitude or assert their perpetual struggle with "actuarial dilemmas." This chapter describes costs and benefits of labor union funds. Despite the lack of employer support that establishment funds enjoyed, union funds offered benefits that were not much less generous. Some critics proposed that union funds were financially unstable, but they set costs and benefits in a prudent manner. Their net effect was to enable sick members to take needed time off work to recuperate. To the extent that the funds worked as intended, then, it appears that Gompers and others' defense of these funds along with the voluntary principles they stood for was justifiable.[2]

The most prominent union leader in Progressive-Era America, Gompers had vowed to fight compulsory government health insurance to the bitter end. The labor movement as a whole was anything but united behind him. Gompers argued that as a potential substitute for union-provided insurance, government insurance would weaken the bond between workers and their union. In the American Association for Labor Legislation, the leading Progressive organization in the fight for government health insurance, Gompers saw "barnacles" hanging on to the labor movement, which was carrying most of the burden of protecting workers. The AALL did not endear itself to labor by failing to consult union leaders when drawing up an insurance proposal for the New York state legislature.[3]

Within the house of labor many saw benefit provision as critical for the particular union that offered benefits but, taken as a whole, insufficient for the welfare of the working class. In 1917 William Green of the United Mine Workers argued that the existing network of voluntary insurance funds was a worthy experiment, "productive of much good," but ultimately inadequate. In his view, it would never suffice for workers' needs. In the same year Pauline Newman of the International Ladies' Garment Workers' Union (ILGWU), a union well known for extensive welfare provisions, urged that labor look beyond its membership: "It is well to forget for the moment the organized small minority and think of the great mass of unorganized workers. That is why my organization is in favor of health insurance and social insurance. We can take care of ourselves, but who are we? A mere hundred and fifty thousand."[4]

Labor officials had good reason to be satisfied with their operations. Members of the Western Miners' Federation saw management of their extensive benefit programs as essential responsibilities of a conscientious union. According to James Lynch, the New York State Commissioner of Labor, "Officials of the great trade unions now recognize the value of benefit features as builders of unions, as conservators of the membership of these unions, entirely aside from their assistance to the members as safeguards against financial loss during physical adversity." Many labor leaders agreed with Gompers that the prime mover in worker welfare was higher wages. Henry Ott, of the Central Labor Council in Cincinnati, testified to the Ohio Health and Old Age Insurance Commission that "if wage-earners were given sufficient wages there would be no trouble. Workers can guard against all contingencies if given sufficient wages."[5]

In their political activity, unions did not divide neatly into proponents and opponents of government insurance according to whether they provided sickness benefits. The ILGWU, which had operated its own benefit funds to aid members who suffered from pulmonary tuberculosis, supported government insurance. The Typographical Union was in a similar situation. It provided unemployment and pension benefits and operated a tuberculosis sanitarium through the national union and, as noted below, sickness benefits through locals. In 1918 the Typographical Union national endorsed compulsory health insurance. Whether they favored government or union sickness insurance, all union officials recognized that there was no third way. Referring to fears of job-lock, Grant Hamilton of the AFL charged that "employer provided health insurance chains workers to their job." Only government or the union could provide health insurance to workers in a way that would maintain their dignity and not infringe on their rights to change jobs.[6]

Union officials debated whether the additional dues required to support a benefit program discouraged workers from joining or whether the financial support provided by sickness and unemployment funds encouraged workers to maintain their membership (and not work for wages below union scale) during hard times. Gompers asserted that the Cigar Makers' benefit operations kept members in the fold during the long depression of the 1890s and urged that other unions offer such benefits to encourage greater solidarity among members.[7]

A substantial minority of unions accepted Gompers's challenge. Of the 117 AFL affiliates that existed in 1904, 28 reported payment of sickness benefits. That number held steady through the next decade. The

1908 federal survey of union funds, which made no claim to completeness, found 346 local funds that offered sickness benefits with 102,800 members as well as 19 national unions with 4,625 local branches that provided sickness insurance. A 1916 survey of New York City benefit societies reported that 11 union funds there insured 20,000 workers, about one-fifth as many as were insured by fraternal societies. State-level investigations into the feasibility of government health insurance revealed that in absolute terms and as a share of organized workers, many were covered by union funds. In California, the share of union workers who were eligible for union sickness benefits was 41 percent; in Illinois it was 34 percent. The Ohio insurance commission estimated that union funds covered 85,000 members; the Illinois commission estimated 140,000 there. Though they were more heavily industrialized than most, if these states were typical, it seems reasonable to suppose that nationwide several hundred thousand workers were eligible for union sickness insurance benefits in the Progressive Era. Relative to a unionized workforce of about three million, perhaps one-fourth of union members enjoyed sickness insurance coverage.[8]

Arrangements between local and national unions in sponsoring sickness benefits fell into three categories. Some national unions paid death and permanent disability benefits and allowed locals to offer sickness benefits. Other nationals paid death, sickness, or unemployment benefits and prohibited locals from paying similar benefits. Some of these nationals included the Cigar Makers, the Deutsch-Amerikanischen Typographia, the Iron Molders, and the Journeymen Plumbers. The third and largest group of national unions that paid benefits allowed locals to pay similar benefits. Some of these nationals included the Typographical Union and the Brotherhood of Carpenters and Joiners. In general, reported one contemporary observer, the more highly developed the beneficiary functions of the national, the less freedom locals were given to provide benefits.[9]

Among local unions there were three basic types of funds, known as local sick benefit insurance, auxiliary mutual aid insurance, and chapel or shop insurance. The St. Louis Typographical Union number 8 provided an example of the first of these. All union members were automatically enrolled in the union's sickness fund, which paid $7 per week to members who had been in good standing for at least six months, after they had been incapacitated for at least two weeks. The second category included funds that were sponsored by the local in which membership was voluntary. For example, at the Chicago Union Printers' Mutual Aid Society, only members of Chicago Typographical Union number 16 could join, and those members received $10 per week for up to twenty-six weeks of sickness in a year. Membership in the third type of fund was open to nonunion members. For example, the Composing Room Relief Association of the *New York World* was founded for compositors, but by 1914 it was open to editors, writers, business office and circulation workers, stereotypers, and mailers. This fund paid benefits of $10 per week for up to twenty-six weeks, and workers who earned more were eligible, on payment of additional dues, for benefits up to $30 per week.[10]

Union funds operated in much the same way as other sickness insurance funds. One difference was the lack of a dedicated payment of dues specifically for sickness insurance. In establishment and other funds such dedicated payments were common. In union funds it was more common for sickness benefits to be financed through general dues payments. To keep the fund solvent in the face of powerful incentives not to work, a series of membership and claim requirements were generally imposed. Typically, union members could not receive benefits immediately but needed to belong to the union for several months before they could file a claim. The median trial period of six months was intended to limit fund vulnerability to adverse selection problems, in which chronically ill workers would join the union to gain immediate access to sickness benefits. Nor could they receive benefits immediately on incapacitating illness or injury; instead they had to wait several days (the median waiting period was a week), and they were limited to a certain number of weeks of benefits in a given year. The waiting period was imposed to reduce exposure to moral hazard, because it forced members to take care of themselves during transient illnesses. Union officials believed, with good reason, that these restrictions effectively kept expenses down. The Iron Molders' treasurer estimated in 1902 that if the union had paid benefits for the first week of illness rather than requiring a one-week waiting period, its spending on sick benefits would have risen by 23 percent.[11]

Union funds had ruled out paying benefits to members for certain ailments, just as other funds had done. Relatively easily avoidable conditions such as venereal diseases, injuries resulting from drunkenness or fighting, and chronic illnesses such as consumption or gastritis were not typically covered. These restrictions were so widely known that few members made claims for such conditions. One union reported that of thirty-two disallowed claims in 1911, only one rejection was for "intemperance."[12] Members generally could not make claims for conditions from which the worker obviously suffered at the time of application. The confinement expenses of female union members were virtually never covered.

Sick benefit payment levels were similar to those in other funds. Typical payments, for example, included $5 to $7 per week in Ohio and $7 to $10 per week in California. According to some unionists, such as J. G. Skemp of the Painters' Brotherhood, "the sick benefit provided by many trades unions is inadequate in amount." But since the modal benefit offered by establishment funds at this time was $5 per week also, union funds offered benefit levels similar to those of other funds of the time. Unions aimed to set the value of sick pay at an intermediate level. If set too high, it gave workers an incentive to take time off when they were really well enough to work. If set too low, sick workers would continue to report to work until they became incapacitated for many weeks. A sizable minority of local funds offered stratified benefit payments. Older members were not turned out, but older applicants were generally either rejected or offered reduced benefits in exchange for reduced dues payments. Similarly, unmarried men and apprentices were paid less in benefits, in part because they were younger and earned less than married journeymen and masters earned.[13]

The duration of sickness benefits was another shortcoming of union-sponsored benefit programs, according to their critics. Skemp complained in 1916 that the inadequate level of sick pay was available for "too short a period." Of 316 local union funds reporting maximum benefit periods in 1908, the median number of weeks for which a worker could draw sick benefits was thirteen. But a few funds offered up to a year's worth of benefits, and a small number (23, or 7.3 percent) imposed no limits on the duration of benefit payments. These figures are quite similar to those for funds sponsored by employers, so union funds should not be viewed as inadequate in a relative sense.[14] In short, great diversity in benefit programs characterized turn-of-the-century union insurance offerings, but on average many of their characteristics were similar to those of establishment and fraternal sickness funds.

The process of making a claim in a typical union sickness fund is illustrative. An example comes from the benefit operations of the Amalgamated Association of Iron, Steel, and Tin Workers. A member who became sick or disabled needed to notify the local union's financial secretary, vice president, or sick committee within a week of onset of the illness or of the injury and then fill out a form describing his ailment. Within two weeks of onset, the worker was examined by the visiting committee of union members and, if they believed it necessary, a physician. The physician attested to the member's medical diagnosis, and the committee attested to his inability to work. The local then paid a benefit that was retroactive one week, leaving the member minus a pay packet for only the first week of his incapacity. The local sent the report of the member's case to the national office, and it was followed by updated reports from the physician. The national then reimbursed the local for the benefit payments.[15]

Not every union operated a sickness fund. Investigation of the characteristics of unions that did illustrates the importance of benefits to union members in ways that have been overlooked. These distinguishing characteristics can be examined in two surveys of union members and unions conducted in Michigan. The first was a survey of individual railroad workers in 1893 that asked the respondents whether they belonged to a union and whether their union provided sick benefits.[16] Of the 1,158 workers who reported membership in a union, 71 percent reported that their union provided sick benefits. What distinguished workers who belonged to such unions from members of unions that did not offer such benefits? Unionized workers who were at elevated risk of accident or ill health were more likely to belong to unions with sickness funds than were workers at low risk of accident or sickness. Table 6.1 describes mean values and results of logit regressions in which the dependent variable was set equal to one if the worker's union offered sickness benefits. Workers were defined as at high accident risk if they reported having suffered an injury in their current occupation. They were defined as having worsening health if they reported their health at the time of the survey as "bad," "fair," or "poor" relative to when they started their cur-

Table 6.1.
Worker characteristics and union benefits, Michigan railway workers, 1893

VARIABLE	MEAN (STANDARD DEVIATION)	MODEL 1	MODEL 2	MODEL 3
Intercept		0.55	0.62	0.55
		(0.54)	(0.53)	(0.54)
Age 20 and under	0.01	−0.62	−0.57	−0.57
		(0.72)	(0.72)	(0.72)
Age 30–39 years	0.41	0.23	0.21	0.21
		(0.17)	(0.17)	(0.18)
Age 40–49 years	0.13	0.39	0.36	0.35
		(0.25)	(0.25)	(0.25)
Age 50 and older	0.04	−0.65*	−0.71*	−0.69*
		(0.36)	(0.36)	(0.36)
Brakeman	0.16	0.80***	0.82***	0.78***
		(0.23)	(0.23)	(0.23)
Conductor	0.17	0.03	0.003	−0.01
		(0.23)	(0.23)	(0.23)
Engineer	0.17	−0.15	−0.26	−0.22
		(0.27)	(0.27)	(0.27)
Fireman	0.10	1.09***	1.02***	1.05***
		(0.29)	(0.29)	(0.29)
Married	0.67	0.37	0.36	0.37
		(0.24)	(0.24)	(0.24)
Widowed	0.01	−0.18	−0.10	−0.12
		(0.92)	(0.96)	(0.92)
Family size	3.63	−0.02	−0.02	−0.02
	(2.27)	(0.05)	(0.05)	(0.05)
Regular earnings	$768.67	−0.0002	−0.0002	−0.0002
	(271.84)	(0.0004)	(0.0004)	(0.0004)
Accident risk	0.14	0.42*		0.40*
		(0.22)		(0.22)

Table 6.1.
Worker characteristics and union benefits, Michigan railway workers, 1893 (*continued*)

VARIABLE	MEAN (STANDARD DEVIATION)	MODEL 1	MODEL 2	MODEL 3
Worsening health	0.25		0.41** (0.18)	0.40** (0.18)
Pseudo R^2		0.06	0.06	0.07

Source: Carter et al., "Codebook . . . Michigan, 1893."
Note: Sample size restricted to union members. Standard errors in parentheses for regression estimates. Estimation method, logit; dependent variable = 1 if member belonged to union that offered sickness benefits and = 0 if respondent's union did not. Dummy variables for city of residence and place of birth included but coefficients not reported. Omitted categories included age 20–29 years, other occupation, single. Regular earnings = annual earnings excluding overtime. Accident risk = 1 if worker reported any on-the-job accident since entering present occupation. Worsening health = 1 if worker reported the effect of his job on current health to be "bad," "fair," or "poor." Correlation between accident risk and worsening health = 0.02.
*significantly different from zero at the 0.10 level; **significantly different from zero at the 0.05 level; ***significantly different from zero at the 0.01 level

rent job. In separate regressions and in Model 3, which included both risk and health variables, the coefficients of accident risk and declining health were all positive and significant. This simple test suggests that railroad unions were particularly likely to provide health insurance to those at high risk of accident and sickness.

Because many unions aimed to provide their members with a variety of benefits, including payments during strikes and unemployment, it would be useful to see which unions were most likely to offer sickness benefits. The other Michigan survey can help illustrate not only which unions offered sickness insurance but to what extent it may have substituted for other benefits such as strike, unemployment, and death benefits or whether some of these benefits were packaged together. This survey was the first statewide canvass of labor unions in Michigan.[17] Local investigators who enjoyed union connections collected the information. The survey examined 222 unions with 17,864 members. Sickness funds could be found in a wide variety of crafts, and in several trades (barbering, machining, and cigar making) all or nearly all locals ran a sickness fund. Overall about one-third of local unions offered sickness benefits, covering about one-third of all unionized workers.

Determining the characteristics of locals that offered sickness insurance yields insight into the way they structured their benefits. Table 6.2 reports estimated values of two regressions. The first considered unions that either did or did not provide sickness benefits, and the second considered factors behind union provision of a variety of benefits: unemployment, strike, burial, and sickness benefits. In general, larger unions offered these benefits. The probability of providing sickness benefits increased with size to a level of nearly four hundred members, much greater than the average local's eighty-one members. Funds with more than four hundred members were less likely to offer sickness benefits, which also tended to come packaged with burial and unemployment benefits, creating a sickness benefit moral hazard among unemployed members in bad financial straits. Locals that offered strike benefits tended not to offer sickness benefits, so that striking workers in these unions were not tempted to claim their sickness benefit in order to make ends meet. The regressions produced no evidence that insurance benefits were tied to wage levels, although the provision of several benefit types required higher dues to pay for them. It appears that unions that offered these benefits were high-cost, high-benefit unions, but not necessarily unions of highly paid workers. It was not simply that these benefits appealed to well-paid workers, nor did workers pay more in dues to obtain sickness benefits. Union insurance benefits appealed to risk-averse workers who wanted to pay higher dues in order to receive a larger package of several kinds of benefits.[18]

Across the nation, unions carefully set the dollar value of their sickness benefits at sustainable levels. The 1908 survey of sickness funds examined local and national union funds and reported local sickness fund operations in detail, including the particular craft of the union. The typical value of union sick benefits at this time has been reported as $5 per week, a sum that was criticized in the contemporary and present-day literature as insufficient to protect a worker's standard of living. The average worker in this sample, though, received about 10 percent more than that (table 6.3), and some unions, such as those for glass workers and the National Association for Letter Carriers, paid more than $6 per

Table 6.2.
Influences on benefit offerings by Michigan unions, 1896

VARIABLE	MEAN VALUES (STANDARD DEVIATION)	MODEL 1: SICKNESS BENEFITS (LOGIT)	MODEL 2: ALL BENEFITS (POISSON)
Intercept		−1.01	−2.36
		(1.33)	(2.36)
	Local union characteristics		
Members (hundreds)	0.81	1.33**	0.40**
	(2.02)	(0.57)	(0.20)
Number of members squared		−0.17**	−0.06**
		(0.09)	(0.03)
Market share	0.73	0.79	0.14
	(0.29)	(0.87)	(0.28)
Strike benefit	0.33	−1.27**	
		(0.58)	
Burial benefit	0.38	0.98**	
		(0.48)	
Unemployment benefit	0.10	3.16***	
		(0.14)	
	Member characteristics		
Dues known	0.97	−2.05*	−0.33
		(1.18)	(0.64)
Dues if known ($ per year)	7.51	0.05	0.03***
	(7.00)	(0.03)	(0.01)
Wage known	0.75	0.96	0.25
		(0.69)	(0.21)
Wage if known ($ per day)	2.01	−0.05	−0.03
	(4.47)	(0.10)	(0.04)

Table 6.2.
Influences on benefit offerings by Michigan unions, 1896 (*continued*)

VARIABLE	MEAN VALUES (STANDARD DEVIATION)	MODEL 1: SICKNESS BENEFITS (LOGIT)	MODEL 2: ALL BENEFITS (POISSON)
Hours known	0.83	−0.76	−0.62
		(2.24)	(0.72)
Hours if known	8.08	0.02	−0.04
(per day)	(3.82)	(0.21)	(0.07)
N	221	190	221
Pseudo R^2		0.27	

Source: State of Michigan Bureau of Labor and Industrial Statistics, *Thirteenth Annual Report.*
Notes: Standard errors in parentheses for regression results. Model 1 dependent variable = 1 if sickness benefits offered; method = logit. Model 2 dependent variable = sum of types of benefits offered (e.g., =1 if only sickness benefits, =2 if sickness and strike benefits, etc.); method = Poisson. Dummies for craft and city are included in both regressions. All barbers and cigar makers' locals provided sickness insurance, and no carpenters' and coopers' locals provided sickness insurance, so these 31 locals were omitted from Model 1. Market share = share of union membership as sum of membership and local nonunion workers in same craft. Dues, wage, and hours known = 1 if union reported average dues charged, wage earned, and hours worked per member; dues, wage, hours if known = interaction of dues known × dues, wage known × wage, hours known × hours.
*significantly different from zero at the 0.10 level; **significantly different from zero at the 0.05 level; ***significantly different from zero at the 0.01 level

week. Standard benefit levels reflected differences in relative earnings, with miners paid the most and barbers the least. "Reduced sick benefits" refers to lower benefits paid in later periods of illness (sometimes in earlier periods) and those paid to older members, the unmarried, and apprentices.[19]

Progressives complained that few union funds offered medical benefits. Only about 2 percent of sampled funds surveyed in 1908 did so. These tended to be large, however, so that the share of covered workers was closer to ten percent or so. The survey conducted by Anna Kalet in New York City also found that only one in eleven union funds offered medical benefits. Another criticism, similar to complaints made of establishment funds, was that the quality of the care rendered by union physicians was closely connected to budgetary considerations. Edgar

Table 6.3.
Mean values and standard deviations of union fund characteristics, 1908

CHARACTERISTIC	AVERAGE BY FUND	AVERAGE BY WORKER
Number of funds	323	323
Number of members per fund	295	1,052
	(473)	(22,833)
Share with medical benefits	0.02	0.10
Sick benefit ($/week)	$5.23	$5.63
	(1.85)	(30.38)
Reduced sick benefit	$4.51	$4.73
($/week)	(2.05)	(37.83)
Waiting period (days)	7.17	7.22
	(4.49)	(72.93)
Maximum benefit period	13.28	12.22
(weeks)	(9.84)	(128.81)
Cases of compensated sick time/member	0.11	0.09

Source: U.S. Commissioner of Labor, *Twenty-third Annual Report.*
Note: The top figure in the cell is the mean or share. Standard deviations of continuous variables are in parentheses.

Sydenstricker, the prominent Public Health Service reformer, wrote that "from the standpoint of these [union] funds the physician's function is to prevent malingering."[20]

Table 6.4 helps disentangle influences on levels of sick pay benefits. Each column shows the results of an ordinary least squares regression in which the value of the sick pay benefit, as measured in terms of dollars per week, for a given union was the dependent variable. Characteristics of the union formed the independent variables. Contrary to criticisms that union sickness funds were ineptly run, given that very few sick funds operated on any kind of actuarial basis, the union funds sampled in 1908 appear to have attended to incentive conflicts. More valuable weekly benefits were associated with longer waiting periods between the onset of illness and the beginning of benefit payments. There was also a trade-off between duration of benefit payments and the value

Table 6.4.
Influences on value of union sick fund wage replacement benefits, 1908

INFLUENCE	WEEKLY SICK BENEFIT		REDUCED WEEKLY SICK BENEFIT	
Intercept	5.35**	5.52**	3.96**	4.21**
	(0.35)	(0.27)	(0.41)	(0.31)
Membership	0.29	0.54*	0.15	0.33
	(0.23)	(0.23)	(0.27)	(0.26)
Age of union	0.009	0.005	0.0056	−0.0028
	(0.010)	(0.010)	(0.012)	(0.011)
Probationary period	−0.034	−0.11**	−0.005	−0.053
	(0.033)	(0.031)	(0.039)	(0.036)
Waiting period	0.079**	0.083**	0.094**	0.10**
	(0.026)	(0.025)	(0.030)	(0.029)
Maximum length of benefits	−0.031**	−0.030**	0.010	0.0063
	(0.011)	(0.010)	(0.012)	(0.012)
Medical benefits	−0.93	−0.47	−0.72	−0.51
	(0.78)	(0.79)	(0.92)	(0.90)
Craft dummies	Yes	No	Yes	No
Adjusted R^2	0.17	0.09	0.07	0.04

Source: U.S. Commissioner of Labor, *Twenty-third Annual Report*.
Note: Standard errors in parentheses. n=323.
*significantly different from zero at the 0.05 level; **significantly different from zero at the 0.01 level

of those benefits. Longer benefit payment periods were associated with smaller weekly benefits. Unions appear to have determined benefit levels and eligibility requirements prudently.

Critics of union funds claimed that their finances were precarious, and in some cases they were. The Brotherhood of Carpenters and Joiners offered permanent disability benefits through its national union and encouraged locals to provide temporary disability benefits. The locals were aware of competition from fraternal insurers and offered sickness benefit levels comparable to those of the Odd Fellows and the Foresters. At fifty cents per month, their dues were lower than those of the fraternals, the intention being to make their insurance a better buy. But many Carpenters and Joiners' locals set dues payments too low to keep their funds actuarially sound and went bankrupt. Other financial difficulties arose in the treatment of chronic illness. A frequent problem of workers in the dusty trades was tuberculosis. The Tunnel and Subway Constructors became insolvent after exhausting their funds on benefits for members who had contracted consumption in the course of their work.[21]

One of the most urgent problems that union funds faced was directly related to one of their most attractive features. As long as a worker maintained his membership in the union he was eligible for sickness benefits. Many unions aimed to make it as easy as possible to maintain that membership while the brother was unemployed so as to reduce the pressure to work for less than union scale. But if he had exhausted his unemployment benefits he could see advantages in claiming a sickness benefit. Even if he was not very ill, sick pay might make the difference between a tight household budget and outright hunger.

On the whole, this connection implies that unemployment rates or payments of unemployment benefits might have been positively correlated with sickness benefit claims for union funds in ways that would not have occurred in establishment funds. Opponents of state insurance claimed that this was an ongoing problem in European sickness insurance. According to Frederick Hoffman, "The sickness curve rises invariably during prolonged periods of unemployment, which is in Germany accepted as evidence of substantial increase in the tendency to malinger and defraud the funds." In fact, European sickness claims did rise during periods of economic recession, although that might also have been due to declining worker health in hard times.[22]

Support for this hypothesis can be seen in the case of an old and large British union, the Amalgamated Society of Engineers, to which 174,253 men belonged in 1914. This union provided both sickness and unemployment benefits. To illustrate some of the forces operating on union sick funds, figure 6.1 shows trends in unemployment claims and sickness claims made by members of this union, as reported by the economic historian T. S. Ashton. It is clear that unemployment and sickness were positively related to each other, the estimated correlation coefficient

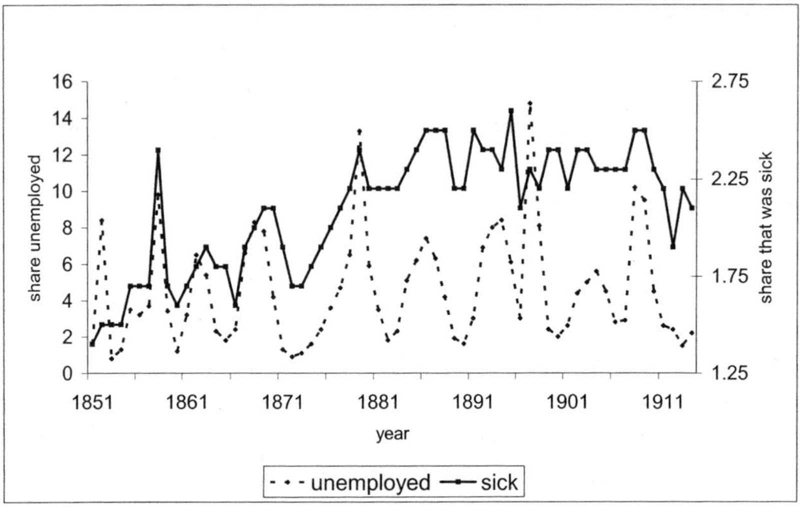

FIGURE 6.1. Sickness and unemployment claims in a British trade union friendly society. (Data from Ashton, "Relation Between Unemployment and Sickness.")

equaling 0.45, significant at less than the 0.001 level. The causes of this relationship were less clear. Low unemployment rates might lead to healthier workers, but Ashton observed that men would be tempted to claim sickness benefit when high weekly earnings were not available. He further proposed that the reduction of sick benefit payments during World War I could not have been due to improving health among the engineers, who worked for days without end to support the war effort. James Riley's findings for British friendly society members were similar. Although the relationship between unemployment and sickness claims was positive and significant, the magnitude was small, and he dismissed unemployment as a major factor in sickness rates.[23]

Contemporary observers reported that American unions that offered unemployment and sickness benefits were subject to the same stresses as were European funds. In America, too, union members who could draw both types of benefits would try to do so, according to these writers. Boris Emmet, a government statistician, testified before the Ohio Health and Old Age Insurance Commission that as a rule "during unemployment the sickness rate increases." According to the Illinois Health Insurance Commission, "Some of the nationals have experienced some difficulty in malingering found in excessive claims presented in times of wide-spread unemployment." Beyond these assertions, though, there has been no evidence to support these claims, which on their own suggest an important weakness of union benefit provision.[24]

It is possible to compare sick benefit payments to membership trends as well as to trends in unemployment benefits in a few particular unions. These case studies can help illustrate the ways in which particular unions managed their funds. They indicate that despite the economic incentive to take time off that sickness benefits offered, union funds managed their benefits carefully. The few sources of available data suggest that American funds did not allow members to claim excess sickness benefits during hard times.

One union that managed sickness benefits carefully was the Cigar Makers' International Union. The Cigar Makers intentionally set out to be a distinctive high-cost, high-benefit union, believing that benefits would encourage loyalty. Both membership and weeks of compensated sickness per worker increased over the quarter century from 1882 to 1906.[25] Gompers drew on reports of such trends when he argued that the availability of sickness benefits attracted workers to the union and discouraged members from leaving. This correlation also suggests that as the union grew it became better able to fund sickness claims, perhaps as a result of learning-by-doing in regard to insurance operations. To see how the Cigar Makers balanced claims on their sickness and unemployment benefits, consider the period that includes the depression of 1893–1897. An increase in both types of payments during those years could suggest the kinds of financial mismanagement that critics of union funds alleged.

Figure 6.2 shows the value of sickness and unemployment benefits paid by the Cigar Makers in terms of dollars per member. This is a far from perfect measure of claims because it misses the number of claims and their length, but it should correlate reasonably well with them. The Cigar Makers' original unemployment benefit consisted of loans to cover travel expenses for out-of-work members who wanted to look for work in greener pastures. Only later did they offer cash payments. The figure shows the sum of the loans and cash payments. For corroboration, figure 6.3 shows much the same pattern for another union that offered both kinds of benefits, the Deutsch-Amerikanischen Typographia. The Typographia had been founded in 1873 for printers of German-

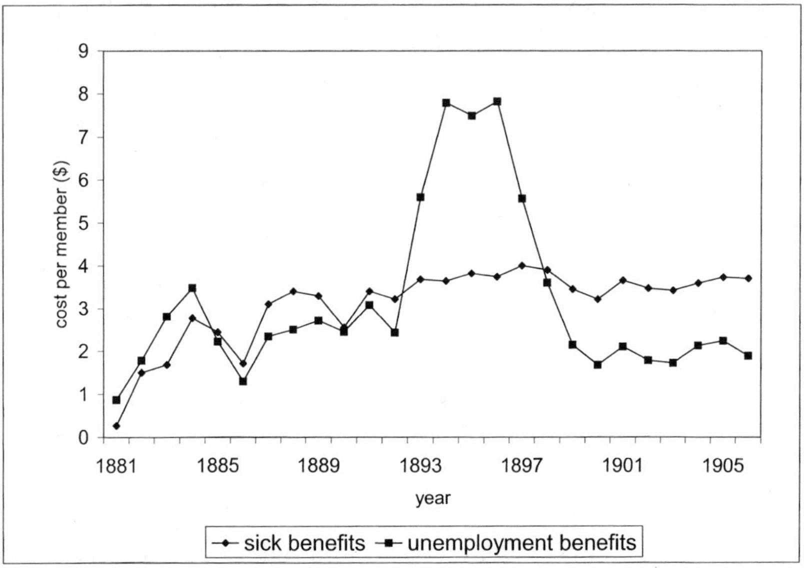

FIGURE 6.2. Cigar Makers' International Union, benefit payments per member (in dollars). (Data from Kennedy, *Beneficiary Features.*)

language publications. Its benefits also consisted of cash payments to unemployed members and additional grants to fund travel to new places of employment.[26]

For both unions an upsurge in unemployment payments in the mid-1890s is clearly seen in the figures, and this trend coincided with the downturn in the business cycle. The magnitude of increase was much greater for the Cigar Makers—unemployment benefit payments per member were on the order of 2.5 times greater during the depression than they had been earlier. A smaller rise can be seen among the German printers. But in neither case did sick benefit payments deviate much from the trend. This was quite different from the case of the British engineers. At a time when each union's reserves would have come under severe strain from unemployment benefit payments, either they refused to pay additional sickness benefit payments or members did not apply for sickness benefit at higher rates. Either way it suggests that union sickness funds were viable longer-term operations that could withstand some vicissitudes of the business cycle.

* * *

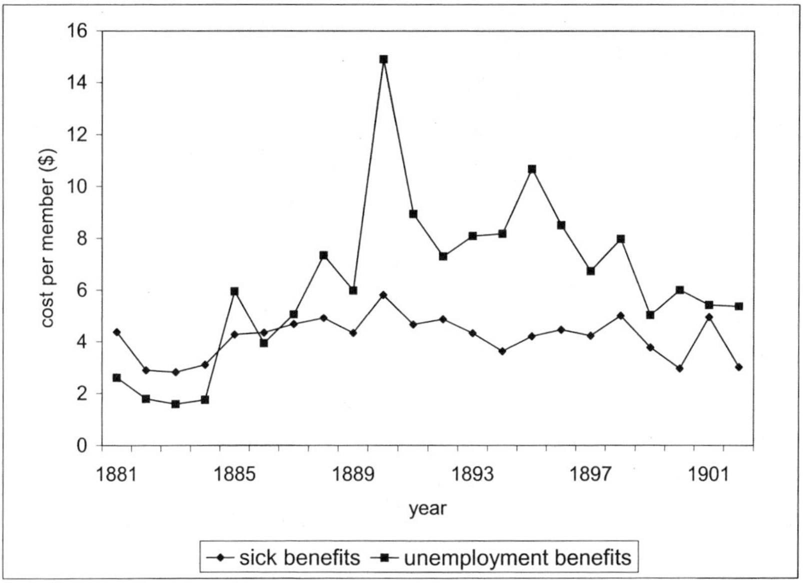

FIGURE 6.3. German American Typographia, benefit payments per member (in dollars). (Source: Kennedy, *Beneficiary Features*.)

The Progressive case against union sickness insurance funds has been summarized in three points. First, inadequate reserves kept funds from fulfilling unexpectedly high demand for their benefits. Second, premiums were too expensive for most workers, and so they covered a small share of union members. Third, the sick pay benefit was "very small" and available for too short a period, and funds rarely offered medical benefits. None of these points withstands close consideration.[27]

The role of reserve funds is ambiguous. Many unions operated benefit funds together with their own finances, so a single account received regular dues and any extra charges for insurance coverage. The union then paid out benefits from the same pot. It is worth thinking about what would happen to union reserves that were supposed to pay unexpectedly high numbers of sickness claims. An official of the United Brotherhood of Leather Workers on Horse Goods reported on the value of a large reserve fund: "An organization without a good reserve fund is helpless in case of strikes or lockouts." Reserves marked for medical benefits could easily be spent on sickness or strike benefits. Unions that aimed to amass a strike fund may have made reserves for sickness insurance a low priority. Also, some union leaders believed that local union funds did not need much in the way of reserves, apparently because peer pressure would keep the greatest threats to financial health, fraudulent claims, to a minimum.[28]

Union funds were not the only sickness funds with relatively low reserves. A 1923 survey of establishment funds found that few funds sponsored by firms carried reserves, though their necessity was a widely known principle of insurance. Even fewer bothered to employ an actuary. Apparently establishment and union funds suffered from similar weaknesses. Establishment funds desired to keep dues to a minimum, but they also believed that large reserves would encourage workers to demand dividend payments or moratoria on dues payments. Faced with relatively short time horizons of insured workers, establishment funds chose to keep low reserves. Perhaps union funds had similar motivations. Fraternal sickness funds were well served by simple financial practices combined with the ability to extract emergency dues payments from members as a last resort. Informal pricing protocols and low reserves characterized all funds in that era, not only union funds.[29]

Regarding the second point, exactly how expensive union benefits were is difficult to assess, since they generally did not collect separate dues for sickness benefits. Table 6.2 reported no relation between union dues and sickness insurance provision, and according to one state commission, "Few could not pay for the insurance if they desired to do so." The cost of operating benefit funds must not have been debilitating for unions because in California and Illinois in the late Progressive Era, 30 to 40 percent of unionized workers enjoyed sickness insurance coverage. Further, benefits were offered to workers in a variety of crafts. It seems quite possible that unions whose members desired sickness benefits were able to operate sickness funds.[30]

Demand for benefits by covered workers may well have been higher than union officials expected, but they managed extra demand capably. During the times in which we would have expected sickness claims to peak and perhaps overwhelm available resources, during the depression of the 1890s, union funds provided a steady level of benefit payments. The Deutsch-Amerikanischen Typographia actually reduced its benefits in July 1894 from $6 to $5 per week to ensure that the treasury would be able to pay the claims made against it.[31] Such prudential and unpopular changes suggest careful management of resources.

With regard to the third point, the value of union-sponsored sickness benefits was sufficient by the standards of the day. Although nobody in the published contemporary literature seemed to think that $5 per week was enough, it was similar to other benefit levels. Union sick pay benefits alone were worth about half again as much as sick pay and medical benefits combined in Germany (see Chapter 3). The actual benefit payments of fraternal and establishment funds were greater than payment levels of the European systems, as idealized by Progressives, and less than the AALL's own ideal benefit payment levels.. These were the very real alternatives to union funds for workers who wanted to buy insurance. All funds provided the same $5 or so per week, so it is not clear that union benefit payments were penurious in any realizable sense.

The motivations of employers and unions in providing sickness benefits may not have differed very greatly. Behind the paternalism of employer rhetoric was a conscious awareness of costs and benefits. Union officials who believed that government insurance was necessary made similar statements. William Green of the Mine Workers claimed (perhaps mechanistically) that "society is vitally interested in promoting and maintaining at the highest standard the efficiency of each worker. Loss of time, inability to work, the removal of each social unit from the field of industrial activity means, in the last analysis, a distinct loss to society at large."[32] The path from insurance to health to greater productivity was evident to all.

Union funds played a unique role among the congeries of sickness insurance operations in turn-of-the-century America. They were an additional expense some unions willingly took on, in part because they believed that benefits increased solidarity, and in part because they believed that the additional expense could be built into their next round of wage negotiations. And these funds grew dramatically in the late nineteenth century. Much later, unions that had specialized in providing health care for workers in particular occupations could maintain their niche. An ILGWU official observed in 1947 that the union's benefit system helped stabilize membership and raised the prospects of growth.

Whether it was politically prudent for Gompers to fight for these funds is a separate question. But the historian Roy Lubove's assertion that "statistics substantiate the criticism that trade union benefit funds were defective by rational economic criteria" could not have been more wrong.[33] Union sickness funds did provide effective and ongoing protection against income loss to the workers who joined them.

CHAPTER SEVEN

Workers' Decisions to Save or Buy Insurance

> The true solution of the situation lies in the education of the individual to provide for himself.
>
> —REINHOLD KOCH, 1912

> The saver is an isolated adventurer. He cares only for himself.
>
> —HOWELL CHENEY, 1919

IN THE LATE NINETEENTH and early twentieth centuries American workers insured themselves against the costs of sickness through fraternal, union, and employer sickness funds. Progressive reformers attacked these arrangements as inadequate. If Progressive proposals for state insurance were to be improvements over the existing arrangements, in what ways were existing arrangements defective? One deficiency that Progressives steadily noted was the inability of workers to save part of their usual earnings in case of income loss due to sickness. According to this argument, the state needed to step in and force workers to insure themselves to protect them from their own fecklessness. Was such compulsion necessary? Were workers really unable to save?

This chapter discusses the ways in which workers chose to insure themselves over the course of the life cycle so as to protect their finances from the effects of extended illness. The statistical evidence presented considerably weakens the Progressive case that workers would not prudently save. A significant part of the working class was able to self-insure against illness by accumulating savings. A key to this explanation that has not previously been discussed is that demand for health insurance varied across the life cycle. Demand was a function of expected health, ability to save, and asset portfolio composition. Workers provided for unexpected income losses in a prudent manner, but in different ways at different times in their lives. In this light, Progressive reforms were not obviously better for the working class, which helps explain their inability to gain any political purchase.

By the late nineteenth century, American workers were nearly the best paid in the world. In 1890, the average American worker earned nearly double what the average French or German worker did and half again as much as the average British worker. In the last decade of the century, real wages for unskilled American workers grew by 7.6 percent, and between 1900 and 1910 they grew another 9 percent. From 1890 to 1910 real German wages grew nearly as fast, at 14.5 percent, but British wages grew only 8 percent and French wages 11 percent. The American economy suffered periodic downturns such as those that took place in the early 1890s and following the Panic of 1907, but the general level of wages was high and the trend upward.[1] To be sure, averages mask distributional differences as well as individual experiences. The breadth of these statistics makes them useful, though, and to know something about the "average worker"—omitting differentials by race, sex, age, union status, and so on—yields an understanding of the American worker's material level of living. By the standards of the day, it was high.

Two reasons for those high American wages were productivity and mobility of labor. In industry, American productivity at this time was about double that of British and German workers. Differences in agricultural labor productivity were much smaller, and in services British workers seem to have been more productive than Americans. Sources of higher levels of American industrial productivity, in turn, included high levels of capital per worker, widespread use of general power technologies such as steam, and a well-educated and mobile workforce.[2] The mobility of the American worker is an important part of this chapter's story.

The fluidity of the American labor market was remarkable. A longstanding characteristic was geographic mobility. Europeans arrived on the East Coast and, joined by ambitious or discontented Easterners, they steadily flowed westward. In addition to the lure of higher wages, local and migrating workers benefited from institutions such as employment agencies and labor exchanges that connected prospective employees with jobs. Easy access to employers who might lure workers away from their current drudgery made movement from one job to another easy, and so workers were quick to seize alternative employment opportunities. Between 1910 and 1920 workers were seven times more likely to quit than to be laid off.[3]

As a result of high turnover rates, a large share of early twentieth-century industrial workers had gained relatively little experience in any one job. By one estimate two-fifths of manufacturing workers had been on the job less than a year; the figure was as high as two-thirds among chemical workers. One difference between the Progressive Era and later labor markets was the decline over time of very short-term employees, known as "floaters," who had the loosest of attachment to their jobs.[4]

Such is our understanding of Progressive-Era labor markets, thanks to the imaginative and diligent work of economic historians who have access to federal census manuscripts, well-organized archives, and powerful computers. We might like to know something about the contemporary understanding of the workforce at that time—work conditions, wages, hours, and the well-being of its members and their families. Social scientists attracted to the Progressive movement were happy to oblige. They wanted to establish that American workers earned very little relative to the cost of living so that government needed to step in and provide insurance to a working class that could not save against the costs of illness.

According to Progressives, what government provision of health insurance would achieve was relatively straightforward. Ultimately, it promised to reduce the incidence of poverty. Irving Fisher claimed that state-supervised health insurance would "indirectly but powerfully tend to reduce poverty." The way in which this would happen, they stated, was that the sickness benefit would keep workers who were on the edge of poverty from losing their independence. Their opponents charged that letting a small share of the working class determine social welfare policy was to let the tail wag the dog. They added that "a large percentage of the cases of poverty caused or accompanied by sickness would not be avoided by compulsory health insurance of the kind that has been proposed."[5]

Progressives asserted that poverty and sickness were linked together via a feedback mechanism. Sickness reduced time on the job in an era when relatively few workers received sick pay and so reduced worker income. They emphasized a high-end estimate that the average worker missed nine in three hundred work days, thus losing 3 percent of his pay. Other estimates suggested that the average cost of medical care was an additional three days' pay. At the same time, poverty caused workers to suffer from inadequate diet and housing, which led to further illness and less time at work.[6] A vicious circle of impoverishment and declining health ensued.

Because reformers lacked much of a statistical context and because they expected that the sicker the working class was perceived to be, the more readily government intervention would be accepted, they cast available estimates in apocalyptic language. To Progressives the available data provided evidence of dire health conditions. The Ohio Health and Old Age Insurance Commission interpreted its 2 percent absence rate as "overwhelming evidence of unnecessarily high mortality and preventable ill-health." The American Association for Labor Legislation noted that although "complete morbidity statistics were lacking," it was sure that "the amount of disability due to sickness among wage-earners is high." Given this level of statistical ignorance, one option was to import estimates from Europe. In 1910 the AALL proposed that if the United States suffered from sickness at the same rate as did Germany, that is, so that workers missed 8.5 days per year, the total loss to the economy must have been nearly $800 million.[7] That figure must have seemed enormous, and it was in fact the equivalent of about 2.5 percent of GDP. If the absenteeism estimates presented in Chapter 4 of six to seven work days in three hundred were accurate, then this estimate was a little high, and it may have overestimated losses since firms could hire temporary employees to fill in gaps, and entrepreneurs and workers in small shops could work extra hours when healthy to catch up. In any case, it was unclear how a state-supervised health insurance program might reduce this figure.

More important for insurance purposes were the financial consequences for unlucky workers who did become temporarily disabled. Those who missed any work at all tended to be off for weeks and weeks. As noted in table 8.6, 20 to 24 percent of workers took sick leave during this period, and among them the average duration of an absence was five to six weeks, meaning that 10 to 15 percent of their annual earnings could be lost. The prospect of an unusual but costly event would be the classic problem to be solved by insurance.

The need for insurance begged the question of government intervention. If insurance was an efficacious means of preventing "dependency," why did workers not obtain it on their own, so as to avoid falling into poverty? The answer given by reformers was that workers earned so little relative to their expenses that they were unable to self-insure by saving, nor could they afford to buy insurance. Rubinow tallied the results of several surveys of the cost of living in his influential 1913 book *Social Insurance*. Table 7.1 summarizes these and other estimates. According to the experts, the minimum income needed to keep the wolf from the door had risen steeply in the previous two decades, from $500 to $900 per year, an 80 percent increase. In nominal terms, however, the full-time weekly earnings of a semi-skilled manufacturing laborer rose only from $8.75 to $10.37, an increase of less than 20 percent. This sounded dire. From another perspective, because the consumer price index was constant during these years, it may have been that the experts had overestimated increases in the cost of living. To compare income and expenditure more directly, Rubinow cited a recent study by Scott Nearing of income in the Northeast and the Midwest that estimated that the typical worker earned between $500 and $700 annually. On a family basis, a federal survey suggested, average household income was about $750, or just $660 in families in which only the father worked. In these cases, claimed Progressives, little would be left over to cover emergencies that disabled the breadwinner.[8]

Medical expenses in particular were supposed to be large and unexpected. But it is not clear that reasonably far-sighted families ignored medical expenses, nor was it clear that they were so large as to threaten family financial well-being. Nearly everyone had some such expenses in a typical year. The 1901 federal cost of living survey estimated that more than three-fourths of families spent something on medical or funeral bills, which resulted in an average expenditure of $26.78. Other surveys found similar results. The New York State Factory Investigating Committee estimated that families with typical incomes spent, on average, $22 per year on physicians, medicines, and hospital expenses, a figure that these researchers then used as a "reasonable allowance" for health care spending in estimating typical family budgets. Chapin estimated that New York City families with incomes between $600 and $1,100 spent only around 2 percent of the total on medical bills, or around $20.

Table 7.1.
Estimates of minimum family income necessary for subsistence

SOURCE	INCOME	COMMENT
Aldrich Committee, 1892[a]	$500 for "laborer's family"	$50 for items other than food, clothing, and rent
John Mitchell, *Organized Labor,* 1903[b]	$600 for "average" family	Rubinow: Estimate for "semi-rural communities."
N.Y. State Conference of Charities and Corrections, 1907[b]	$700–800 if no emergencies	$825 for family with 3 children in Manhattan
Robert Coit Chapin, *Standard of Living,* 1909[a]	$900 for "normal" standard of living	

[a]Chapin, *Standard of Living,* pp. 5, 246.
[b]Rubinow, *Social Insurance,* pp. 30–32.

Later in the Progressive Era, Ohio and Pennsylvania families devoted between $20 and $40 to medical, dental, and eyeglass-related expenses. In Washington, D.C., white families earning between $600 and $900 spent about $25 and those with incomes between $900 and $1,200 spent $42 on medical bills. Black families in each earnings category spent a third to a quarter less on health care. In general, medical expenses were relatively small because, compared to our day, medicine was cheap and inefficacious.[9]

The inability of workers to save for such events while employed was a critical supposition of the Progressive agenda. The physician Alexander Lambert recommended that health insurance be made compulsory because "most wage-earners live on a wage from which they can store up but little to protect them against any individual misfortune." Howell Cheney, a textile executive who provided this chapter's epigraph, declared that it was "unquestionably proven" that workers would not save against sickness voluntarily. Progressives criticized savers for their *lack* of prudence and trust in their fellow man. Cheney went on to praise workers who had obtained insurance, which indicated a belief in cooperation with others. Sounding like a proto-Keynesian, Rubinow wrote that "thrift may become a positive vice" if workers saved so much that they reduced spending on necessities. The ability of workers to save for such contingencies was, therefore, a "myth." Fundamentally, Progressives believed that workers were too dull to recognize their need for savings. In John Lapp's view, "All experience shows that the bulk of the people are not forehanded enough to see the necessity for insurance."[10]

Of two ways to smooth consumption over time, saving and borrowing, attentive reformers noted that workers could and did borrow in a pinch. Chattel loan brokers, who accepted movable (non–real estate) collateral, remedial loan societies (an alternative to chattel lenders promoted by private foundations), and Morris Plan banks, which specialized in small loans with jointly liable co-signers, all lent money to low-income workers burdened with the costs of sickness. Reformers interpreted the need for such capital market institutions as a sign of labor market failure, but their existence also reflected the adaptability of the capital markets of that time.[11]

Income levels that workers needed for a comfortable standard of living varied, according to the experts, and Progressive reformers chose their rhetoric so as to emphasize the advantages of government insurance. They put claims that only the tiniest of gaps appeared between income and expenses in the forefront of their case. The AALL announced in the subtitle of an article in its magazine, "Savings of Wage-Earners Are Insufficient to Meet This Loss." Present-day historians have accepted these arguments without further investigation. This chapter investigates whether the claims can be supported with historical evidence.[12]

The rest of this chapter has a fairly narrow purpose. It is to show that, by and large, workers who wanted to obtain insurance did so, and many of those who were not insured chose that status freely.[13] Workers generally *could* save against income loss due to bad health and did save when they needed to. Given these points, a simpler explanation of the failure of Progressive health insurance reform proposals can be offered. Rather than having been sunk by the political efforts of a few, they were not obviously an improvement, on net, for the many.

It is possible to insure against nearly any adverse event. Generally speaking, as the probability of the event increases and the value of the loss decreases, people self-insure via savings (think of the breakdown of a household appliance), but for events with a small probability but large potential loss, insurance is preferred (think of property losses due to a house fire). Where the choice was between savings and insurance only, analysis can be relatively straightforward. In the present day, such analysis is complicated considerably by social insurance in the forms of Medicare for the old and Medicaid for the poor. Because their coverage is not only costless but means-tested, they reduce the need to save against medical expenses twice over. This effect of social insurance on precautionary saving has been confirmed in numerous studies.[14] Thus, whether savings and insurance can act as substitutes might be seen more clearly by using historical data that were collected in an era before social insurance was common.

The notion that Progressive-Era social insurance would reduce the incentive for workers to save in advance of injury or illness has been explored in the historical literature. Shawn Kantor and Price Fishback studied the effect of state-mandated workmen's compensation on savings. They estimated the value of a typical worker's compensation claim by state and found that the value and availability of such insurance induced a decline in savings of about 25 percent. Michael Palumbo found evidence among workers in 1890 Maine that precautionary savings helped families self-insure against income variation. In this study savings had different effects on various kinds of insurance. After treating private insurance purchases (benefit society membership, union membership, and life insurance) as endogenous, he concluded that only the latter two were associated with decreased probability of savings.[15]

These studies indicate that workers saved in precautionary fashion, but the focus of the current chapter is on the related issue of demand for health insurance. In the absence of Medicare and Medicaid, it should be easier to test whether precautionary savings influenced this demand. But evidence has been hard to produce. Palumbo estimated a first-stage probit for benefit society membership that omitted savings on the right-hand side. Although this was a reasonable econometric strategy, it still left the savings-insurance connection unaddressed. Robert Whaples and

David Buffum examined benefit society membership among Michigan furniture workers in 1889. They, too, did not include savings as an explanatory variable. In their study of fraternal society insurance George Emery and Herbert Emery found indirect evidence for self-insurance via savings.[16] They did not have direct estimates of member savings, however, but inferred precautionary savings from patterns in members' ages. This chapter provides the first estimates of historical demand for health insurance as a function of savings.

A recent study shed considerable light on savings and health insurance. Laurence Levin analyzed demand for private, supplementary health insurance by present-day elderly Americans who were already covered by Medicaid or Medicare. He found that demand for such insurance was increased by ill health, confirming the presence of adverse selection, and by illiquidity of asset holdings, *ceteris paribus*. "Precautionary motives are both ubiquitous and important," he concluded, having observed the "economically sensible" behavior of the elderly.[17] These studies indicate that there is good reason to suspect that Progressive-Era workers might have self-insured instead of obtaining insurance. Such economically sensible behavior can help us understand the nature of demand for health insurance a century ago.

The primary sample analyzed in this chapter consists of men who worked in the agricultural implement and iron industries in Michigan in 1890.[18] The survey was published in two parts. One covered establishments in Detroit and the other, slightly larger, covered plants elsewhere in Michigan. Because both surveys asked the same questions they could be combined into a single sample of 8,835 workers. Table 7.2 provides descriptive data. About one-fourth of these workers belonged to benefit societies, which could have been sponsored by their employer or fraternal group or their union. As described in Chapter 4, other surveys conducted at this time also found that 25 to 30 percent of respondents had joined benefit societies. A little more than 10 percent of those in benefit societies belonged to more than one. Sick pay benefits for those in societies were worth about $6.50 per week. The average annual earnings of workers who belonged to benefit societies was $562, or a little more than $10 per week—close to the average estimated by Progressive

Table 7.2.
Descriptive statistics regarding samples of Michigan agricultural and iron workers 1890

	MEAN VALUES (STANDARD DEVIATION)		
	DETROIT	ELSEWHERE	POOLED
Member of at least one benefit society	1,120	1,121	2,241
Share of sample belonging to at least one benefit society	0.29	0.23	0.25
Member of one benefit society	956	976	1,932
Member of two benefit societies	138	139	277
Member of three benefit societies	17	6	23
Member of four or more benefit societies	9	0	9
Average value of benefits, full sample	$1.88 (3.77)	$1.48 (3.18)	$1.65 (3.46)
Average value of benefits, society members	$6.56 (4.35)	$6.46 (3.48)	$6.50 (3.94)
Aged 20 or younger	0.22	0.14	0.17
Aged 20–29	0.41	0.36	0.38
Aged 30–39	0.23	0.26	0.24
Aged 40 or older	0.14	0.24	0.20
Married	0.50	0.64	0.57
Family size	2.81 (2.13)	2.88 (1.85)	2.85 (1.98)
Share reporting any sick time	0.06	0.29	0.19
Annual earnings	$460 (237)	$473 (197)	$467 (215)
Share with any savings ("amount saved aside from payments on home")	0.19	0.35	0.28
Savings, full sample	$28.31 (98.89)	$44.45 (87.13)	$37.27 (89.15)

(continued)

Table 7.2.
Descriptive statistics regarding samples of Michigan agricultural and iron workers 1890 (*continued*)

	MEAN VALUES (STANDARD DEVIATION)		
	DETROIT	ELSEWHERE	POOLED
Savings among those with any savings	$145.82 (159.47)	$127.42 (105.80)	$133.07 (125.01)
Share with any wealth ("present worth")	0.82	0.86	0.84
Wealth, full sample	$590.72 (1,204.72)	$777.03 (1,002.91)	$694.39 (1,100.85)
Wealth among those with any wealth	$718.28 (1,293.52)	$902.41 (1,027.13)	$822.82 (1,153.41)
Owns home	0.19	0.32	0.26
n	3,919	4,916	8,835

Sources: Carter et al., "Codebook . . . Detroit, 1890," "Codebook . . . Outside of Detroit, 1890."

reformers. The replacement rate of sick pay benefits was close to the two-thirds recommended by the AALL, so that covered workers were eligible for what was later asserted to be an adequate amount of sick pay.

Figure 7.1 illustrates the way in which health insurance coverage, health, income, and wealth varied over the life cycle. A steady increase in wealth accompanied aging, in part because of a steady level of savings that added to that wealth. The sickness incidence variable was taken from two questions that asked the respondent, first, how much time he had missed from work in the preceding year and, second, the reason for that lost work time. This variable was set to 1 if the respondent gave sickness, accident, or other ill health as a reason for missing any work, even if it was combined with other explanations such as "laid off" or "short hours," and set to zero otherwise. This curve shows that men missed work due to ill health more often as they aged. Given accumulating wealth and increasing incidence of sickness, it seems reasonable to expect that the share of respondents who belonged to a benefit society

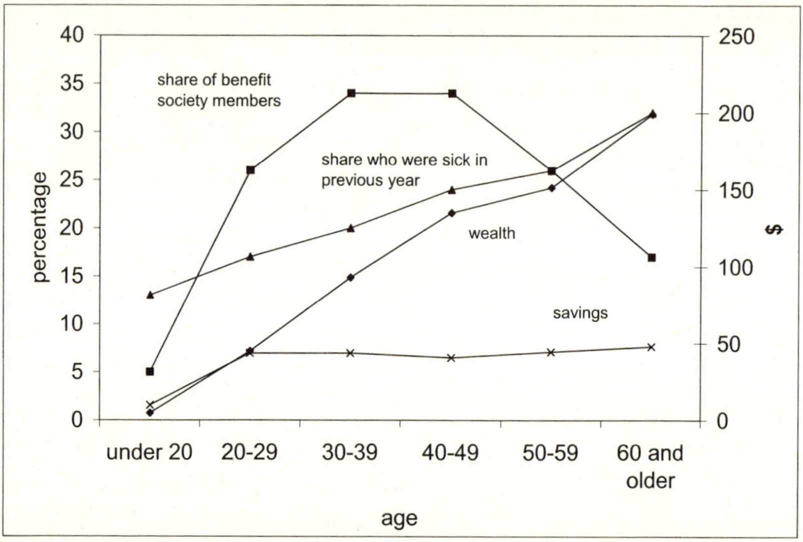

FIGURE 7.1. Characteristics of Michigan iron workers by age. Savings reported as "amount saved aside from payments on house." (Data from Carter et al., "Codebook . . . Detroit, 1890"; "Codebook . . . Outside of Detroit, 1890.")

would also increase with age. After all, the need for sickness benefits increased among older and therefore sicker workers, and so did their ability to pay for such insurance. But the rate of coverage among those aged sixty and older was only about half the rate of those in their forties. Because annual earnings of workers in their sixties were only 10 percent below the earnings of workers in their forties ($506 versus $558), something other than sickness rates and affordability of insurance was influencing demand. That something was precautionary savings that varied during a worker's life cycle.[19]

A series of regressions of the demand for insurance examined the role of savings in that determination. The surveys asked three questions regarding insurance coverage that allowed for regressions of three different measures of demand. The most direct measure was whether the worker belonged to any benefit society, and so in table 7.3 a simple binary variable for benefit society membership was regressed on variables that described the respondent, his job, his family, his finances, and his residence. The other measures of insurance coverage included the number of benefit societies to which a worker belonged and the value of

Table 7.3.

Regressions of health insurance coverage on savings and wealth

	LOGIT REGRESSIONS MEMBER OF BENEFIT SOCIETY = 1; OTHERWISE = 0					
	A	B	C	D	E	F
Age under 20	−1.21***	−1.22***	−1.28***	−1.21***	−1.19***	−0.96*
	(0.14)	(0.15)	(0.32)	(0.14)	(0.15)	(0.51)
Age 30–39	0.16**	0.24***	−0.03	0.16**	0.30***	0.10
	(0.08)	(0.08)	(0.18)	(0.08)	(0.10)	(0.29)
Age over 40	−0.01	0.13	−0.39**	−0.01	0.17	0.77**
	(0.09)	(0.10)	(0.20)	(0.09)	(0.11)	(0.33)
Married	0.34***	0.36***	0.34***	0.35***	0.30***	0.35***
	(0.09)	(0.09)	(0.09)	(0.09)	(0.09)	(0.09)
Family size	0.04**	0.04**	0.05**	0.04**	0.04**	0.05**
	(0.02)	(0.02)	(0.02)	(0.02)	(0.02)	(0.02)
Any sick days	0.24***	0.23***	0.22***	0.24***	0.24***	0.12
	(0.08)	(0.08)	(0.08)	(0.08)	(0.08)	(0.09)
Annual earnings	1.84***	1.84***	1.65***	1.78***	1.71***	1.48***
	(0.18)	(0.18)	(0.19)	(0.18)	(0.18)	(0.19)

(continued)

Table 7.3.

Regressions of health insurance coverage on savings and wealth (*continued*)

	LOGIT REGRESSIONS MEMBER OF BENEFIT SOCIETY = 1; OTHERWISE = 0					
	A	B	C	D	E	F
Owns home	0.28***	0.30***	0.29***	0.31***	0.28***	0.28***
	(0.07)	(0.07)	(0.07)	(0.08)	(0.08)	(0.07)
Savings/100	−0.05	0.12**	0.17**	−0.02	0.17**	0.92***
	(0.03)	(0.05)	(0.09)	(0.03)	(0.08)	(0.29)
Savings*		0.50*	−0.04			
Age under 20		(0.26)	(0.20)			
		−0.19***	−0.14			
Age 30–39		(0.07)	(0.12)			
		−0.34***	−0.28**			
Age over 40		(0.08)	(0.13)			
Wealth/100				−0.02	0.17**	0.92***
				(0.03)	(0.08)	(0.29)

Wealth*					0.33	−0.44
Age under 20					(0.64)	(0.73)
					−0.20**	0.08
Age 30–39					(0.07)	(0.40)
					−0.22***	−1.09**
Age over 40					(0.07)	(0.45)
Goodness of fit	0.21	0.21	0.21	0.21	0.21	0.21

Source: Carter et al., "Codebook . . . Detroit, 1890"; "Codebook . . . Outside of Detroit, 1890."

Note: Standard errors in parentheses. Models A and D lack finance-age interaction variables; Models B and E include interaction variables; Models C and F represent instruments for savings using weeks of work missed for reasons other than sickness, its square, its cube, and its quartic. First-stage regressions are reported in Appendix B. Member of benefit society=1; Method: logit. Intercepts and dummy variables were included in regressions but not reported here. They included (number of categories including the omitted ones) city of residence (12), occupation (13), number of employees in establishment (5), and country of birth (6). Goodness of fit statistics: For logit=McFadden pseudo R^2; for Tobit=log likelihood; for Poisson=Pearson χ^2 /d.f.

*significantly different from zero at the 0.10 level; **significantly different from zero at the 0.05 level; ***significantly different from zero at the 0.01 level

weekly sick pay benefits. These formed dependent variables in other regressions that produced substantially the same results. To illustrate the robustness of this model in relation to the specification and the nature of the dependent variable, these results are presented in Appendix B.

Variables describing worker characteristics found relationships similar to those found in previous studies. The inverse-U-shaped proportion of coverage to age in Regression C was similar to that found in other contemporary samples. Married workers were far more likely to carry health insurance, and as their families grew the probability of being insured also grew. A worker who had taken any sick days off in the previous year was significantly more likely to belong to a benefit society, although this had no effect on the number of benefit societies or the expected value of benefits. This suggests that if sick workers tended to join a benefit society, adverse selection may have been a problem for sickness funds. But the tendency of such workers not to join additional benefit societies suggests that adverse selection was not a great problem. Benefit society membership was a strongly normal good: as incomes increased, the probability of membership, the number of societies, and the value of benefits all increased significantly.[20]

The most important variables referred to the respondent's financial status. They included questions about savings ("amount saved aside from payments on house"), wealth ("worth"), and whether the worker owned his house. Each regression included a variable for home ownership. The coefficient of this variable was consistently significant and strongly positive. The effect of home ownership, *ceteris paribus,* may be interpreted in light of present-day findings described above. Holding a large share of one's assets in a house represented a substantially illiquid position. Insurance compensated for that illiquidity by providing cash in case of an adverse event. So the results were comparable to the effect of illiquid asset holding on the demand for health insurance in the present.[21]

Table 7.4 offers estimates of the likelihood of particular characteristics to induce (or discourage) benefit society membership. Average values of other variables were used in the regression equation, and then the value of the variable of interest was changed to see how powerful that variable was in influencing insurance coverage. Among young workers, the effects of marriage plus one child (as opposed to bachelorhood) and of having an average amount of wealth (as opposed to no wealth) were about the same. Each increased the probability of having health insurance by about five percentage points. Among workers in their thirties, marriage plus three children increased the probability of being insured by 12.4 percentage points relative to bachelors. The effects of income and prior illness were small but detectable. After age forty, consistent with figure 7.1, the addition of average wealth acted to reduce the probability of insurance by about five percentage points.

The subtle effect of savings or wealth on demand for health insurance is a key part of this chapter. Regressions A (on savings) and D (on wealth) simply included a variable for savings (wealth), which was not significant. That did not mean, however, that there was no relation between savings and demand for insurance. Life cycle theory, in its various formulations, predicts changing propensity to save at different ages. Regressions B (on savings) and E (on wealth) interacted savings and wealth with age groups to see how saving and wealth-holding at different ages might affect demand for insurance. This strategy revealed important relationships. Among workers older than thirty, the interaction of savings and age suggests that increased savings with age reduced the demand for health insurance. This is strong evidence of precautionary savings as a substitute for insurance, and it helps explain the pattern seen in figure 7.1. But it is reasonable to suppose that savings and health insurance purchases were determined jointly, which leads to a statistical problem known as endogeneity, which could bias these parameter estimates if, for example, a worker decided to reduce his savings after joining a benefit society.

One way to manage this problem is to substitute an estimated value for the savings variables by the use of an instrumental variable. Finding an appropriate instrument in a historical data set requires a generous dose of luck, which seems to have been delivered. The question regarding missed work time asked for the reason. Those who reported being sick or injured formed the share reporting any sick time. The instrument became the number of weeks of work missed for reasons other than sickness. This variable should have been correlated with savings, since most of those missed weeks were due to unemployment, shop closure, and the like, causes that imply missed pay packets and thus lower savings. But because these absences were not health-related they should

Table 7.4.
Estimated probabilities of health insurance coverage

WORKER DESCRIPTION	WITHOUT CHARACTERISTIC	WITH CHARACTERISTIC
Under 20, unskilled, unmarried, no wealth, not a homeowner and . . .	Not absent due to sickness in previous year: 0.020	Absent due to sickness in previous year: 0.023
Age 20–29, woodworker, not a homeowner, and . . .	Not married: 0.097	Married with 1 child: 0.144
Age 20–29, woodworker, married with 1 child, not a homeowner, and . . .	No wealth: 0.099	Average wealth: 0.144
Age 30–39, machinist, average wealth and earnings, a homeowner and . . .	Not married: 0.312	Married with 3 children: 0.436
Age 30–39, machinist, married, 3 children, average wealth and earnings, a homeowner and . . .	Not absent due to sickness in previous year: 0.430	Absent due to sickness in previous year: 0.459
Age 30–39, machinist, married, 3 children, average wealth, a homeowner and . . .	90 percent of average earnings: 0.416	110 percent of average earnings: 0.455
Age 40 or older, machinist, married, 2 children, average earnings and wealth, and . . .	Not homeowner: 0.253	Homeowner: 0.310

Table 7.4.
Estimated probabilities of health insurance coverage (*continued*)

WORKER DESCRIPTION	WITHOUT CHARACTERISTIC	WITH CHARACTERISTIC
Age 40 or older, machinist, married, 2 children, average earnings and probability of being a homeowner and . . .	No wealth: 0.315	Average wealth: 0.268

Note: All variables not mentioned in column 1 set equal to average values (average wealth and earnings set equal to average for that age). Estimates based on Model F, table 7.3.

not have been related to the demand for health insurance (and hence to the error term in the original specification). Regressions of savings on this variable, its square, its cube, and its quartic produced predicted values that made reasonably good instruments.

Regressions C and F were estimated with the predicted values of savings and wealth. The main effect of the instrumental variable estimation was to flatten the effects of savings or wealth by age until the age of forty and older. That is, the instrumental variable regressions clarify that precautionary saving that substituted for health insurance was concentrated in the oldest age group. This pattern also appeared in the regressions of number of benefit societies and value of benefits on the same independent variables, making these results robust among the Michigan workers.[22] It is noteworthy that the same results appear in the wealth regressions because the instrument, weeks missed in the preceding year for reasons other than sickness, did not predict the cumulative variable of wealth nearly as well as it did the more recent flow variable of savings. In general, the regressions indicate that older workers increasingly substituted savings or wealth for health insurance as they aged and their health deteriorated. Why would they do that?

A key to the answer lies in a question asked in a different survey of Michigan workers. In 1889 the Michigan Bureau of Labor and Industrial Statistics published the results of a survey of furniture industry workers

Table 7.5.
Age and tenure at employer, Michigan furniture workers, 1889

YEARS AT EMPLOYER	UNDER 20	20–29	30–39	40–49	50 AND OLDER	TOTAL
0–1	531	492	237	108	42	1,410
1–5	714	985	506	270	146	2,621
5–10	42	298	234	144	71	789
10 or more	0	45	114	71	70	300
Total	1,287	1,820	1,091	593	329	5,120

Source: Carter et al., "Codebook . . . Michigan, 1889."

that asked many of the same questions as in the survey of agricultural implement and iron workers. One question in the former that was not asked in the latter was how long the respondent had worked for his current employer. Similar questions have provided evidence that short-term workers formed a large share of the contemporary labor market.[23] According to Table 7.5, a small but important share of older workers had spent relatively little time with their current employer. Among all workers aged forty and older, 16 percent had worked at their current employer for a year or less.

The importance of worker age and tenure on the job can be seen by considering the difficulties that confronted newly hired older workers when they tried to join benefit societies. In 1908, as a screen against selection problems, the average probationary period of employment required before a worker could join a sick fund was seven weeks, with a standard deviation of 8.3 weeks.[24] Over a period of several weeks a new hire could be observed closely to see if he was, for example, consumptive, and thus a bad risk. From the perspective of the funds, this was a rational requirement. From the perspective of a worker, though, it meant that those new to their jobs, the committed and floaters alike, could not obtain health insurance right away. This problem was particularly acute for older workers because many funds opened their ranks only to new hires who were no older than forty or forty-five.

Tenure on the job was an important determinant of insurance coverage. Figure 7.2 shows membership in sickness funds by age for sev-

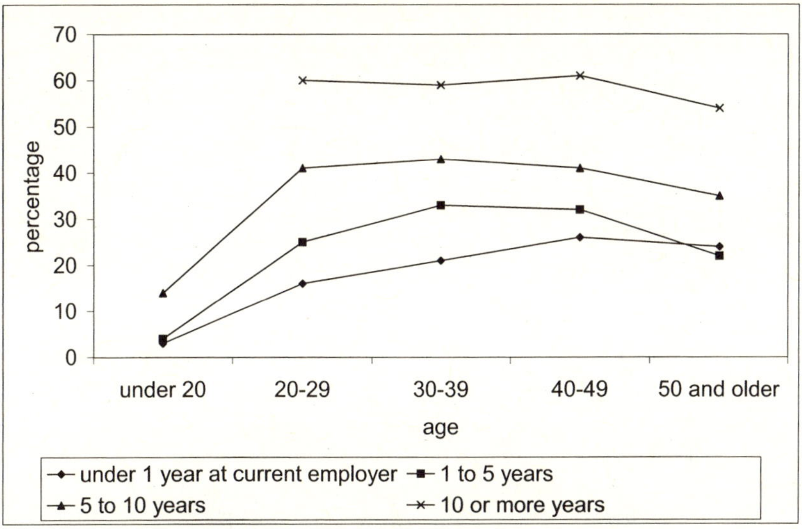

FIGURE 7.2. Share of Michigan furniture workers in benefit societies by tenure at employer in years. (Data from Carter et al., "Codebook . . . Michigan, 1889.")

eral tenure cohorts. The share of furniture workers who belonged to at least one benefit society was, at 23 percent, very close to that of agricultural implement and iron workers. Employees with five to ten years' experience at their employer were much more likely to belong to a benefit society than those with less than five years' experience. Among workers with at least ten years' tenure at their employer the majority belonged to a benefit society.

Probationary periods and age maximums were well-known characteristics of sickness funds. Because all parties knew of these restrictions, they could plan their financial activities ahead of time, taking these restrictions into account. Table 7.6 shows savings patterns among new furniture workers (those with less than two years at the employer) by age group (younger or older than forty) and benefit society membership.[25] The effect of the latter on savings depended greatly on the age of the worker. It was sought by better-paid workers who were also likely to save. Among younger workers, benefit society members were more likely to save and to save more than did nonmembers. Completely different patterns obtained among new hires aged forty and older. Older workers who did *not* belong to benefit societies were more likely to save than

Table 7.6.

Savings among new hires by benefit society membership and age

Years with current employer	Benefit society members			Non–benefit society members		
	N	Value of savings ($)	Share with any savings	N	Value of savings ($)	Share with any savings
			Workers under 40 years of age			
One year or less	147	29.75	0.27	1113	12.60	0.14
One to two years	140	30.34	0.26	784	11.25	0.15
Total of two years or less	287	30.03	0.26	1897	12.04	0.15
			Workers 40 and older			
One year or less	38	12.50	0.11	112	16.04	0.13
One to two years	39	19.87	0.18	110	39.42	0.23
Total of two years or less	77	16.23	0.14	222	27.63	0.18

Source: Carter et al., "Codebook . . . Michigan, 1889."

were benefit society members, and to save more. The share of nonmembers with savings was 29 percent greater (18 versus 14), and the value of their savings was 70 percent higher. The particular group of new workers that was likely to save and to save more if they did not (or could not) join a benefit society was older workers. That is, precautionary savings typified the strategy of older workers who had recently been seeking work and who knew they might be excluded from benefit society membership once they found it.

Progressive reformers promoted compulsory government-supervised health insurance as a solution to the problem of sickness among workers. They believed that just when the practice of medicine was becoming efficacious it was also becoming too expensive for workers to benefit from it. One result was that the sick workers who might benefit from medical attention were losing income owing to avoidable absences and in any case were paid too poorly to be able to save against income loss due to sickness. In the format advanced by the AALL, compulsory health insurance would be directly paid for mainly by parties other than the worker, making it a kind of forced savings that would protect otherwise improvident workers.

If workers could not save at all or would not do so in the absence of health insurance, perhaps the Progressive reforms would have represented humane policymaking. But if workers prudently purchased insurance after assessing the costs and benefits to them, the reforms would have been a step backward. This chapter suggests that there were three types of workers. Young men in their twenties were in excellent health and so had little interest in purchasing insurance that they did not expect to need. Working men between twenty and forty years old did buy such insurance. They especially wanted it if they were married, once they had started their families, and if they were better paid than most workers. And the majority of those with at least a decade's tenure with their employer had obtained health insurance.

The third group, consisting of older workers, exemplified rational responses to difficult constraints. As they aged, the chances that they would miss some time from work because of sickness increased steadily. At the same time, if they quit, if they were fired, or if their employer failed and they needed to start over at a new firm, they could obtain health insurance only with difficulty. So they chose the best available alternative for income in case of lost work time: they saved. If they could not join a benefit society, they saved more than did men in their age cohort who did belong to one. The best explanation of the patterns of demand for insurance and of savings shown in this study is that these men were saving in precautionary fashion.

If this behavior was in fact typical of industrial workers, it suggests that the Progressives misdirected their concern. They intended for government insurance to cover a larger share of the labor force, but that share would have increased anyway with the decline of very short-term labor and the steady increase in wages. As it was, the large share of workers who were not insured included young people who did not want to buy insurance because they did not expect to need it and older people who had saved in anticipation of lost income. Workers' decisions regarding insurance were reflected in the rare episodes in which they could express their opinions such as the three-to-one defeat of the California referendum and the 1919 survey conducted in Utica, New York, which found near-universal rejection of the idea. The private provision of health insurance may have survived Progressive assaults because most people saw it to be, however flawed, better than the proposed alternative.

CHAPTER EIGHT

Workers' Decisions to Work or Stay Home Sick

> SOCRATES: In a well-ordered state every man has a job to go to, and therefore lacks time to spend continually being ill.
>
> —PLATO *Republic*, bk. 3

> The question of moral hazard looms up at every point in the consideration of the general subject of sickness insurance.
>
> —REINARD KEELOR, 1912

THIS CHAPTER and Chapter 7 test assertions made by Progressive reformers regarding actions of workers covered by sickness insurance and those who were not covered. The previous chapter concluded that, contrary to claims made by reformers, workers could save for the rainy day of illness that prevented them from working. The present chapter tests the claim that insured workers were not subject to moral hazard. Moral hazard is the tendency of insurance to remove an incentive to prevent the insured-against event, which thereby increases the probability of its occurrence. The primary moral hazard associated with sickness insurance was the decision to take time off from work. An insured worker was compensated for work time lost to sickness, and an uninsured worker was not. According to Progressives, workers who were offered sick pay benefits when ill would return to work as soon as they were physically able rather than malinger in order to get more benefits. Their opponents believed that sick pay would induce workers to take more time off than otherwise.

To see whether workers were subject to the moral hazard of unnecessary sick pay, this chapter tests for correlations between sick pay and absenteeism in two types of data. First, it compares absence among workers with and without sickness insurance, and then it analyzes absence among members of funds that offered varying levels of sick pay benefits. What emerges is a more complex story than the Progressive-Era activists imagined. Paid sick leave did create an absenteeism moral hazard. Its magnitude was open to question because the results suggest that it was small among individual workers but great according to sickness fund records. Consistent with the claim of their fundamental competence, sickness funds countered this tendency because they understood a particular principal-agent problem: they hired their own physicians to rein in excessive absenteeism. The net effect over time was to increase the incidence of absenteeism among insured workers but to reduce the average duration of any given absence. This left unchanged the overall number of days missed by an average worker. The stability in prevalence rates among privately insured American workers contrasted with increasing absence among compulsorily insured Europeans and decreasing rates among the less stable voluntary European networks, as illustrated in Chapter 3.

The question of how to manage work duties when ill is an old one. Perhaps the first reference occurs in book III of Plato's *Republic,* in which Socrates and Glaucon discuss how artisans and the wealthy resort to different strategies when sickness strikes. The industrious carpenter, observes Socrates, does not waste his time on elaborate therapies when ill but aims to return to work as soon as he can, in part to minimize loss of income but mostly because he is too conscientious to neglect his work for long. Glaucon notes that the rich really are different in this regard; when ill they are willing to engage in an eclectic variety of treatments precisely because they have no job to return to and thus have plenty of time and money to spend. Although Socrates is usually understood to imply that the artisan's behavior is a consequence of his virtue, the artisan's goal is sometimes translated as "profit."[1]

Progressives who argued against the existence of moral hazard in health insurance were Platonists. They believed that a worker who needed to take time off would not be swayed by a sickness benefit that was less than his usual pay to absent himself for longer than necessary. The worker simply understood his duty and would report to work because that was what a worker did with his time, just as in Socrates' day. Further, because existing sick benefits were so scant, an uninsured worker and one who belonged to a sickness fund suffered nearly equally when ill. Uninsured workers faced no incentive to miss work without sick benefits. Ergo, insured workers had only a small incentive to do so. Progressives argued further that medical benefits were also less valuable than they may have appeared. Few funds paid for medical care, and workers simply would not attend charity hospitals when they needed to. Combining the presumed incompetence of private funds with the large share of the workforce that was sick on any given day, the only solution, reformers concluded, was government provision of health insurance.[2]

Opponents of reform argued that government sickness insurance in the European style would aggravate an obvious problem of moral hazard. To make sick pay available to all was to court disaster. More workers would malinger if they could do so on the government's dime. Until now, no study has tested for evidence of moral hazard in such private insurance as existed in early twentieth-century America. Were workers completely oblivious to the incentive created by sick pay, as the Progressives insisted, or, as their opponents claimed, were they all too aware, and happy to take time off even if they could maintain only part of their income flow?[3]

The most important part of the sickness fund benefit package was the sick pay that provided some measure of security. "Cash benefits are thought of first when health insurance is mentioned," reported the Ohio Health and Old Age Insurance Commission, implying that workers were doing the thinking. The effect of those benefits was the subject of debate. To Progressives, limiting sick benefits to a fraction of the worker's usual pay sufficed to discourage unnecessary absenteeism. Rubinow scoffed at the idea that fractional sick pay would induce a moral hazard: "We must think the workingman a great deal less susceptible to physical discomfort and bodily pain than ourselves, if we believe that the few dollars of weekly allowance will reconcile him to disease or injury."[4]

Malingering, which was constantly discussed, if only to deny that it was a problem, is what economists recognize as moral hazard. Absenteeism cost the worker his lost wage; sickness insurance reduced those costs; therefore, more valuable sickness insurance benefits and greater coverage would lead to increased absenteeism. Progressives' rhetoric emphasized that their opponents misinterpreted moral hazard and thus overlooked the therapeutic powers of rest. Karl de Schweinitz, general secretary of the Philadelphia Society for Organizing Charity, lamented that "only too often, however, the sick throw away their chances for speedy cure by continuing to work because they cannot afford to lose pay by staying at home." Paid sick leave, according to this view, had powerful abilities to improve workers' health.[5]

Opponents claimed that many benefit recipients really could work but preferred absence with less income thanks to their sickness funds. The Health Insurance Commission of the State of Illinois concluded, "Certainly an employee is less apt to pretend to be sick if he does not receive payment for the waiting period. If he does receive payment he is likely to remain away from work a day or two longer to fill out the time necessary to receive benefits." According to this view, widespread malingering posed a threat to productivity and worker morality in general. Developing their argument, opponents protested that a worker who went to work to avoid losing a day's pay was to all appearances well enough to work. They argued that insurance benefits would lead to widespread feigning of sickness to the extent of wrecking the finances of a government insurance program. Referring to bizarre cases that came before state workmen's compensation boards, they cited instances in which workers burned and bit themselves in hopes of qualifying for benefits. Employers generalized from such extremes to claim that "the majority of labor today, will do as little [work] as they possibly can." Acknowledging such potential problems, Rubinow purported to know methods of administrative control that would limit malingering and fraud but claimed that they were too complicated to describe in his five-hundred-page book.[6]

Opponents of government insurance suggested that Europe provided examples of worker malingering following the introduction of government health insurance. They publicized statements by Ferdinand Friedensburg, a German insurance official turned critic of his country's system, who claimed that social insurance had caused "universal degradation and demoralization" of the working classes, a point which, as Rubinow noted, was not really subject to statistical verification. Among the most prominent opponents of Progressive insurance reforms was the Insurance Economics Society. Testifying before the Ohio Health and Old Age Insurance Commission, the society's chairman, William Gale Curtis, claimed that European sickness insurance programs were riddled with moral hazard problems. He stated that the share of workers claiming sick pay and the overall number of days missed had increased sharply. Curtis blamed these increases on malingering rather than justifiable sickness. Alexander Lambert, a physician who supported the American Association for Labor Legislation, acknowledged that "whenever compulsory health insurance has gone into operation there has appeared an amount of sickness that has surprised even the physicians working among the poor." He explained that insurance enabled the poor to afford necessary medical attention and so increased absenteeism was a sign that the insurance system was performing its duties well.[7]

The Progressive case against the existence of a sick benefit moral hazard had an uphill climb because existing insurers did indeed find that the value of benefits and prevalence of claims were positively correlated. Insurers as disparate as the Manchester Unity in Great Britain, the Cigar Makers' International Union, and various railroad funds all found that more valuable sickness benefits caused an increase in compensated sick time. Nonetheless, Progressives made three arguments to the contrary. First, they claimed that attributing increased absenteeism under government insurance to moral hazard was a fallacy of composition. Expansion of coverage by government insurers would bring workers who had been screened out of private insurance precisely because of their high-risk status into the risk pool. The newly covered workers would then make claims at higher-than-average rates and thereby increase overall claim rates. For example, if the state were to insure previously uncovered women workers, average claim rates would rise because women were more likely to make claims than men. Referring to the supply of benefits, the Ohio commission also suggested that funds that were on firmer financial bases might be able to underwrite more generous benefits for absenteeism than the current system allowed.[8]

Second, Progressives argued by assertion that there was no absenteeism moral hazard associated with better sick pay. In many public statements, advocates of state-provided insurance argued that malingering simply would not be the problem their opponents (who were equally lacking in firm evidence) claimed it would be. Their gratuitous assertions, though they modestly acknowledged gaps in the understanding of incentives created by social insurance, left the reform program open to effective counterarguments. Warren and Sydenstricker claimed that requiring workers, employers, and the government all to pay into health insurance accounts ensured that it was in the interest of all three parties to prevent malingering—but this strategy would leave the responsibility for preventing it in nobody's hands in particular. The Ohio commission, while acknowledging that "we know very little about malingering at present," still claimed that "the fear that obligatory health insurance will increase malingering is however an exaggerated one, due in part to failure to understand the nature of malingering." A New York hospital executive concurred that the "extent of malingering is exaggerated for political effect." Rabbi Maurice B. Hexter of Cincinnati testified to the Ohio commission that "the danger from malingering was overestimated." But if the phenomenon really was little understood, why was this fear exaggerated rather than underestimated? Progressives may in part have trimmed their sails for rhetorical reasons, but their statements indicate that they did not acknowledge moral hazard as a potential problem for government-financed insurance.[9]

Third, Progressives claimed that labor supply was wage-inelastic. According to this argument, discounted sick pay of less than 100 percent of a regular pay packet would not alter the number of days a worker was willing to toil in a year. Fractional sick pay would remove the incentive of workers to malinger simply because it would reduce the claimant's income. Ignoring the possibility that some workers might prefer no work with some income to a full week at full pay, Progressives repeated many times that two-thirds pay would not cause malingering. The AALL was certain that sick pay "offer[ed] a direct financial incentive to return to work as soon as possible, an incentive which would be absent if full wages were paid during illness." Some businessmen agreed that fractional sick pay could be offered without causing malingering but believed that close monitoring of claimants was necessary as a counterweight. The National Industrial Conference Board reported that only the few sickness insurance funds that offered sick pay of two-thirds of wages or more risked encouraging malingering. Funds that offered more generous sick pay needed to exercise the "strictest supervision . . . over all benefit claims" to keep malingering under control. That supervision worked for some firms. A publishing plant in Pennsylvania that provided full sick pay found little " 'soldiering' to draw benefits" thanks to close monitoring of sick members by the fund's visiting committee.[10]

Supervision was conducted by visiting committees and by physicians. Investigating committees were composed of fund members who visited claimants in their homes and then reported to the fund managers their opinion of the claimant's condition. Committee members were not typically paid for their efforts, although they were reimbursed for transportation expenses. Although some claimants were happy to have the company, others despised overt attempts of visitors to act as "detectives whose only duty it is to try to detect malingering." The effectiveness of the committees depended in part on the proximity of workers' residences to the plant. Visitors were especially good at identifying claimants who visited their favorite local tavern in violation of fund rules. Other claimants, especially in workforces consisting of single men, welcomed social interaction with co-workers. These visitors provided care and companionship that their sick co-workers would otherwise have gone without. Visiting committees also occasionally stood up for fellow fund members and persuaded fund managers to overrule a physician who had ordered a co-worker back to work.[11]

Besides monitoring by co-workers, another form of loss control was to require a certificate of disability signed by a physician. Contemporaries recognized that the outcome of a worker's request for a certificate depended on who paid the doctor. The primary allegiance of physicians paid by the sickness fund was common knowledge. According to a reformer in New York City, "The sort of physician supplying this certificate is considered important because, it is argued, a private physician may be in some cases more lenient than a lodge or society physician." That was because the private physician worked for the patient. The benefit society physician had less need to keep his patient happy precisely because he worked for the insurance fund. He knew that if the benefit society believed he certified claimants too easily, it would fire him. As a result, insured workers faced the prospect of being hectored into returning to work too soon by a doctor who was in the insurance fund's pocket. On calling for the local physician's help, Finley Peter Dunne's Mr. Dooley was mercilessly interrogated by Dr. O'Leary: "What d'ye mane be tyin' up wan iv th' gr-reat industhrees iv our nation be stayin' away fr'm wurruk f'r a day?"[12]

A benefit society physician held considerable authority over fund members. A claimant who refused to be examined could be denied benefits. The fund physician was also saddled with the responsibility of keeping members away from quack doctors who might certify the claimant too quickly and then prescribe a useless course of treatment that would keep him sick and draining fund coffers. In some cases the fund's physician was asked to recommend lighter duties that would fit the sick worker's diminished capacities.[13]

The society physician carried out a variety of duties with a particular goal in mind. Although limited in therapeutic efficacy, the physician's labors held considerable value—but not to the insured worker. The primary beneficiary of the physician's services was the fund. From the insurers' perspective there was little doubt as to the physician's main job: get the worker back to work. To some extent, this was a humane goal because the worker's return indicated a recovery of health. But all parties recognized the financial consequences as well. The Ohio Health and Old Age Insurance Commission recommended that sickness insurance include medical benefits "to restore disabled workers to their original working power as completely and as quickly as possible," so that "the drain upon the funds may be stopped at the earliest possible moment." Providing medical attention to incapacitated fund members, noted the NICB, would do much "to arrest development of disability and thereby lessen the amount that the association might otherwise have to pay out in benefits." Even in union funds "the physician's function [was] to prevent malingering," rather than to provide diagnostic and therapeutic services.[14]

Between widespread fear of malingering and a mechanistic view of the medical arts, the ambiguity of the relation between sickness insurance and absenteeism in the minds of contemporaries is understandable. Progressives claimed that companies would benefit from government sickness insurance by contrasting it with current problems of absenteeism. The Ohio commission observed that industry suffered from the "inefficiency of workers due to sickness." Absence disrupted production processes, and sick employees who came to work anyway worked less efficiently and might pass their disease on to co-workers. Although some absenteeism data existed, the commission felt unable to "make any definite estimate" of the value of such losses, but even so it assured the reader that "it is apparently large."[15]

The potential effect of health insurance on those large losses was unclear. On one hand, it might increase absenteeism by rewarding malingerers. On the other, insurance enabled workers to begin to rest early in the course of an ailment, thereby preventing it from becoming much more serious. Reformers observed that workers could be dogged in their persistence at work despite physical disabilities, reporting that "anyone familiar with the poor knows with what grim determination half-sick workmen labor." Employers had learned from workmen's compensation that having injured workers treated more quickly could lead to a shorter spell of absence and reduce their overall financial liability. Workers with sickness benefits could opt to recuperate at home, presumably in less time than if they continued to work in order to maintain their income. Amy Maher of the Consumers' League testified to the Ohio commission that "malingering under health insurance is apparent, not real. People were availing themselves for the first time of medical care and perhaps, a few days rest, which had been impossible before."[16] This chapter's statistical analysis indicates that Maher's were among the most insightful of contemporary comments.

The combined effect of moral hazard, the recuperative power of rest, and required physician approval of absenteeism was unclear at that time. Some employers believed that on net, sickness insurance caused absenteeism to decline and productivity to increase. A New York City manufacturer reported that it had recouped the costs of its benefit association through diminished absenteeism. The Bureau of Labor Statistics claimed that sickness funds and other such "welfare work" reduced sickness and accident rates. Investigators for the NICB concluded that the influence of benefit funds on absenteeism was generally for the better. A steel mill in Illinois reported that "the effect of our association upon absenteeism has been salutary," thanks to inquiries by visiting committees. In addition, labor turnover decreased, and overall productivity increased. A Pennsylvania printer attributed reductions in absenteeism to the requirement of a waiting period before benefits were paid.[17]

Other firms, however, believed that sick funds increased absenteeism, not so much because of malingering per se but because of the strategic behavior of some workers who subscribed to more than one fund. The prospect of sick pay that exceeded an ordinary pay packet offered an irresistible moral hazard for workers who had so strategized. Still other employers concurred with Progressive reformers and reported that sick benefits that were worth less than a regular wage had no effect on absence.[18] Contemporary observations by informed participants suggest that sickness insurance had different effects at different firms. What is needed is a way to identify the most common effects, the major tendencies, of such insurance benefits on absenteeism in the widest number of cases, while taking into account the differences across workers, firms, and sickness funds. That way is by means of regression analysis.

A statistical test for moral hazard is relatively simple; interpretation of its results is less so. A few surveys taken in the late nineteenth century asked whether a worker belonged to a benefit society; if so, how valuable his weekly benefit was; and how many days he had missed in the previous year due to sickness. If the value of a worker's benefits and his proclivity to miss work were positively correlated across several samples of workers, holding constant as many of their characteristics as possible, then we can conclude that moral hazard was present. Whether that relationship was due to workers absenting themselves at times when in some sense they were healthy enough to work—a kind of unworthy absence—or whether, as Amy Maher proposed, insurance enabled truly sick workers to take necessary time off, we cannot say. Without recourse to second opinions by physicians (themselves problematic, given the principal-agent problem discussed above), there is no way to distinguish between such worthy and unworthy motivations in any case. If no statistical relationship is found, the case for an absenteeism moral hazard due to sickness insurance would be weakened considerably.

Whether the root motivation was recovery or slacking, the influence of sickness insurance on worker behavior expressed itself in absence from work. Absenteeism data for this study were collected from two types of sources, each with its own particular strengths and weaknesses. One included state labor bureau surveys of workers, and the other a set of federal surveys of sickness funds. The only labor bureau surveys with more than a few hundred respondents that asked about both absenteeism and the value of sickness benefits were those of Michigan iron and agricultural implement and furniture manufacturing workers in 1889–1890 (these formed the basis of Chapter 7's analysis) and the more general California survey of 1892.[19] These surveys included members and nonmembers of benefit societies and reported the value of ben-

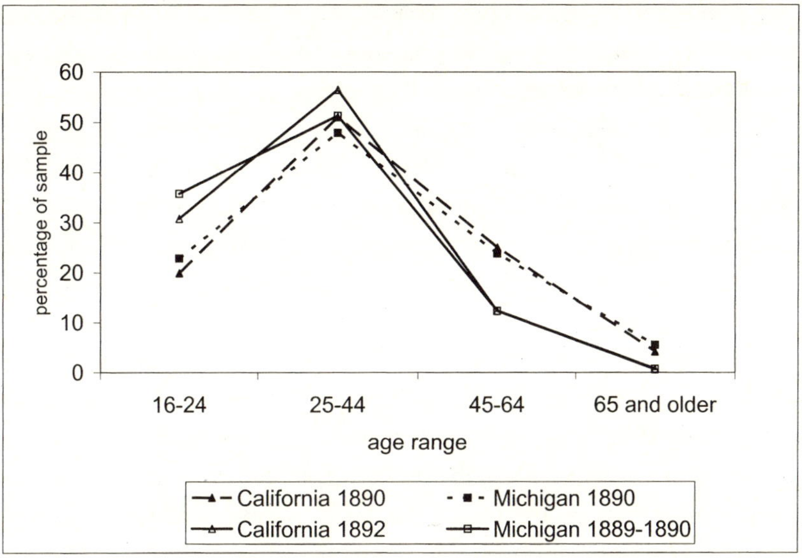

FIGURE 8.1. Age distributions of survey respondents and the gainfully employed according to the 1890 Census. (Data from Carter et al., "Codebook . . . Detroit, 1890"; "Codebook . . . Outside of Detroit, 1890"; Carter et al., "Codebook . . . Michigan, 1889"; Carter et al., "Codebook . . . California, 1892"; Lee et al., *Population Redistribution*, pp. 521, 533.)

efits for members; therefore, we can compare measures of absenteeism in relation to the value of sick benefits, with benefits for nonmembers set equal to zero.

The representativeness of these surveys is worth considering. Figure 8.1 shows the age distribution of male respondents to the surveys compared to estimates of the age distributions of gainfully employed men in the 1890 Census. The distributions were roughly similar, and in particular the difference between the two states within each sample was small. Although the surveys involved a higher proportion of young workers than appeared in the Census, the difference could have been due to inclusion in the Census of disproportionately older agricultural workers among the gainfully employed. The age distributions in the two surveys are similar to each other.

The state labor bureau surveys provide a rich body of information about individual workers, but they are largely silent with regard to characteristics of sickness funds. For these the 1908 Commissioner of Labor survey of sickness funds is invaluable.[20] The federal survey published responses by company-sponsored sickness insurance funds ("establishment funds") and railroad funds to questions about number of members, income, and benefits, eliminating the name and geographic location of the fund but identifying the industry. Published results also included information about the share of members in funds who made a claim in the previous year and the number of days for which a fund paid sick benefits, as well as the value of dues payments and benefits. Information about claim eligibility requirements included the length of the probationary membership period and the length of the waiting period between onset of ill health and eligibility for sick pay. Unfortunately the federal survey did not report age distributions of fund members.[21]

All these surveys provide an opportunity to test whether and how sick pay, medical benefits, and fund characteristics influenced worker absenteeism, which can be measured in three different ways. *Prevalence* of absenteeism is represented by the number of days missed per worker-year, *incidence* (sometimes referred to as *frequency*) by the number of workers who reported any absence due to sickness relative to the sample size (individual-level data) or who made claims relative to number of fund members (fund-level data). In both cases *duration* is prevalence divided by incidence, yielding the average number of all sick days per worker who missed any sick days (individual-level data) or the average number of compensated sick days per claimant (fund-level data). Variation in prevalence could have been due to variation in incidence, duration, or both.

An obvious influence on a worker's tendency to miss work due to ill-health was his age. Common sense suggests that older workers were at higher risk of sickness, a hypothesis borne out by the data. Figure 8.2 shows the incidence of absenteeism in the Michigan and California samples by age of the (male) respondent. Michigan workers clearly displayed an increasing frequency of absence (which could have been due to illness or injury) as they aged. The same tendency appeared among Californians but was slightly flatter.[22]

The industry in which a worker toiled influenced the absenteeism rate. Figure 8.3 shows incidence rates of compensated absence in several industries as reported in the Commissioner of Labor survey. This survey did not include absence spells that concluded before the worker qualified for benefits. Given that bias, it is clear that absence rates varied con-

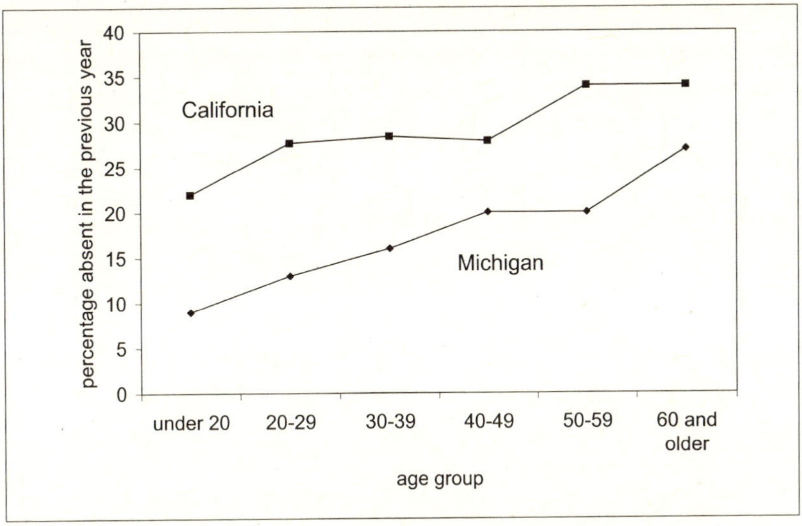

FIGURE 8.2. Incidence of sickness among men by age. (Data from Carter et al., "Codebook . . . Detroit, 1890"; "Codebook . . . Outside of Detroit, 1890"; "Codebook . . . Michigan, 1889"; "Codebook . . . California, 1892.")

siderably by industry. Fewer than one in five workers in printing and lithography and in electrical apparatus manufacturing (1,937 and 7,339 covered workers, respectively) received sickness benefits in the year preceding the survey, whereas in iron and steel and in agricultural implement manufacturing (30,365 and 7,948 workers, respectively) nearly half did so.

To investigate effects of sickness insurance coverage while controlling for individual and fund characteristics, regression analysis is fundamental. The measure of absenteeism for Michigan workers was the same as the one used in Chapter 7. The state labor bureau asked whether a worker had missed any work days in the previous year and the reason for the absence. Some responses to the latter question limited themselves to reporting only sickness or injury, but many responses combined health with other considerations such as "sickness and no work" or "sickness and vacation." Because it is impossible to determine the number of days missed due to each cause, the number of days missed due to sickness per worker and per sick worker cannot be estimated with the Michigan

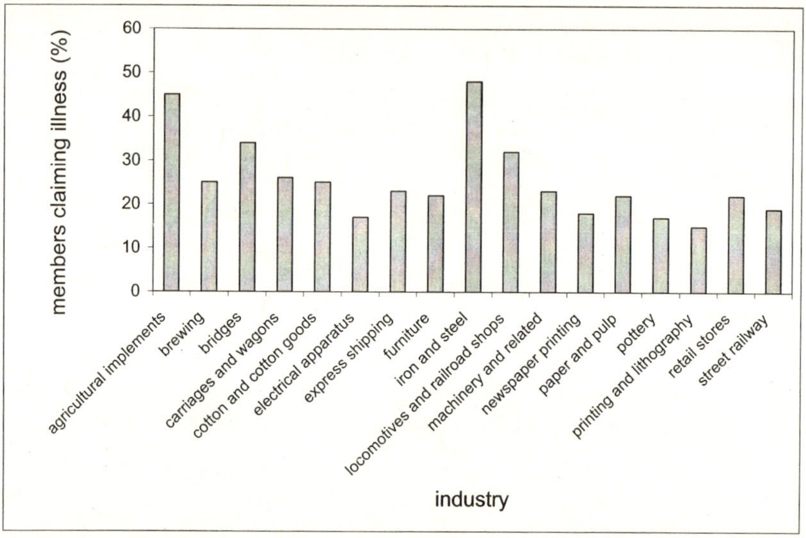

FIGURE 8.3. Risk of sickness by industry, 1908. (Data from U. S. Commissioner of Labor, *Twenty-third Annual Report.*)

surveys. The surveys did report the value of sickness benefits and the worker's usual earnings, and these permit analysis of the effects of both the absolute value of benefits and the replacement rate (value of sick benefits divided by wages) on the incidence of sickness absence. Because the three Michigan surveys asked similar questions, they could be pooled into one large data set.

Table 8.1 shows mean values of Michigan workers' characteristics. The median worker was twenty-seven years of age, married, and had been born in the United States. On average he earned about $40 per month, which was consistent with other estimates of worker income at the time.[23] Among covered workers, the average value of benefits was more than $6 per week, which was about 54 percent of his regular pay. About 25 percent of the sample belonged to benefit societies.

Two logit regressions shown in table 8.1 investigated the effects of age, industry and location, nativity and family status, income, and benefits on the incidence of absence. Risk of absence increased with age, although the effect was not large even after age fifty. A man in his fifties was about 4 percent more likely to be absent due to sickness than a man in his twenties with identical characteristics.[24]

Sick pay benefits were estimated two ways: in absolute terms (dol-

Table 8.1.
Influences on incidence of absence in Michigan

INFLUENCE	MEAN (STANDARD DEVIATION)	MODEL 1 (STANDARD ERROR)	MODEL 2 (STANDARD ERROR)
Intercept		−1.06***	−1.08***
		(0.10)	(0.10)
Married	0.54	0.26***	0.26***
		(0.08)	(0.08)
Number of dependents	1.76	−0.004	−0.004
	(1.99)	(0.02)	(0.02)
Born in United States	0.54	0.22***	0.22***
		(0.05)	(0.05)
Less than 20 years of age	0.20	−0.18**	−0.18*
		(0.09)	(0.09)
Age 20–29	0.37	Omitted	Omitted
Age 30–39	0.23	0.09	0.09
		(0.07)	(0.07)
Age 40–49	0.12	0.24***	0.24***
		(0.09)	(0.09)
50 years old or older	0.07	0.31***	0.31***
		(0.10)	(0.10)
Detroit iron and agricultural implement workers	0.33	−1.38***	−1.67***
		(0.07)	(0.07)
Other Michigan iron and agricultural implement workers	0.35	Omitted	Omitted
Furniture workers	0.37	−1.36***	−1.36***
		(0.06)	(0.06)
Monthly earnings	$40.29	−0.006***	−0.006***
	(17.82)	(0.002)	(0.002)
Value of sick benefit (mean: among those covered)	$6.37	0.013*	
	(3.65)	(0.0078)	

Table 8.1.

Influences on incidence of absence in Michigan (*continued*)

INFLUENCE	MEAN (STANDARD DEVIATION)	MODEL 1 (STANDARD ERROR)	MODEL 2 (STANDARD ERROR)
Replacement rate (mean: among those covered)	0.54 (0.22)		0.18* (0.10)
Pseudo R^2	0.11	0.11	

Sources: State labor bureau surveys of Michigan iron, agricultural implement, and furniture workers, 1889–1890. See Carter et al., "Codebook . . . Michigan, 1893"; "Codebook . . . California, 1892"; "Codebook . . . Detroit, 1890"; "Codebook . . . Outside of Detroit, 1890"; "Codebook . . . Michigan, 1889."

Notes: Dependent variable = 1 if respondent reported any absence due to illness in previous year. Mean value of dependent variable = 0.147. N = 14,018. Method: Logit. Omitted categories include age 20–29, worker in iron and agricultural implement manufacturing outside Detroit, born outside the U. S., single or widowed.

*significantly different from zero at the 0.10 level; **significantly different from zero at the 0.05 level; ***significantly different from zero at the 0.01 level

lars per week) and relative to the worker's usual income. If workers who believed they were at higher-than-average risk of making claims were especially likely to join benefit societies, endogeneity would result, a problem with no obvious solution in terms of instrumental variables.[25] In order to mitigate such problems, the value of benefits rather than a dummy for benefit society membership was employed. Estimated benefit coefficients suggested that a sick pay moral hazard existed. Coefficients of both absolute and relative values of sick pay benefits were positive and significant, indicating that the relation between sick pay benefits and absence was robust to the way benefits were measured. The magnitude of the effect was not very large in the Michigan case. Granting an average level of benefits to a worker who previously had none would only increase the probability of absence by one percentage point. The evidence indicates a significant but small moral hazard of sick pay for covered workers in Michigan.

The California survey offers a richer set of variables with which to measure absenteeism and its influences. The scholars who digitized this sample acknowledged a lack of representativeness with regard to ethnicity and union membership in the original sample but "concluded that the sample is reasonably representative of the manufacturing labor force as a whole except for a slight overrepresentation of brewery and construction workers and of workers in light manufacturing." The California survey was the only one of the digitized state surveys to include men and women, ask specifically about the number of work days missed due to sickness, and provide a dollar value of sick pay benefits.[26] Table 8.2 provides mean values of variables used in this analysis. The overall length of the workday was about 9.6 hours, typical for the time. Among the 26 percent of the sample who were eligible for sick pay benefits, the replacement rate was a little more than half, very similar to the Michigan surveys. Only about 5 percent of the California sample reported eligibility for medical benefits.

Results of logit regressions of incidence of absence appear in table 8.2. In these regressions, as in table 8.1, the dependent variable was set equal to one for respondents who reported any work days lost due to illness and zero otherwise. The California results are largely consistent with those from the Michigan analysis. Coefficients of the value of sick benefits, whether estimated in absolute terms or relative to wages, were positive and significant, again suggesting a degree of moral hazard. The relationship was robust to absolute and relative measures of sick benefits, as well as inclusion and exclusion of the self-reported health variable that gauged baseline well-being. The magnitude of the sick pay effect was larger in California than in Michigan: granting average sickness benefits to a worker who previously had none increased the probability of absence by 5.5 percentage points, a not inconsequential increase from a base of 28 percent. The magnitude of the effect of the same change in replacement rate terms was 4 percent. To summarize, as in Michigan, more valuable sickness benefits raised the probability of at least one absence, which is consistent with the hypothesis that sick pay induced moral hazard.[27] The effect of longer workdays was to increase the probability of absence, which supported the common Progressive claim that worker exhaustion was in part behind what they saw as excessive absence rates.[28]

Because the California survey reported days missed due to illness alone, it is possible to estimate influences on the prevalence and duration of this type of absence (table 8.3). Duration can be approximated by

Table 8.2.

Influences on incidence of absence in California

FACTOR	MEAN VALUES (STANDARD DEVIATIONS)	MODEL 1	MODEL 2	MODEL 3	MODEL 4
Intercept		−1.94***	−1.98***	−2.34***	−2.38***
		(0.53)	(0.53)	(0.55)	(0.54)
Male	0.80	−0.49***	−0.49***	−0.46***	−0.46***
		(0.14)	(0.14)	(0.14)	(0.14)
Married	0.31	0.18	0.19	0.20	0.21
		(0.13)	(0.13)	(0.13)	(0.13)
Number of dependents	0.96	−0.001	−0.0001	−0.02	0.01
	(1.66)	(0.03)	(0.03)	(0.04)	(0.03)
Age unknown	0.02	−0.86**	−0.89**	−1.01**	−1.03**
		(0.43)	(0.43)	(0.45)	(0.45)
Age less than 20 years	0.25	−0.02	0.003	0.09	0.11
		(0.13)	(0.13)	(0.14)	(0.14)
Age 20–29	0.39	Omitted	Omitted	Omitted	Omitted
Age 30–39	0.20	0.04	0.04	0.05	0.05
		(0.13)	(0.13)	(0.13)	(0.13)
Age 40–49	0.10	0.09	0.09	0.08	0.08
		(0.16)	(0.16)	(0.17)	(0.17)

Age 50 or older	0.06	0.41**	0.40**	0.34	0.33
		(0.21)	(0.21)	(0.21)	(0.21)
Length of workday	9.50	0.09**	0.09**	0.09*	0.09*
(hours)	(1.07)	(0.05)	(0.05)	(0.05)	(0.05)
Self-reported bad	0.11			1.17***	1.17***
health				(0.13)	(0.13)
Weekly wage	13.39	0.00009	0.003	0.003	0.007
	(7.03)	(0.009)	(0.009)	(0.009)	(0.009)
Value of sick	9.07	0.03**		0.03**	
benefit (mean:	(3.13)	(0.01)		(0.01)	
among those					
covered)					
Replacement rate	0.56		0.37**		0.38**
of sick pay	(0.19)		(0.18)		(0.19)
(mean: among					
those covered)					
Eligible for medical	0.05	0.20	0.22	0.20	0.23
benefits		(0.20)	(0.20)	(0.20)	(0.20)
Pseudo R^2		0.03	0.03	0.05	0.05

Source: Carter et al., "Codebook . . . California, 1892."

Note: N = 2872. Method: Logit. Mean value of dependent variable = 0.28. Standard errors in parentheses for regression results. Dummies were included for industry, years in California, and years at employer but were not reported here to save space.

*significantly different from zero at the 0.10 level; **significantly different from zero at the 0.05 level; ***significantly different from zero at the 0.01 level

Table 8.3.

Influences on prevalence and duration of absence in California

FACTOR	DURATION OF ABSENCE (LOG OF DAYS ABSENT IF ANY DAYS ABSENT)	DURATION OF ABSENCE (LOG OF DAYS ABSENT IF ANY DAYS ABSENT)	OVERALL ABSENCE RATE (NUMBER OF ABSENT DAYS IN YEAR)	OVERALL ABSENCE RATE (NUMBER OF ABSENT DAYS IN YEAR)
Method	OLS	OLS	Tobit	Tobit
Intercept	1.59***	1.56***	−71.12***	−71.99***
	(0.52)	(0.52)	(14.48)	(14.47)
Male	0.12	0.11	−8.43**	−8.63**
	(0.14)	(0.14)	(3.71)	(3.71)
Married	−0.10	−0.11	3.10	3.22
	(0.13)	(0.13)	(3.46)	(3.45)
Number of dependents	0.03	0.03	−0.29	−0.25
	(0.03)	(0.03)	(0.92)	(0.92)
Age unknown	−0.17	−0.18	−21.57*	−22.12**
	(0.48)	(0.48)	(11.22)	(11.22)
Age 19 or less	−0.09	−0.08	3.55	4.03
	(0.13)	(0.13)	(3.61)	(3.63)
Age 20–29	Omitted	Omitted	Omitted	Omitted
Age 30–39	0.10	0.09	3.66	3.59
	(0.12)	(0.12)	(3.38)	(3.38)

Age 40–49	0.43***	0.42***	8.98**	8.94**
	(0.16)	(0.16)	(4.35)	(4.35)
Age 50 or	0.14	0.15	11.17**	11.08**
older	(0.20)	(0.20)	(5.55)	(5.55)
Length of	0.02	0.03	2.10*	2.10*
workday	(0.04)	(0.04)	(1.21)	(1.21)
(hours)				
Self-reported	0.66***	0.66***	38.10***	38.00***
bad health	(0.11)	(0.11)	(3.41)	(3.41)
Weekly wage	0.02	0.02*	0.13	0.21
	(0.01)	(0.01)	(0.24)	(0.24)
Value of sick	0.005		0.64**	
benefit	(0.01)		(0.31)	
Replacement rate		0.24		9.58*
of sick pay		(0.18)		(4.95)
Eligible for	–0.33*	–0.38**	0.28	0.45
medical	(0.18)	(0.19)	(5.41)	(5.42)
benefits				
Adjusted R^2	0.11	0.11		
N	809	809	2872	2872

Source: Carter et al., "Codebook . . . California, 1892."

Note: Standard errors in parentheses. White tests indicated homoskedastic residuals. Dummies were included for industry, years in California, and years at employer but were not reported here to save space.

*significantly different from zero at the 0.10 level; **significantly different from zero at the 0.05 level; ***significantly different from zero at the 0.01 level

days missed per worker who missed any days. In this case, sick pay benefits had no effect at all on duration. If malingering is defined as staying away from work a few days longer than necessary thanks to the availability of sick pay, there is no evidence of malingering here. Medical benefits significantly reduced the duration of illness, holding constant the absolute or relative value of sick pay benefits.[29] Workers who were ill at some point in the year prior to the survey and who were eligible for medical benefits from their sickness fund experienced spells of illness that were one-third shorter than those endured by workers without medical benefits.

The remaining two models report influences on the prevalence of absence as measured by days of work missed due to illness for each respondent. Because only 28 percent of the sample reported any lost work days, the large proportion of zeroes in the dependent variable indicated the estimation of Tobit models. The most important result was that the tendency of higher sick pay to increase days missed was significant. Membership in a sickness fund did influence worker absenteeism. Sick pay increased the probability of an absence, and medical benefits reduced durations of sickness spells. These results provide evidence supporting the hypothesis that sick pay created a moral hazard. Because all workers needed physician certification of their absence, but only those with medical benefits were seen by a doctor paid by the insurance fund, these results also support the hypothesis that the identity of the principal for whom the physician served as agent, whether insurer or worker, mattered.

These results are so striking that it is worthwhile asking whether they can be replicated. The answer is yes. The data for the next set of regressions are from the 1908 Commissioner of Labor's survey. Although the survey could not include information about workers who were not members of funds, absence measures were comparable to those in the individual worker surveys: incidence (claims per member), duration (days per claim), and prevalence (days per member). In addition, effects of fund characteristics as well as benefit levels can be estimated. Average values of available variables appear in table 8.4.[30]

The Commissioner of Labor's report listed characteristics of railroad funds separately from establishment funds. Railroad funds covered

Table 8.4.
Mean values of U.S. Commissioner of Labor survey (weighted by membership)

FACTOR	ESTABLISHMENT FUNDS: REPORTED	ESTABLISHMENT FUNDS: CORRECTED FOR WAITING PERIOD[a]	RAILROAD FUNDS
Days lost to sickness per worker	4.99 (2.13)	6.76	9.40 (3.01)
Share of workers reporting any absence	0.20	0.33	
Cases per worker	0.23 (0.22)		0.53 (0.16)
Days lost per case	25.33 (11.55)	20.30	18.21 (10.76)
Number of members	691 (1,992)		56,718 (48,372)
Age of fund (years)	12.16 (8.48)		21.74 (9.55)
Employee-managed	0.39		0.03
Jointly managed	0.46		0.97
Firm-managed	0.15		0.00
Voluntary membership	0.70		0.77
Compulsory membership	0.30		0.23
Trial period (weeks of membership with no benefits)	3.61 (8.25)		1.43 (12.17)
Waiting period (days of sickness before benefits)	5.86 (3.44)		5.04 (2.27)
Maximum weeks of benefits per year	18.61 (9.85)		50.05 (18.50)
Medical benefits available	0.42		n/a

Table 8.4.
Mean values of U.S. Commissioner of Labor survey (weighted by membership) (*continued*)

FACTOR	ESTABLISHMENT FUNDS: REPORTED	ESTABLISHMENT FUNDS: CORRECTED FOR WAITING PERIOD[a]	RAILROAD FUNDS
Maximum sick pay	6.25		16.33
($ per week)	(2.42)		(4.99)
Minimum sick pay	4.06		2.35
($ per week)	(1.87)		(1.62)
N (funds)	394		29
N (workers)	272,134		262,747

Source: U.S. Commissioner of Labor, *Twenty-third Annual Report.*
Note: Since these means were weighted by fund membership, the proportions represent the share of workers (not of funds) with the given characteristic. Standard deviations in parentheses.
[a]Assumes distribution of absence durations as in the California worker sample.

nearly as many workers as establishment funds but were few in number: there were only twenty-nine of them. The small number of funds followed from the number of railroads, and the number of covered workers is large because a few of the funds were huge. It also was a function of the highly developed culture of corporate welfare in the railroads, which in turn stemmed in part from the geographically far-flung nature of their operations. Railroad workers became ill or injured long distances from home, in areas with few residents and no medical services.[31]

Fund level regression results appear in table 8.5. Again the value of sick benefits influenced worker absence rates and did so in ways similar to those seen in the individual-level regressions, suggesting robust relationships between benefits and absenteeism. Increases in the minimum value of sick pay significantly raised the frequency of claims in establishment and railroad funds. An increase of one standard deviation in the lower level of sick benefits induced an 11 percent increase in the share of establishment fund members who made claims and a 32 percent increase among railroad fund members. For both kinds of funds, this effect was strong enough that minimum levels of sick pay were significantly and positively related to overall days missed per worker. For both kinds of funds, variation in sick pay left duration of sickness unaffected. Similar to the results for the California survey with regard to individual workers, availability of medical benefits reduced the average duration in establishment funds by 15 percent. In fund-level data the effect was strong enough to reduce overall prevalence. The consistency of these findings is noteworthy. In four independent data sets—Michigan workers, California workers, establishment sickness funds, and railroad sickness funds—similar relationships between sickness fund benefits and absenteeism rates appeared. Sick pay increased frequency of absences, and medical benefits reduced their duration.

Medical benefit coefficients provided evidence of a principal-agent problem. Medical benefits might have enabled a sick worker of limited means to have greater access to a physician than if he had to pay for the doctor visit himself, but that cannot explain all the present results. Nearly all workers had to be examined by a physician in order to get their initial claim approved, and that approval had to be renewed by the physician every week or two that the worker claimed to be incapacitated. In funds that did not provide medical benefits, approved claims led to cash payments that were intended to cover medical bills. Physicians must have examined about the same proportions of workers with and without medical benefit coverage.[32]

A better explanation for these results is that the medical benefit coefficients reflected a principal-agent problem in which the identity of the employer of the physician influenced the length of the worker's absence. When the worker paid his physician out of pocket (perhaps in part with sickness benefits), the physician was more likely to approve the worker's claim and allow more compensated sick days. When the insurance fund paid the physician, he was more likely to do the fund's bidding and get the worker back to his job sooner. The ambiguous pronoun referent in a statement by a Rhode Island foundry executive was telling. In his experience, the fund's physician "tends to bring the man back to work as soon as he is able."[33]

As many Progressives believed, an important therapeutic effect of sickness insurance benefits was the ability to take time off when moder-

Table 8.5.

Fund-level regressions weighted by membership size

LOG OF:	ESTABLISHMENT FUNDS			RAILROAD FUNDS		
	DAYS MISSED PER MEMBER PER YEAR	CLAIMS PER MEMBER PER YEAR	DAYS MISSED PER CLAIM	DAYS MISSED MEMBER PER PER YEAR	CLAIMS PER MEMBER PER YEAR	DAYS MISSED PER CLAIM
Intercept	1.36***	−1.89***	2.41***	−0.05	−3.08***	2.93***
	(0.14)	(0.14)	(0.14)	(0.90)	(0.67)	(0.96)
Number of members	0.02	−0.05***	0.05***	0.01	0.03**	−0.01
	(0.02)	(0.02)	(0.01)	(0.02)	(0.01)	(0.01)
Number of members squared	−0.05	0.18***	−0.15***	−0.05	−0.14*	0.08
	(0.06)	(0.06)	(0.05)	(0.10)	(0.08)	(0.08)
Employee management	−0.05	−0.11	0.02	−0.72*	−0.70**	−0.05
	(0.06)	(0.06)	(0.05)	(0.35)	(0.26)	(0.29)
Voluntary	0.04	0.20***	−0.07	0.83**	0.69**	0.16
	(0.06)	(0.06)	(0.05)	(0.33)	(0.24)	(0.28)
Age of fund	0.008***	0.013***	0.0005	0.004	−0.004	0.007
	(0.003)	(0.003)	(0.002)	(0.01)	(0.009)	(0.008)

Trial period	−0.003	−0.009**	0.002	−0.11*	−0.11**	−0.01
	(0.004)	(0.004)	(0.003)	(0.06)	(0.05)	(0.05)
Waiting period	−0.02*	−0.04***	0.001	0.02	0.03	−0.01
	(0.01)	(0.01)	(0.009)	(0.08)	(0.06)	(0.06)
Maximum						
benefit	0.001	0.002	0.0003	0.02	0.03**	−0.01
period	(0.002)	(0.002)	(0.002)	(0.02)	(0.01)	(0.01)
Medical	−0.15***	0.004	−0.15***			
benefits	(0.005)	(0.05)	(0.04)	n/a	n/a	n/a
Maximum sick pay	−0.01	0.01	−0.01	−0.07	−0.12*	0.05
	(0.01)	(0.01)	(0.01)	(0.08)	(0.06)	(0.06)
Minimum sick pay	0.04***	0.06***	0.01	0.19**	0.20***	−0.004
	(0.01)	(0.01)	(0.01)	(0.09)	(0.07)	(0.08)
Log claim			−0.45***			−0.03
rate		(0.04)			(0.23)	
Industry dummies?	Yes	Yes	Yes	n/a	n/a	n/a
Adjusted R^2	0.40	0.57	0.38	0.78	0.90	0.72
N	394			28		

Source: U.S. Commissioner of Labor, *Twenty-third Annual Report*.

Note: White tests indicated homoskedasticity in all regressions. Standard errors in italics.

*significantly different from zero at the 0.10 level; **significantly different from zero at the 0.05 level; ***significantly different from zero at the 0.01 level

ately ill. The negative and significant coefficient on the claim rate as an independent variable in the establishment fund duration regression suggests an important role for rest that resembled past findings regarding Europe and present findings for the United States. The higher the number of claims filed, the shorter the average absence, holding constant the length of the waiting period. The easier it was for workers to take time off when moderately ill, it seems, the less likely it was that a spell would develop into a grave illness from which a worker needed weeks and weeks to recover.[34] Amy Maher's testimony to the Ohio Health and Old Age Insurance Commission, described above, was fundamentally correct.

The information asymmetries that plagued European systems were present in American programs as well, but establishment funds seem to have used effective methods to mitigate these problems. Sickness funds encountered adverse selection. According to table 8.5, workers in establishment or railroad funds who joined their funds voluntarily were more likely to experience an absence. This is consistent with voluntary funds' drawing in a disproportionate share of high-risk members. One way to deal with this problem was a probationary or trial period in which a new fund member was ineligible for benefits. The effect of a trial period was to screen out high-risk applicants, since longer probationary periods were associated with significantly lower frequency of absenteeism.[35] Longer waiting periods also reduced the frequency of absenteeism in establishment funds, exactly as expected. In general, fund characteristics that were intended to relieve problems of selection bias and moral hazard—medical benefits, waiting periods, trial membership periods—all seem to have worked effectively.

As noted above, some employers believed that their firm's sickness insurance program caused absenteeism to decline and productivity to increase, whereas others reported increasing absenteeism due to their sick fund's benefits, and still others found no relationship between benefits and absenteeism. The analysis presented in this chapter is consistent with the idea that expanding private insurance had considerable influence on absence patterns but affected them in such a way that the two most direct effects cancelled each other out. Increases in sick pay benefits and coverage raised the frequency of absence, and expanding medical benefits would have reduced the duration of such spells. Although the shift from a relatively solid base of worker and fund surveys to interpretation of national trends is a speculative leap, the story it tells is a consistent one and worthy of consideration.

Broad surveys of American workers during the Progressive Era all found roughly similar rates of prevalence of absenteeism. Table 8.6 shows estimated values of absenteeism measures culled from a variety of sources during the Progressive period and later. This period was marked by stability. Twenty to 25 percent of workers missed any work at all due to sickness in a typical year, and those workers missed five to six weeks. On net, a typical worker missed six to seven days in a given year due to ill health—far fewer than the ten to fourteen days, or as much as 5 percent of the work year, that some reformers claimed. With three hundred days in the work year, the Progressive-Era estimates shown in table 8.6 indicated a prevalence rate of about 2 percent. Business executives and reform opponents, who backed that rate, were closer to the mark than were Progressive activists.[36]

Trends in incidence and duration after the Progressive Era were consistent with a story of insurance benefits and absence behavior as outlined above, combined with an increase in the value of benefits and an expansion of coverage. According to table 8.6, over the course of the 1920s the incidence of absence rose by about 50 percent (from one-fourth to one-third), and duration declined by about one-third (from between twenty-five and thirty-five days to seventeen days per claiming worker). During this period typical weekly sick pay benefits increased in value by half, the availability of medical benefits expanded, and the share of firms providing such benefits grew.[37] If the parameters I have estimated are correct in sign, these trends would have led to higher incidence rates and briefer durations of absence throughout the 1920s, and they did, as table 8.6 reports. The growth of both private sick pay and medical benefits during this period led not to increased malingering but to a steady share of the work year lost due to sickness. Whether government insurance could have done the same is open to speculation.

The statistical analysis presented in this chapter indicates that private health insurance in the Progressive Era was in fact subject to moral hazard. Workers who were eligible for higher rates of sick pay, whether

Table 8.6.

Mean values of sickness absence measures (men only)

YEARS	1888–1899	1912–1916	1915–1917	1928–1931	1987
Prevalence	6.62	6.11	7.17	6.04	3.44
Incidence	0.24	0.23	0.20	0.36	0.40
Duration (in days)	28.17	26.17	36.51	17.00	8.61
N (workers)	5,968	81,607[a]	55,157	8,956	4,992

Sources: Data for 1888–1899 are from state labor surveys, available at http://www.eh.net/databases/labor/. Michigan (stone workers), 1888; California, 1892; Kansas, 1895, 1896, 1899; Maine 1890. Data for 1912–1916 are from Collins, "Economic Status and Health," from records of the Workmen's Sick and Death Benefit Society. Data for 1915–1917 are from Frankel, "Comment," pp. 642–643, from Metropolitan Life Insurance Company surveys for white males aged 15–64, number sick and unable to work in Boston, North Carolina, Rochester, Trenton. Data for 1928–1931 are from Collins, "Cases and Days of Illness," from the Committee on the Cost of Medical Care survey. Data for 1987 are from Vistnes, "Gender Differences," from the National Medical Expenditure Survey.

Note: Prevalence is measured by days missed owing to ill health per worker-year. Incidence is measured by cases per worker (1912–1916, 1928–1931) or share of workers reporting any days off (1888–1899, 1915–1917, and 1987). Duration is measured by days missed per sick worker.

[a]Worker-years of exposure.

measured in dollars or as a share of their usual wage, were more likely to miss work due to sickness. The sickness insurance funds that underwrote such absenteeism were aware of this incentive and aimed to reduce its effect by imposing various rules on eligibility for benefits. The most important, and the one most widely understood to be effective at the time, was the requirement that claims be approved by a physician. Funds that paid physicians to make these assessments found that they ended compensated absence spells sooner than doctors who were paid by the worker-claimant. By such methods, private funds were able to maintain a constant level of absence, in terms of days missed per worker, throughout the era.

The effects of sick pay and medical benefits on absenteeism address important political claims of the day. We can never know how viable Progressive health insurance reform proposals would have been, but we can compare the workings of the insurance operations that actually existed to characteristics of Progressive proposals and then speculate on what might have happened under hypothesized state insurance programs.[38] Progressive reformers who wanted state governments to provide health insurance in place of private sickness funds claimed that the sickness benefits they advocated would not induce a moral hazard. In the AALL proposal, sickness benefits were to be paid at two-thirds the worker's usual wage, a higher replacement rate than most insured workers actually enjoyed, thereby inducing more absence. While some advocates, such as members of the Ohio Health and Old Age Insurance Commission, understood that physician willingness to certify workers as incapacitated was a critical part of managing moral hazard, their proposals did not reflect this understanding. Their opponents' claim that moral hazard was a problem that the Progressives had failed to address was valid.

Existing insurance funds recognized moral hazard and aimed to counter it with a variety of strategies, including approval of claims by a fund-employed physician, probationary membership periods, and waiting periods before claims were paid. Progressive proposals downplayed the importance of the first of these, omitted the second, and reduced the third to only three days. Indeed, these proposals seem to have intentionally obfuscated compensation and supervision of physicians, hoping to bring them on board during the campaign for government insurance and then address these issues after the fact. But what Progressives saw as finesse others saw as confusion.[39] The omission of cost controls may have made political sense because the Progressive goal was, more or less, to compensate a larger number of workers for longer spells of absence, at higher rates, and to provide medical care for them as well. But to do so created incentives for ever greater spending, and Progressive proposals failed to show much awareness of the need to check these incentives or budget for their consequences.

The failure to persuade legislators and voters that reformers had adequately reckoned the costs of expanded insurance may help explain why their proposals gained no political purchase. Progressives suffered credibility problems with legislators and voters who recognized the disconnect between claims that moral hazard would not be a problem and persistent evidence that it was already a problem. By contrast, a deeper if informal understanding of conflicting incentives enabled private sickness insurance funds to provide a modest but very real degree of income security to their members. By the end of the Progressive Era, benefit societies had survived reformers' efforts to replace them and continued to go about their business.

PART THREE INNOVATION AND DECLINE

CHAPTER NINE

Insured Workers' Health in the Great Depression

Larger firms selectively fired more, and more expertly, than the average firm did. Employing many at identical work, they knew which workers were least productive. Whom they laid off.

—STANLEY LEBERGOTT

AT LEAST UNTIL THE END of the Progressive Era, this book has contended, industrial sickness funds served the workers who belonged to them well. Today, such funds form a small part of the network of American health insurers. The point at which sickness funds went from being major players to minor players was not the Great Depression proper (1929–1932) but the later 1930s. This chapter explains why, paradoxically, the Depression was beneficial for sickness funds, though not for their members. The paradox emerged from a sharp decrease in absenteeism during the Depression. This was a sign of improving health of the workforce, to be sure, but not of an overall increase in the well-being of the working class. Rather, expulsion of unemployed members from sickness funds produced this artifact, which brings into sharp relief the greatest shortcoming of workplace-based health insurance: its failure to protect workers who simultaneously experienced loss of health and of employment.

The first broad-based and consistent American time series of compensated sick leave began in 1920 and continued until 1952. This series stemmed from quarterly surveys of industrial sick benefit societies conducted by the U. S. Public Health Service and published in their *Public Health Reports*. The impetus behind these surveys was a concern during the World War I era that increasing absenteeism was limiting production of war matériel. The surveys were intended to provide systematic measures of absence to test whether that was the case. Although the war ended before the first absenteeism investigations were carried out, the surveys began anyway and continued for three decades. The reports carried the bylines of only two Public Health Service statisticians: Dean Brundage, who worked on them until 1938, and William Gafafer thereafter. Collection of the surviving data under the direction of only two men over the course of three decades should enhance their consistency.[1] The measure of absenteeism reported was the share of covered workers who experienced a spell of sickness absence long enough to qualify for benefits from their sick fund. Because most funds imposed a one-week waiting period during this time, such spells had to last a minimum of a week for the investigators to count it.

It is natural to inquire whether a time series of sickness rates that includes the Great Depression might have some relation to unemployment rates, as in union benefit operations (described in Chapter 6). As noted there, Progressive-Era observers believed that there was a close connection between sickness and unemployment. Depression-era researchers found that the incidence of sickness was greater among the poor than among the rich, and uncovered evidence for an increase of hospitalization among those on their way down—the newly poor and the unemployed. It was unclear how much was due to decreasing physical health and how much to newfound qualifications to receive means-tested charity care.[2] Because broad-based time series statistics of absenteeism do not extend back into the Progressive Era, we cannot assess the unemployment-absence relationship then, but the interwar period does allow such a comparison.

Figure 9.1 reports the annual unemployment rate as well as the incidence of absence due to sickness. It shows a strong inverse relationship between absenteeism and unemployment rates. As unemployment increased in the sharp but brief recession of 1920–1921, absenteeism declined. For the rest of the prosperous 1920s unemployment was low, and absenteeism was relatively high. As the Great Depression began, unemployment climbed to its peak at 25 percent, and absenteeism decreased by one-third. When the recession-within-the-Depression struck in 1937–1938, producing the upward-pointing "tooth" in the unemployment rate,

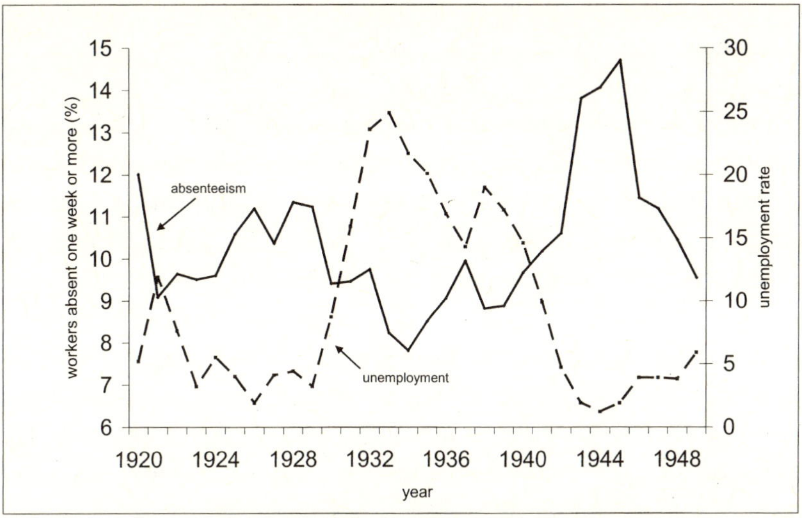

FIGURE 9.1. Sickness absence and unemployment among men. (Data from Brundage, "Sickness Among Industrial Employees"; Gafafer and Frasier, "Frequency of Disabling Illness"; Gafafer, "Sickness Absenteeism"; U.S. Public Health Service, Public Health Reports, various years; U.S. Bureau of the Census, *Historical Statistics.*)

absenteeism moved in the opposite direction. Low unemployment rates during the war years were reflected in high rates of absenteeism. The immediate postwar years saw slight increases in unemployment. Absenteeism fell by about one-third from 1945 to 1949. Confirming the visual relationship, the estimated correlation coefficient was –0.73 for the entire period, significant at the 0.001 level.

The degree to which absence rates reflect sickness as opposed to economics is unclear. In this case circumstantial evidence suggests that absence rates correlated with genuine ill health. The relation between sickness and absenteeism was supported by the particular case of influenza. It was the greatest single cause of absence and accounted for much of the variation in overall absence rates. In 1928 influenza accounted for a quarter (25.7 percent) of all recorded absenteeism. From 1928 to 1934 incidence of absence due to overall respiratory sickness, which included influenza, declined 52 percent, and this decline accounted for 74 percent of the overall decline in absenteeism during those years. Influenza alone accounted for more than half (54 percent) of the overall decline. No other cause accounted for as much as 10 percent of it.[3]

Given the importance of influenza in absenteeism trends, one way to test how closely the absenteeism series reflects levels of worker health is to estimate how closely absenteeism rates tracked some "true" level of influenza incidence and severity. But that cannot be done. Any statistical noise or physical malingering in the general morbidity series is likely to show up in the influenza morbidity series as well. What can be done is to compare absenteeism due to influenza to mortality from influenza.[4] If national mortality rates reflected the true incidence of influenza, and workers attributed much of their absenteeism to influenza when the influenza mortality rate was low, the discrepancy would suggest data quality problems. As things turned out, at least regarding influenza, workers seem not to have malingered during the Depression. In figure 9.2 the two series tracked each other closely until the late 1930s. After that point, mortality continued to decline while absenteeism rose sharply during the war, for reasons discussed below. Workers may have been unusually badly disabled by influenza during the war, but before then trends in absence due to influenza were similar to trends in influenza mortality ($r=0.46$; $p=0.01$; from 1921 to 1938, $r=0.78$, $p<0.001$). There is no evidence in these data that workers took more time off due to influenza than they needed to during the Depression. This in turn suggests that the absenteeism series reliably measures worker health. The larger question of the source of the relation between health and unemployment pictured in figure 9.1 remains.

The best explanation for this relation is that during the Great Depression employers decided to retain or fire workers, in part, according to their health. Three sorts of evidence support this claim. First, ill health was associated with job loss early in the Depression. Second, as the Depression went on the health of the unemployed as a group worsened relative to the health of the employed. If less healthy workers were leaving employment to become unemployed, they suffered doubly owing to the third point of evidence: once workers lost their jobs, they lost their sickness insurance coverage as well. Thus, the sickness benefit funds discussed in the *Public Health Reports* samples covered an ever-healthier workforce.[5] In sum, the relation between unemployment and absenteeism as pictured in figure 9.1 was an artifact of the sampling process. Rather than showing improving health of workers, it provides

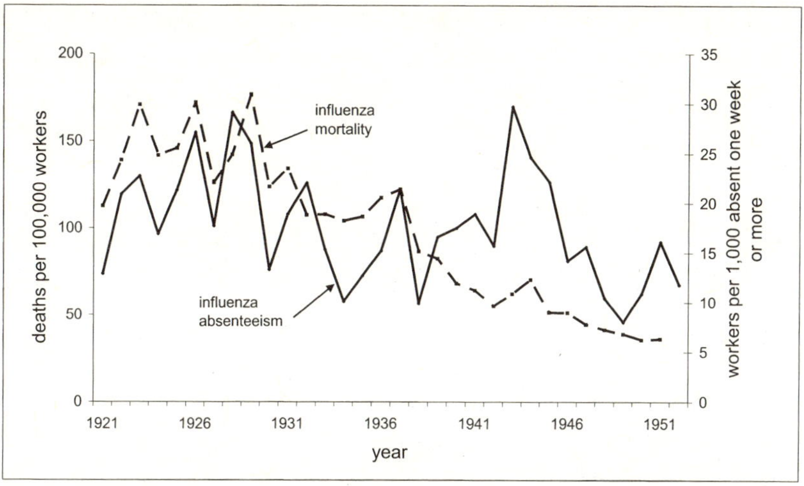

FIGURE 9.2. Absenteeism and mortality due to influenza. (Data from Brundage, "Sickness Among Industrial Employees"; Gafafer and Frasier, "Frequency of Disabling Illness"; Gafafer, "Sickness Absenteeism"; U.S. Public Health Service, Public Health Reports, various years.)

evidence that sickness funds let down their weakest members just when they needed the fund's support the most.

Worker health influenced the timing of Depression-era job loss, according to an unusual survey conducted in Minneapolis, St. Paul, and Duluth between 1932 and 1934. Respondents reported on their health and employment status and, if applicable, when their unemployment began.[6] Investigators classified those unemployed before January 1, 1931, as long-term unemployed and the rest as the more recently unemployed. The long-term unemployed suffered from a variety of physical conditions at higher rates than did the more recently unemployed, who in turn suffered at higher rates than the employed.

Table 9.1 reports the results from one of the survey's most general findings: whether the respondent suffered from "defects probably reducing efficiency" at work. Among skilled men, 26 percent of the long-term unemployed suffered from productivity-reducing health problems, 22 percent of the short-term unemployed were so labeled, and only 10 percent of the employed were. Among semiskilled men these shares were 14 percent of the long-term unemployed, 6 percent of the short-

Table 9.1.

Health and timing of unemployment in Minnesota, 1932–1934: percentage of respondents reporting physical defects likely to reduce efficiency

	MEN			WOMEN		
TYPE OF OCCUPATION	UNEMPLOYED BEFORE 1/1/31 (%)	UNEMPLOYED AFTER 1/1/31 (%)	EMPLOYED (%)	UNEMPLOYED BEFORE 1/1/31 (%)	UNEMPLOYED AFTER 1/1/31 (%)	EMPLOYED (%)
			All ages			
Professional and business	25.7	11.3	9.9	26.3	5.3	10.8
Clerical	24.3	11.4	12.7	21.7	10.6	9.3
Skilled	25.9	22.3	10.4	—	—	—
Semiskilled	14.1	6.2	3.3	—	—	—
N	445	579	399	88	104	306
			Ages 25–44 years, inclusive			
Professional and business	21.0	6.2	9.9	30.8	6.3	16.0
Clerical	25.0	44.3	10.4	22.5	10.9	11.1
Skilled	19.1	19.6	4.4	—	—	—
Semiskilled	11.5	5.0	0.0	—	—	—
N	183	267	281	53	62	160

Scurce: Diehl, "Physical Condition."

term unemployed, and 3 percent of the employed. The source of these patterns was something other than different age distributions by employment status, because similar ratios obtained among those aged twenty-five to forty-four in the sample. Further, since these defects included conditions such as hearing loss that were unlikely to have been exacerbated by unemployment, it appears that the ill health caused the unemployment and not vice versa. The Minnesota investigators concluded, "The individual with physical handicaps is more likely to become unemployed than the one who is in better physical condition."[7]

Second, declining absenteeism was not wholly due to reduced malingering by workers whose health was steady over time. If that had been so, the employed and the unemployed should have been about equally healthy, and they were not. The results presented in this chapter do not correspond with popular opinions at the time, when it was believed that workers were malingering more during the Depression. In part, one business executive reported, this belief followed from a last-hired, first-fired policy that caused younger workers to be laid off first and older, less healthy workers to be retained. Further, he claimed, fixed sickness benefits of five to seven dollars per week became ever more attractive in a time of deflation, which led some business observers to propose that absenteeism was increasing during the Depression. This hypothesis is plausible, but there is no evidence in these data to support it.[8]

Different probabilities of job loss for a worker in poor health and one in good health influenced the collective health of the unemployed relative to the employed as the Depression dragged on. A series of surveys that sampled large groups of Americans reported growing differentials in relative health of these groups. These surveys did not ask the same questions over time, and so their results cannot be compared directly to each other. But each asked about disability days, which were days in which the respondent was unable to perform his usual activities due to illness, and about employment status. Although the unemployed would not have experienced work-loss days for obvious reasons, the employed and unemployed alike could suffer disability days. Comparing the incidence of disability days among the employed and the unemployed within each survey yielded a measure of the relative sickness of each group, and that relative measure can be tracked over time. Table 9.2 shows the results of these estimates.

Table 9.2.
Comparison of the employed and the unemployed by health status

TIME	SAMPLE NAME AND SIZE	MEASURE	RATIO (UNEMPLOYED SICKNESS INCIDENCE RATE/EMPLOYED RATE)
		Short-term disability	
1928–31	Committee on the Costs of Medical Care: 8,758 families; 39,185 individuals	>=1 disabled day in preceding year; employed vs. unemployed + not in the labor force	1.01
Spring 1933	Health and Depression Studies:11,511 families	>=1 disabled day within 3 months of survey; family with full-time employed adult vs. family with no adults employed full-time	1.25
1935–36	National Health Survey: 971,620 workers	Disabled on day of survey; employed vs. unemployed	2.23

May 1942–February 1943	Monthly Report on the Labor Force: 55,000 persons aged 14 and older	Disabled for at least one day in week of survey; employed vs. unemployed	5.84
February 1949	Current Population Survey: 25,000 families	Disabled on day of survey; employed vs. unemployed	2.18
		Long-term disability	
1935–36	National Health Survey	1 or more chronic diseases and disabled less than 1 year; employed vs. unemployed; men aged 20–34	1.23
1935–36	National Health Survey	1 or more chronic diseases and disabled less than 1 year; employed vs. unemployed; men aged 35–64	1.78

Sources: Collins, "Cases and Days of Illness"; Perrott and Collins, "Relation of Sickness to Income"; Hailman, "Prevalence of Disabling Illness"; Sanders and Federman, "Prevalence of Disability"; Woolsey, "Estimates of Disabling Illness."

In the beginning of the Depression, the employed and those not employed (these included the unemployed and those out of the labor force) were equally likely to have experienced a disability day in the previous year. According to the Committee on the Costs of Medical Care, which studied public health issues from 1928 to 1931, about one-third of employed and unemployed men suffered days in which they could not work or pursue their usual activities.[9]

Once the Depression was under way, potential health problems appeared to be sufficiently urgent to commission another survey. The Public Health Service and the Milbank Memorial Fund jointly conducted the Health and Depression Studies in the spring of 1933. The questions concerned families' living standards (including income levels) before the Depression began in 1929. According to this survey, in the midst of the Depression the unemployed were somewhat sicker than the employed. Among families with a full-time wage earner, 123 family members per 1,000 persons reported some disabling illness in the previous six months. Among those with only part-time wage earners, the rate was 160 per 1,000. Among those with no wage earners, the rate was 182 per 1,000.[10]

Concern about the health consequences of the economic depression led to the National Health Survey of 1935–1936. It dwarfed previous efforts in scope, ambition, and consequences, and from this grew the National Health Interview Survey, which continues to the present. Two and a half million Americans, comprising a one-in-thirty sample of urban residents plus an additional one hundred and forty thousand rural residents, were surveyed during the winter of 1935–1936. Coding the response schedules alone occupied a workforce of one thousand for more than a year. The survey reported that by 1935–1936, health differentials by unemployment status had grown to the point where the unemployed were more than twice as likely to be sick as the employed. In the full sample of 971,620, the ratio of unemployed to employed workers who were disabled on the day of the survey was 2.23 for men. Again, the increase in this ratio was not an artifact of differences in age composition. Among men between the ages of twenty-five and thirty-four the ratio of unemployed men who were disabled on the day of the National Health Survey to employed men was 2.17. Nor was it completely an artifact of differential duration of illness by employment status. Among men between the ages of thirty-five and sixty-four who reported suffering from a chronic condition but were disabled for less than a year, the ratio was 1.78. One reason why the unemployed were so much more likely to have been unable to work was the incidence of chronic conditions such as cardiovascular, renal, and nervous diseases and rheumatism, which were more common among the unemployed.[11] Although these conditions could have raised the probability of job loss, they probably were not made worse by long-term unemployment.

The third point supporting the selective retention hypothesis appeared in longstanding membership requirements of sickness funds. Workers who lost their jobs generally lost their sickness insurance coverage shortly thereafter. This lack of portability was criticized by the Progressives, and it remains a shortcoming of the present-day system. Workers in the early 1920s understood the potential problems that this rule created, and they reported a willingness to pay extra for sickness benefits that would continue for a few weeks or months after leaving an employer. Table 9.3 reports on the time between job loss and loss of insurance coverage. In most funds termination of coverage was immediate, except later in the Depression for members thought to be on temporary layoff. One result of loss of coverage was to magnify the effect of selective retention on the absenteeism series presented in figure 9.1. Less healthy workers were at high risk of unemployment, and once unemployed they were at high risk of losing their insurance. The two relationships led directly to the paradoxical claim that the Depression improved the health of the average insured worker. From the institutional perspective, the flow of less healthy workers out of employment by firms and out of coverage by sickness funds meant that both firms and funds dealt with ever-healthier workers as the Depression worsened. This differed from the British situation studied by Ashton and later Whiteside, in which unemployed workers remained members of their friendly society or were covered by national health insurance. Some unemployed workers in Britain found it easier to draw sickness benefits than unemployment benefits, and so they did.[12]

The idea that the war brought prosperity has been thoroughly dispelled.[13] Low levels of unemployment masked the increased risk of harm for those in the armed forces, whose meager pay did not reflect the dangerous environments in which they served. On the home front, too,

Table 9.3.
Continuation of benefits

	1931: SICKNESS FUNDS ONLY		1937: ALL BENEFIT SOURCES	
PERIOD	DURING LAYOFF	AFTER (PERMANENT) SEPARATION	DURING LAYOFF	AFTER (PERMANENT) SEPARATION
Immediate loss of coverage	73	85	29	71
Up to 1 month	9	n/a	21	6
32 days to 6 months	10	n/a	28	7
Indefinite	6	n/a	7	5
Other	2	n/a	15	11
N	388		731	

Sources: NICB, *Present Status,* pp. 50–53; Sayers et al., "General Aspects," p. 1575.

the average work week increased in duration, and time at work stretched into the night. Workplace injury rates in manufacturing rose by a third from just before the war in 1940 to their peak levels in 1943. Figure 9.3 shows work injury rates in manufacturing, stone quarrying, and railroads. It appears that a long-term decline in injury rates ended in the depths of the Depression. In manufacturing and railroads, injury rates increased over the course of the war. This figure and the detailed analysis of Higgs may still understate the increase in physical ill health on the home front. The absenteeism series, which excludes workplace injuries that were covered by workmen's compensation, and the sickness surveys fill this gap.

Absenteeism soared during World War II (see figure 9.1), in part because of exhaustion among workers performing extra shifts with few days off. Inexperienced and physically unwell workers moved into jobs after being unemployed or out of the labor force. The reduction in physical capacity of the workforce was clear to many observers. Concerning

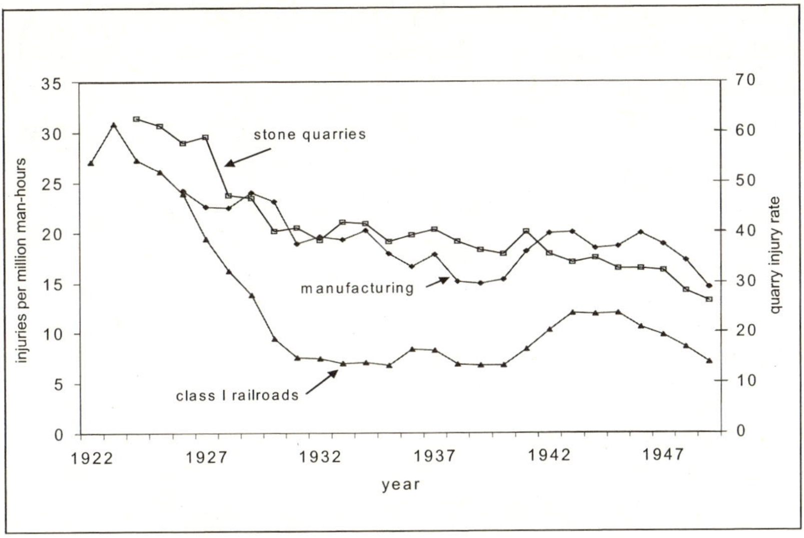

FIGURE 9.3. Workplace injury rates. (Data from U. S. Bureau of the Census, *Historical Statistics* ser. D 1029, 1034, and 1036. "Class I railroads" excludes injuries resulting in fewer than three days of absence.)

workers who came to General Motors in 1942–1944, Alfred Sloan recalled, "The sheer numbers [of new hires] were distressing enough; but in addition, the workers we got were generally at a very low level of industrial skill. Many of them were not physically fit; many, especially the women, had no industrial experience at all."[14]

These workers, many of whom were originally not in the labor force because factory work was too physically demanding for them, altered sickness rates during the war. From the 1934 trough, absenteeism nearly doubled to its peak in 1945 (figure 9.1). As with the decline in absenteeism during the Depression, nearly all of the change was due to increases in sickness rather than to nonworkplace injuries. Absence due to influenza more than doubled, and absence due to respiratory conditions more generally accounted for about half the increase in wartime absence. Particularly large increases in neurasthenia (250 percent) and bronchitis (200 percent) could well have been due to general exhaustion. These relatively unimportant sources combined accounted for only about 12 percent of the increase, as did increased absenteeism due to more general digestive illness and heart and circulatory illness.[15]

Sickness surveys support the claim of diminishing health on the home front. In 1942 the Social Security Board arranged with the Works Progress Administration and later the Census Bureau to include questions about sickness in four surveys conducted between May 1942 and February 1943. The sickness fund surveys reported that employed workers became much more likely to miss several consecutive days during the war (figure 9.1). The Social Security Board estimated that the few who were unable to find work were nearly six times more likely to be sick than were the employed (table 9.2). In addition, the average duration of illness among the unemployed was longer, at 6.1 days, than for the employed, at 3.7 days. Different age distributions among the employed and unemployed played a role because the employed were probably younger than the unemployed. Still, among those between the ages of twenty-five and forty-four, the share of male workers who reported sick was 1.8 percent in 1935–1936 but 2.2 percent in 1942–1943, an increase of 20 percent among prime-aged workers.[16] In that sense, even controlling for age, the workforce was less healthy during World War II than during the Depression.

Overall, the time series evidence indicates that worker absenteeism behavior was closely tied to the state of the macroeconomy. In the prosperous 1920s, absenteeism was relatively high. During the Depression, absenteeism rates fell because the workforce came to consist of ever-healthier workers. The war years saw the healthiest of young workers enter the armed services, and those who stayed behind to toil in production of war matériel worked very hard indeed and were subject to increasing sickness and accident rates. A hidden benefit of postwar prosperity was a return to prewar sickness and accident rates, and the decline in unemployment also meant for many workers a return to sickness insurance coverage.

During the Depression years, perhaps surprisingly, the national network of establishment sickness funds remained largely intact. Union funds struggled because of the simultaneous pressures on their treasuries from workers who were unemployed and those who were sick or desperate to claim sickness. Many folded. Establishment funds seem to have held up better. As Chiaki Moriguchi noted, the largest and best known of firms that practiced welfare capitalism maintained their benefit operations as best they could. Those subject to the hardest blows of the slump could keep those benefits intact through policies that stressed internal discipline. The Depression did not cause the end of industrial sickness funds as viable health insurance providers. Advances in a competing technology did, as Chapter 10 shows.[17]

CHAPTER TEN

Actuarial Science and the Decline of Sickness Funds

The industrial accident and health insurance business, though twenty years old, is still in its infancy.

—REINHOLD KOCH, 1912

Very little group health and accident insurance, as such, has been written either in Illinois or in the United States as a whole.

—HEALTH INSURANCE COMMISSION OF THE STATE OF ILLINOIS, 1919

IF THE GREAT DEPRESSION failed to kill off industrial sickness funds, then what did? In Chapter 9 I observed that discharging the least healthy employees had salubrious effects on sickness funds' finances. Thus did sickness funds prove their resilience in the face of a severe and sustained financial shock. What they could not withstand was the development of a technologically superior alternative, namely, actuarially sound group health insurance. Even enthusiastic proponents of government insurance acknowledged that a great strength of sickness funds was their ability to get members to accede to close scrutiny while receiving benefits. Commercial insurers recognized the powerful effects of such capabilities on the bottom line precisely because they lacked such powers. According to the Health Insurance Commission of the State of Illinois, there were plenty of group health and accident insurance executives who "doubt[ed] as to its eventual success. They fear[ed] that the problem of simulation and malingering [would] be difficult to meet."[1] At the time of the Progressive-Era debates about government health insurance, the viability of group health was very much in question.

In order for commercial insurers to overcome the informational advantages of sickness funds, they would need a superior technology. The technology used by insurers to transform inputs (premiums) into outputs (promises of benefits) depended on the state of actuarial science. Commercial insurers worked to create and improve actuarial technology that was specific to group health from the time of the Progressive health insurance debates to the mid-1930s. Initially, several insurers believed that they had the appropriate technology at hand in the form of sickness tables from the Manchester Unity friendly society in Britain. These data, however, failed to take into account the incentive consequences of sick pay benefits; that is, the tables had not accounted for moral hazard and so underestimated sickness rates, a recipe for insolvency.

This chapter describes the development of actuarial methods that gave commercial insurers decisive superiority over industrial sickness funds. I describe these methods as "technology" to recognize their role in the production of insurance. As in any other industry, technology is the means by which factors of production are transformed into a finished product. Before the development of reasonably accurate actuarial technologies, commercial insurers and sickness funds both operated by educated guesswork. The actuarial technology available to insurers was far below the capabilities it would later attain, so neither type of insurer suffered a particular disadvantage in that regard. The ability of sickness funds to maintain a close watch over sick members, both for caring and for monitoring purposes, and to inspire feelings of personal investment in the funds among their members, gave them a substantial advantage over commercial insurers. Comparison of both providers' costs and benefits reveals that the funds were closer to what actuaries supposed were ideal levels of premiums and benefits than were the insurers. Eventually advances in actuarial science gave insurers the technology to overcome that gap and ultimately surpass sickness funds in simple cost-benefit terms. In economic terms, the story is simplicity itself: when sickness funds offered the better deal, workers chose to be insured with them, and when group health became the better deal, it captured a larger share of the insured workforce. In historical terms, concentration on the political role played by these insurers has obfuscated their role in a critical episode in the history of technology, which this chapter helps reveal.

* * *

The ability of industrial sickness funds to continue operations for decades after the Progressive period is evidence of their structural soundness. The eventual decline of establishment funds was not due to Depression-induced financial crises. Indeed, fund managers used a variety of prudential strategies to keep their operations solvent during the Depression. Some sought to relieve members of the burden of dues payments by suspending them and dipping into reserves instead. Others reduced benefits.[2] Few establishment funds experienced dire financial crises, and measures of fund activity peaked in the late 1930s, after the worst of the Depression had passed. The advent of technologically superior group health insurance, thanks to the growing sophistication of actuarial science, caused the decline of workplace-based sickness funds. Group health grew in places where sickness funds had never taken hold and accounted for nearly all the spectacular increases in the number of Americans with health insurance coverage.

In Progressive-Era debates about health insurance, there were really only two alternatives: the government and the sickness funds. Progressives acknowledged that commercial health insurance existed, but it was such a minor player that it was hardly worth criticizing, as the epigraphs to this chapter suggest. Within a few years of the Progressives' defeat, however, commercial insurers began rapidly to expand their health insurance offerings. At the same time, the humble sickness funds poked along, losing market share but not membership in absolute terms until after World War II.

The conventional historical view of the rise of commercial health insurance generally omits the transition from sickness funds to group insurance in favor of analyzing the repeated failures of the government to enter and dominate the market. According to the standard history, new commercial insurance ventures appeared, but they appeared from nowhere. Rather suddenly, insurers were able to offer group disability insurance to pay for sick leave in the 1920s, group hospitalization in the 1930s, and group medical and surgical in the 1940s. One historian proposed that the rise of group insurance in general was an attempt to redeem the industry from bad publicity created by the corruption and scandals that led to the Armstrong commission's investigations of 1905–1906.[3] That would explain at least some of the insurers' motives, but not their ability successfully to introduce each type of insurance at each particular time. How did commercial insurers expand so quickly—and why did it not happen sooner? The growth of group health insurance and the decline of mutual sickness funds offer a case study of the success of a superior technology.

An insurance contract protects the buyer from financial losses due to an event that might not happen at all (for example, fire insurance) or that will certainly happen but at a random time (for example, life insurance). Beginning from a fair bet in which the premium is exactly equal to the expected value of the claim (that is, the value of the claim multiplied by the probability of the event), the insurer adds "loads" to the premiums to compensate for administrative expenses and unexpected contingencies. In general, the brighter the line between an event and a nonevent, the smaller the load. For example, life insurance is a relatively straightforward kind of contract because death is easy to distinguish from life. As accident insurance developed, insurers learned to distinguish on-the-job accidents from other accidents or illnesses, although, as noted above, it was not always easy to distinguish whether, say, a hernia was the result of a worker's current employment duties or if it was a preexisting condition (and hence not covered).

From this perspective it should be apparent that insurance companies are producers, even if their product is not tangible. What they produce is a promise to pay benefits on the occurrence of the covered event. In order to make those payments, they take in premiums from people to whom future payments have been promised, contingent on occurrence of that event. In order to transform those premiums into benefit payments, they typically invest their incomes in a way that will generate interest, dividends, or capital gains until the insured makes a claim. If an insurance market is reasonably competitive, the premiums necessary to fund a dollar's worth of benefits will be ground down to the competitive price. Insurance is, however, distinguished from other markets by the severity of informational asymmetries, which has led to a degree of state regulation greater than is found in most other industries. The point is that competition will have the same effect on insurers as it will on other producers: to make it difficult to hold onto high levels of profits.

One sign of competitiveness among insurers was the speed with which they adopted new technologies. JoAnne Yates has documented the rapidity with which life insurers adopted Hollerith punch card–counting machinery. Already in 1910, the Medico-Actuarial Mortality Study, jointly conducted by the Actuarial Society of America and the Association of Life Insurance Medical Directors, employed such technology to estimate tables that were critical for the development of group life insurance. The ability of commercial insurers to analyze such data was in part a result of the fundamentally more clear-cut nature of life insurance, and in part due to their willingness to buy new hardware technologies. The constraining factor in the creation of group health insurance was not the hardware; it was production of the actuarial models behind the software.[4]

By late in the Progressive Era, insurers had accumulated some experience in writing health policies—but only on individuals. These policies appealed mostly to high earners and not to wage workers. Many actuaries thought that insurmountable costs of monitoring beneficiaries would prevent health insurance from ever becoming more than a boutique product for the upper middle class. Because the actuarial landscape was largely unknown, loads were large and premiums expensive. Actuaries disagreed about the importance of different risk factors. Those familiar with life insurance emphasized the role of age, whereas casualty actuaries who had gained experience in workmen's compensation systems identified a policyholder's industry or occupation as requiring more attention. Further, insurers aimed to manage severe problems of adverse selection in two ways. First, they required applicants to pass a medical examination in order to obtain a policy in the first place. Second, to protect themselves from extremely costly and unexpected claims, they stipulated in each policy that they could cancel it at any time, for any reason. The difficulties in managing selection problems in individual health insurance and reinsurance can also be seen in two decades' worth of complaints about its unprofitability.[5]

Typical sickness benefits in individual health policies were not very different from those offered by sickness funds—$5 per week for total disability, and often with no limit on the number of weeks. This transformed the contract into something closer to long-term permanent disability insurance. One actuary estimated from his own research that a yearly premium of a little less than five dollars, which included a load of a little more than a dollar, should have been adequate to pay a sickness benefit of five dollars per week for a maximum of fifty-two weeks. This policy offered the same premium and benefit levels for nearly the entire working life of the insured, beginning at age twenty and continuing to age sixty-five. Except for the fifty-two-week maximum, these parameters were close to those of contemporary industrial sickness funds. For commercial policies beginning when the worker was forty, when it became difficult to join sickness funds, the yearly premium was a little more than seven dollars, again including a 30 percent load, which was much more than sickness funds charged in dues. Apparently, when sickness funds that charged equal dues payments regardless of age excluded new members in their forties and fifties, they were imposing an actuarially sound policy.[6]

In the 1890s insurers began to experiment with group life insurance, which they likened to buying insurance wholesale. The employer was the wholesaler who set the terms of the insurance with the insurance company and then turned around and distributed policies to workers. Usually but not always the employer paid all the premiums. To prevent the employer or the insurer from cherry-picking the best risks for the pool and excluding higher-risk workers, New York legally required a tradeoff that suited all parties. Other states followed suit. For workplaces with at least fifty workers, a minimum of 75 percent of those workers had to participate in the group policy for it to become active, and once that had occurred, none of the workers at that workplace (somehow defined) could be excluded. Once insurers started to develop group health insurance as a product with important similarities to group life, the same laws were taken to be applicable to it.[7]

If the legal framework was reasonably settled for group health by the precedent of group life, the actuarial framework was anything but settled. The few companies that sold individual (also called "commercial" or "personal") health insurance had collected a variety of statistics on premiums, claims, benefits, and reserves. Little of it was of any use, for two reasons. First, the cancellability clause negated the usefulness of individual statistics because group health was noncancellable. Thus frequent claimers who would have had their individual policies cancelled continued in group health pools, but how they would have continued to claim (or not) was unknown once their individual policies had been cancelled. "All companies have made a free use of the cancellation clause," complained one actuary; doing so negated the predictive value of the statistics they had collected. Whether it was "possible to apply actuarial science to the problem at hand," he continued, was not at all clear. Further, the tendency of underwriters to individualize each policy led actuaries to doubt the usefulness of individual statistics for forecasting claim behavior in standardized group health policies. How could individual records be aggregated to form a coherent whole?[8]

Second, individual and group health policies were aimed at different ends of the market. Individual health was marketed to the middle and upper middle classes. The whole point of offering group health was to insure large numbers of workers with one contract, primarily by selling policies to large companies, many of them pioneers in welfare capitalism. The first group insurers could try to base their premium and reserve policies on the individual experience of white-collar workers, but that was a pool with different environmental risks than the blue collar workers who were the likely market for group health.

Commercial insurers would only be able to expand health coverage through group insurance if they could develop an actuarially based pricing scheme. What the actuaries lacked was not primarily the mathematical models that would let them forecast claims and, given premiums and benefit values, profits, although actuarial analysis of health insurance without a cancellation clause proved somewhat difficult. What they lacked were statistics that would enable them to estimate parameters for those models.

One possibility was to rely on the 1907 tables of the Manchester Unity friendly society. Actuaries debated whether the results of the tables, drawn up just before passage of the 1911 National Insurance Act in Great Britain, were applicable to the American situation. To match the British pool as closely as possible to the sorts of Americans who were likely to buy individual health policies meant employing tables A, H, and J, those dealing with agricultural and white-collar workers. Initially these were believed to be adequate for purposes of writing individual policies. A natural experiment of sorts occurred when the Metropolitan Life Insurance Company issued a group health policy to employees of its home office. It then compared the results to those of the 1907 Manchester Unity experience. Overall rates of sickness claims in the two sources were close, but that similarity masked sharp differences by time period that cancelled each other out. With a one-week waiting period, Metropolitan Life claims were 29.5 percent below those of the Manchester Unity from the second to the fourteenth week, and from the fourteenth to the twenty-seventh week Metropolitan Life claims were 58.3 percent greater. One analyst concluded in guarded language, "It is not suggested that sickness rates in this country are likely to follow very closely the Manchester Unity."[9]

These differences suggested that an American sickness table was necessary for group health insurers, but none was available. Miles Dawson's pre–World War I studies of the Brotherhood of Locomotive Engineers and employees of the Westinghouse Air Brake Company gave a broad base of sickness insurance statistics. These tables, Dawson found, corresponded reasonably well with those of British friendly societies, but they failed to inspire much actuarial research in themselves.[10]

Some life insurers believed they could piggyback health coverage onto group life insurance as a way of increasing its attractiveness. In 1912 the Equitable Life Assurance Society developed such a rider when Montgomery Ward and Company asked it to provide group insurance to several thousand employees in Chicago and Kansas City. Ward already had an employee benefit society, however, and when offered the group health insurance to replace it few workers accepted. The offer of group health insurance was withdrawn.[11]

At this point and later, demand for group insurance was reduced by the availability of a sickness fund. Sickness funds were well known. As late as 1919 group insurance was "still in the experimental stage" and, as with individual policies, the experiments produced some Frankenstein monsters. "The policy became more of a literary and insurance monstrosity than the product of scientific underwriting," wrote one actuary, who described such policies as "crude and incomplete" with a baffling array of special clauses that various client firms had requested. With actuarial soundness still in the future, group health insurers poorly estimated the parameters of the policies they sold. In order to compensate, they refused payment of claims "on the slightest technicality." Given the precarious nature of this product and general contentment with sickness funds, by the time of the Progressive-Era debates the Health Insurance Commission of the State of Illinois could report, "So far little has been accomplished in the attempts that have been made to develop the use of group health and accident contracts in the United States."[12]

The first useful tables for group health insurers appeared two years later, in 1921. Because group policies were noncancellable and sold to large firms that employed blue-collar workers, some adjustments needed to be made to the Manchester Unity tables, and they were not small adjustments. First, E. E. Cammack imposed some results from the period following passage of the National Insurance Act in an attempt to simulate the effects of noncancellability. Cammack later made a further adjustment to correct the Manchester Unity practice of recording subsequent attacks of the same disease as new cases. That was not enough, however, because it resulted in premiums far too small to pay for the benefits claimed by American workers with group health policies. Gross premiums to cover the first week of disability were increased by 30 percent, and those to cover later weeks were increased by 10 percent, which was still insufficient. A year later each type of premium was increased by a further 25 percent, indicating that the initial Manchester Unity rates fell short by 62.5 percent for the first week's premiums and 37.5 percent for later weeks. The newly adjusted rates became standard for the next several years. Actuaries speculated that one reason the Manchester Unity tables underestimated sickness rates was that they had failed to account for the moral hazard of health benefits to induce additional claims. Cammack's adjustments partly corrected for this problem.[13]

The consequences for the market for worker health insurance can be gauged roughly by the appearance of new insurers. A National Industrial Conference Board survey of insurers in 1925 found that 78 percent of group insurers had been founded in the previous five years, but 75 percent of workplace benefit societies dated back to the period before 1920. A Public Health Service survey conducted between 1930 and 1934 inquired about initial dates of insurance availability at 731 plants covered by either benefit societies or group insurance. Of 218 mutual benefit associations that answered this question, 183 (84 percent) had begun before 1925, but 95 percent of 141 plants that obtained coverage through group health insurers had initiated that coverage after 1925. Group insurers found it hard to dislodge sickness funds but relatively easy to grow in virgin soil. Rather than displacing benefit societies, they entered new plants that had not previously offered insurance benefits to employees. Metropolitan Life's group accident and health division scored ever larger successes in the 1920s: International Paper in 1923 (4,915 covered employees), Armour and Company in 1926 (16,727), and General Motors in 1928 (180,682).[14]

Ongoing actuarial research enabled such growth in commercial group health insurance. American actuaries were reaching beyond the experience of insurers overseas (Cammack's adjustments to the Manchester Unity tables) or unrepresentative aggregated statistics from individual health policies (for example, Hiram Messenger's early studies of the Travelers' Life Insurance Company records) to achieve greater levels of precision and utility. In 1927 actuaries published tables based on claim experience at Aetna from 1920 to 1925 and Metropolitan Life from 1923 to 1926. These offered "the only published data giving the actual experience under policies of Group Accident and Health Insurance," and the quick turnaround time indicated how anxious insurers were to realize these technological advances. These tables still contained flaws, however, in that many of the sickness data, as distinct from claims data, were maintained by the employer of the insured group. Information about sickness events that did not result in claims was not made available to the insurer. As a result, insurers continued to set premiums and benefits without a standard table for disability and accident "suitable for insurance purposes" until well into the 1930s.[15]

Establishment funds managed the tumult of the Depression quite well. The 1931 NICB survey found that only 33 of 431 benefit associations had been dissolved in the years just prior to the survey. Further, although group insurance grew during the 1920s, it still did not displace existing sickness funds to any great degree. Of those 33 benefit societies only 17 were specifically suppressed in order to switch to group insurance. Nor did the benefit societies have high failure rates later in the Depression. A 1934 NICB survey of benefit availability disclosed surprisingly little change over the course of the previous few years. Of 233 polled firms, 162 offered group life insurance (an unspecified number of which policies included health benefits), a net increase of 3 since 1929. The number of firms offering sickness benefits through a mutual association had declined only slightly, from 128 to 123, in the same period.[16]

The Depression created difficulties for large commercial life insurers, as can be seen in the incentive conflicts triggered in many group life policies. Many included an option to convert the death benefit to a disability-type insurance that would in effect pay a pension if the worker were totally disabled before retirement age. The moral hazard was evident to workers, and permanent disability rates soared along with unemployment rates after 1929. The Equitable reported that whereas the ratio of actual to expected permanent disability in 1926 was 94 percent, in 1930 it was 158 percent. In the same period the ratio of actual to expected deaths increased from 92 to 96 percent. Like individual health policies, this was another once-promising idea that lost money for insurers. They quietly removed the disability clause from standard group policies.[17]

During the 1920s and into the 1930s, sickness funds maintained a great degree of stability despite aging business methods. The technology they depended on had changed little in decades. Commercial insurers' actuarial technologies were becoming superior to the funds' old rule-of-thumb customs, and their great advantages—personal knowledge of fund members and co-workers, their current health, and the veracity of their claims—were fading in importance because of these actuarial advances. In order to benefit from improvements in actuarial science, sickness funds became increasingly likely to consult actuaries regarding their finances. Fewer than 5 percent had ever been examined by actuaries in 1916, but in 1931 twenty-four percent of funds at least tried to set their dues and benefit payments by actuarial standards. It was too little and too late.[18]

In 1937 Gilbert Fitzhugh announced the estimation of tables compiled specifically for group health insurance and derived from a wide base of American experience. The Fitzhugh article was a landmark. It formed the basis of estimates required by the Mailler-Condon Law, an attempt in New York state to extend worker's compensation to nonoccupational disabilities in 1950, and it continued to be cited into the 1970s. The paper's data source was the work of a special committee of the Actuarial Society of America charged with producing a sickness table based on pooled statistics from several different insurance companies, which were adjusted for reporting practices unique to each insurer. Total life years of exposure for white males equaled 2,479,896. By contrast, the previous set of American tables (with data from Aetna) from the early 1920s was based on only 71,000 life years of exposure.[19]

Fitzhugh reported on estimated expected durations of claims, differences between male and female morbidity rates, and load factors to account for insurers' costs. The greatest differences in compensated sickness rates between the newer study ("intercompany investigation") and the Keffer tables (based on Aetna's information) appeared in policies providing benefits from the fourth day of an ailment through twenty-six weeks (sickness rates were greater by 17 percent in the intercompany investigation) and those running from the eighth day to the thirteenth week (rates were lower by 15 percent in the intercompany investigation). The result of the intercompany project could be seen in a table of estimated monthly premiums for policies with a variety of characteristics. New premiums were lower than the old by an average of 6.4 percent for policies that paid benefits after a three- or seven-day waiting period. This was the payoff of actuarial research: the ability to reduce premiums while maintaining profitability by eliminating poorly estimated expected loss values.[20]

The increasing ability of group insurance to deliver benefits comparable to those of sickness funds at a comparable price was evident. In the early 1920s sickness funds provided the better deal. Typical group health benefits consisted of two-thirds pay during incapacitation for a maximum of twenty-six weeks, with a one week waiting period. In order to avoid insuring short-term workers, some employers imposed a probationary period of three to six months. A basic annual premium rate (before loading) to obtain an indemnity of $10 per week for a maximum of twenty-six weeks was $12.94. This seems to have been more expensive than the alternative. In rough terms, establishment funds paid a benefit of one-third less ($7 per week) for half as long (thirteen weeks) but did so for less than half the premium ($6 per year). To maintain competitiveness, benefit societies increased their sick pay. By 1931 the median sick benefit in a sample of 228 associations was nearly $9.00 per week; the median dues payment of 218 reporting associations was still between fifty and sixty cents per month.[21]

In qualitative terms group health insurance was becoming a better bargain by the early 1930s, as shown in table 10.1. Recall that insurers would generally issue a group policy to a particular employer only if at least three-quarters of employees participated. The assurance of a wider pool enabled the insurers to accept poorer risks in the knowledge that the pool contained better risks as well to balance them out. Thus, far more group plans accepted members without age limits than did benefit

Table 10.1.

Characteristics of mutual benefit associations and group health insurance coverage, 1930–1934

	Mutual Benefit Association		Group Health Insurance	
Characteristic	N	Plants with MBAs answering yes to this question (%)	N	Plants with GHI answering yes to this question (%)
Plants with each benefit	306	100	320	100
Workers in covered plants	387,070	100	149,320	100
Voluntary coverage	233	77	233	73
No age limits to initiating coverage	128	42	267	83
Exclusion of persons with chronic diseases	172	56	32	10
Exclusion based on medical examination	100	33	9	3
No occupational exclusions	206	67	302	94
No probationary period from hiring to beginning coverage	111	36	11	3
No waiting period from beginning coverage to eligibility	145	47	34	11
Pregnancy benefits	3	1	187	58

Source: Sayers et al., "General Aspects."

associations (83 percent to 42 percent), and far fewer group plans rejected employees who wanted to join but were chronically ill (10 percent to 56 percent) or who failed a medical examination (3 percent to 33 percent). Workers covered by group insurance were also much more likely to enjoy pregnancy benefits, a particular issue with Progressives and historians.[22]

By the end of the 1930s cost and benefit differentials between benefit societies and group insurance policies had narrowed considerably. A 1938 survey by the NICB found that the 60 percent of benefit societies that set their terms in fixed amounts charged a median rate of fifty to fifty-nine cents per month in dues and provided a median weekly sick benefit of ten to eleven dollars, for a median of thirteen weeks. By this time more than a quarter of the 279 societies offered some kind of medical benefit that went beyond a visit to a physician who would assess the sick worker's eligibility for benefits. Among the 144 firms that offered group insurance, only about one-fourth set their terms in absolute amounts. These amounts were virtually the same as for benefit societies. With a seven-day waiting period, a ten-dollar-per-week indemnity would cost sixty cents per month, down from more than a dollar per month in the early 1920s.[23]

The upshot of the growing ability of group insurers to price their product so as to make it a better deal than sickness fund benefits was that group insurers came to dominate the market. The period of transition appears to have been the 1930s, according to a series of surveys of firms by the NICB. Frank Dobbin analyzed benefit provision questions in these surveys (see figure 10.1). In the late 1920s the share of surveyed firms that enabled employees to join a mutual benefit association was about one-third, a proportion that rose slightly by the mid-1930s but then declined steadily to about one-eighth in 1946. During the same period the share of plants that offered group health insurance increased steadily from about one-sixth in 1928 to two-thirds in 1946. Like the rest of the economy, group insurance in general grew after 1932, but after 1935 group health insurers in particular never looked back.[24]

A broader picture emerges from an independent source: insurance company data (see figure 10.2). Combined with a 1939 analysis by the Social Security Board, the data show that sickness benefits appear to have been provided to about five million workers by insurance company

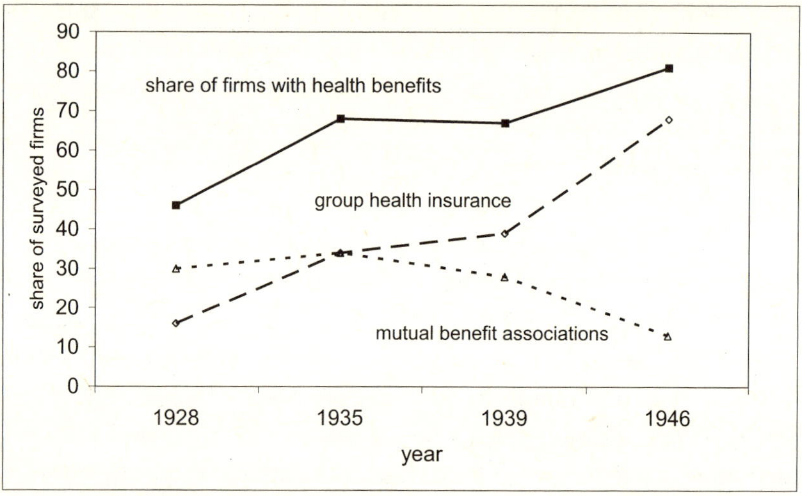

FIGURE 10.1. Health benefit provision and source. (Data from Dobbin, "Origins of Private Social Insurance," p. 1427, citing NICB surveys.)

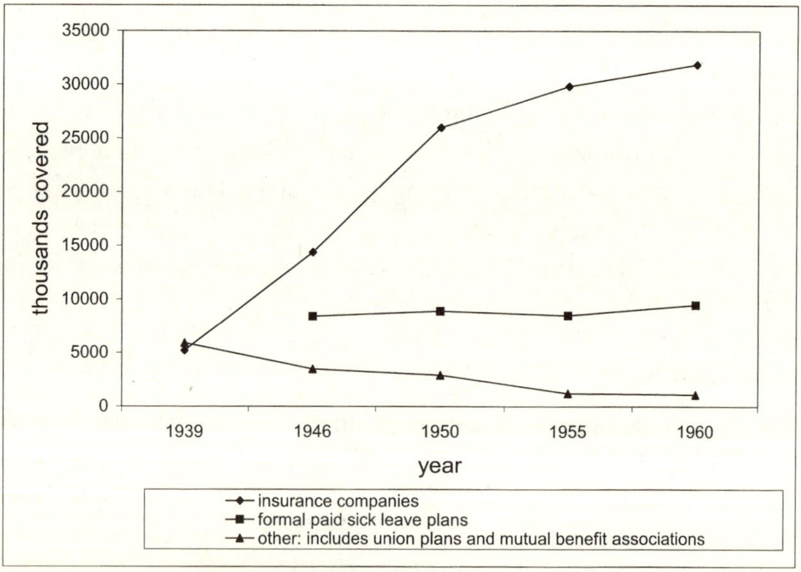

FIGURE 10.2. Trends in sources of cash sickness benefits. (Data from Otey, "Cash Benefits"; Follman, "Development and Significance of Group Health Insurance.")

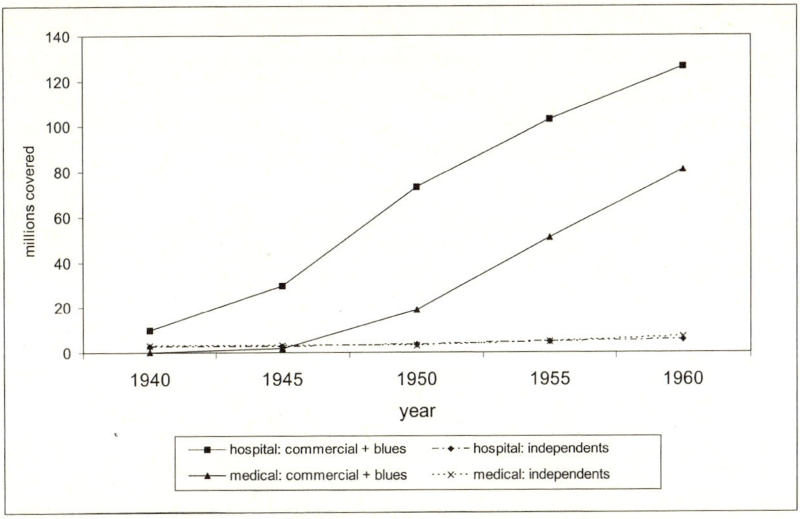

FIGURE 10.3. Trends in hospital and medical insurance coverage by source. (Data from Follmann, "Development and Significance of Group Health Insurance.")

policies and to another five million by union and establishment sickness funds. About a third of workers received sick pay through their employer, which effectively self-insured by this practice. Although sick leave paid directly by the employer was relatively common for office workers, experiments with providing it to shop floor workers had begun by the 1920s. By 1950, the number of workers who enjoyed paid sick leave benefits had about quintupled in comparison to the previous decade. Only about 8 percent of workers obtained sick pay benefits from a benefit society. Beginning during World War II, a growing number of workers were enrolled in group health and accident plans through collective bargaining agreements negotiated by their union.[25]

The growing tendency of commercial insurers to dominate the market for medical and hospital benefits was even more evident (see figure 10.3). From 1940 to 1960 the number of Americans with relatively simple medical coverage for physician visits rose from 3 million to nearly 88 million. Similarly, the number of those with hospital insurance coverage increased from 12 million to 132 million. For both types of coverage, increasing enrollments in commercial group health policies and Blue Cross and related plans accounted for nearly all these dramatic in-

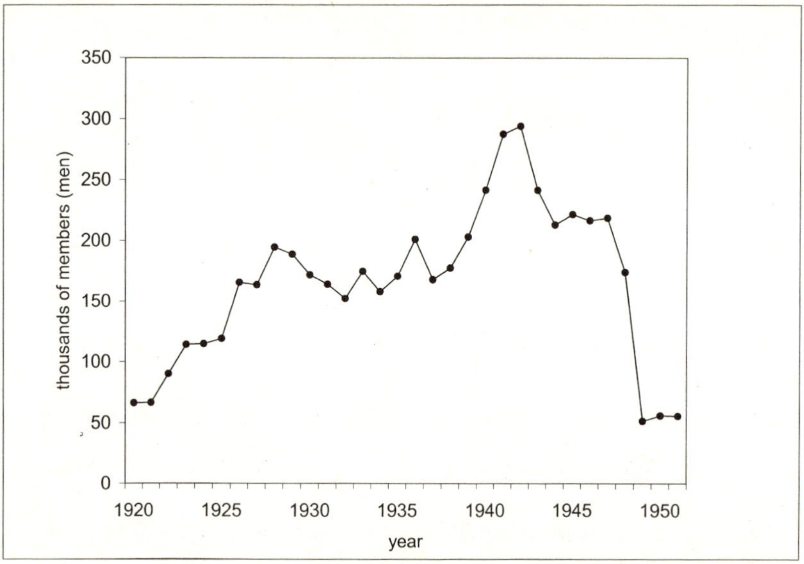

FIGURE 10.4. Enrollments in sickness funds surveyed by the Public Health Service. (Data from Public Health Reports for 1921–28 [January 17, 1930], p. 109; 1929–31 [May 25, 1934], p. 616; 1932–36 [September 2, 1938], p. 1564; 1937–46 [October 24, 1947], p. 1540; 1947 [November 12, 1948], p. 1490; 1948–49 [November 24, 1950], p. 1557; 1950 [March 1953], p. 354; 1951–52 [November 1953], p. 1053.)

creases. Individual and family health policies grew to account for about a tenth of the medical insurance market and a quarter of the hospital market by 1960. Independent plans, which included establishment, union, and fraternal sickness funds, shrank as a source of such insurance, declining to only 4 percent of the hospital insurance market and 8 percent of the medical insurance market by 1960.[26]

During this period few firms suppressed benefit societies in order to replace them with group insurance. Indeed, a 1927 report indicated that a sizable minority of firms that offered group insurance (mostly life insurance) required employees to join the company's mutual benefit association as a condition of obtaining the group insurance. Most of the growth in group insurance occurred in firms previously lacking in benefits, so the overall picture is one of expanding access to insurance benefits broadly defined. The NICB survey of 1938 found results very similar to its 1931 survey. Relative to the 279 firms with benefit societies, only 32 firms had recently discontinued their sick funds, and of those only 12 did so in

Table 10.2.
Enrollments in sickness funds according to federal surveys

YEAR	NUMBER OF MEMBERS	SOURCE
1908	322,000	U.S. Commissioner of Labor
1916	556,000	Bureau of Labor Statistics
1926	750,000	Bureau of Labor Statistics
1939	1,200,000	Social Security Board

Sources: U.S. Commissioner of Labor, *Twenty-third Annual Report,* p. 389; Emmet, "Operation," p. 17; U.S. Department of Labor, "Health and Recreation," p. 59; Otey, "Cash Benefits," p. 32.

order to offer group health insurance instead. In terms of absolute numbers, benefit associations held their ground until World War II. Figure 10.4 shows trends in membership in sickness funds that were surveyed by the Public Health Service for their quarterly absenteeism reports. Except for a decline in the Depression years, enrollments in surveyed funds increased until the early 1940s. The NICB surveys reported that sickness funds enjoyed general stability during the Depression. They had problems, to be sure, but not ones that caused widespread insolvencies.[27]

These trends in numbers of funds and insurers were consistent with trends in the numbers of covered workers. Four surveys specifically aimed to examine sickness funds between 1908 and 1939 (table 10.2).[28] The figures reported in the table included only workers covered by sampled funds, so they do not represent the total number of covered workers. Still, the increase in the number of covered surveyed workers is unmistakable. At the same time, group insurance was growing faster, leaving sickness funds with an ever smaller share of the market. In 1939 the Social Security Board estimated that benefit associations had enrolled 1.2 million workers—compared to 2.2 million in group accident and health plans. The history of health insurance after World War II belonged to group policies issued by commercial insurers and nonprofits such as Blue Cross. Owing to the actuarial advances such insurers supported and from which they benefited, the day of the industrial sickness fund was past.

* * *

Because so much attention has been focused on the role of the government in health insurance in the early twentieth century, the transformation of the private sector on the supply side has been overlooked. In the first two decades of the century, far more workers chose to be insured by industrial sickness funds and fraternal societies than by individual or group policies from commercial insurers because the sickness funds could deliver reliable coverage more cheaply. At the time of the Progressive-Era debates, few insurance executives would have foreseen the coming expansion of group health insurance. By developing better actuarial technology through the 1920s and 1930s, commercial insurers achieved their eventual dominance over the mutual benefit societies.

The history of technology is filled with innovations that, from our vantage point, offered superior productivity but failed to overtake existing technologies for many years, perhaps decades. Sailing ships, for example, continued to ply waters around the world well into the age of steam because they had particular advantages, such as using nearly their entire hull for cargo space rather than coal. Industrial sickness funds, in a similar way, were able to keep a large share of the health insurance market in America well into an age of increasing actuarial sophistication. Their advantages in controlling dubious claims surpassed the actuarial cost advantages of the insurers until decades after the commercial insurance firms had entered the market. Their eventual recession into a small corner of the market should not imply a fundamental lack of competence. Instead, it suggests that a measure of respect is due the sickness funds because it took so much to overcome their substantial advantages.

CHAPTER ELEVEN

Succession in the Forest of Health Care Reform

> The development of the voluntary means of providing insurance for the workman resulting from the changed conditions of the past few years will have a permanent effect upon the social insurance movement in this country and will postpone the day when social insurance of a compulsory character will be considered as necessary by the wage earning class, the employer, or the public in general.
>
> —BENEDICT FLYNN, 1920

A THEORY in ecology proposes that, given an area with a particular soil type, climate, rainfall, and initial composition of plant species, it should be possible to forecast the future composition of plant species in that area. The succession of certain species may occur because of random shocks to the area such as fire, and it may occur because the previously dominant species were not in a sustainable equilibrium but, as it were, contained the seeds of their own obsolescence. Beeches and maples that thrive in the shade may come to succeed sun-loving oaks and hickories by forming a canopy over the latters' saplings, leaving them unable to mature. In the extreme case, a proper model of succession would unlock the mystery of the future completely. Although the oaks and hickories might be surprised by the growth of their successors, we observers, informed by our model, would have expected the triumph of the new species all along.[1]

A theory of history with many similarities to succession is historicism. In one version of historicism, a complete knowledge of the past along with its trajectory to the present would allow us to forecast the future. An actual future that differed from the modeled future could only have missed the mark by the entry of an outside force into our completely modeled world. Perhaps that random force would be indifferent to human pursuits, and perhaps it would not be so benign. Two and a half decades ago, an essay charged recent historians of the Progressive debates about health insurance with historicism. Scholars had been writing the history of health insurance in America, wrote Daniel Fox, as if in the natural course of events government insurance would have succeeded the patchwork of private insurance providers that existed in the early twentieth century. Since it did not, a force external to the natural process must have perturbed it to the extent that the expected government insurance was unable to materialize. Playing the role of destructive fire in this metaphor was the now-familiar alliance of physicians, insurers, labor, and employers more generally. In explaining why the United States lacked compulsory government insurance, Fox argued, these historians had written histories of what never happened, rather than the history of what had happened. He concluded that this manner of writing history was on its way out.[2]

Fox's historiographic analysis was insightful, but his forecast was wrong on a grand scale. Of the making of books about America's lack of national health insurance there has been no end. These recent works have been historicist in varying degrees of fidelity.[3] The resulting histories have overlooked how widespread and effective industrial sickness funds were. I hope this book will help restore these institutions to their place in the history of health insurance and financial history more generally. I have tried to avoid taking the neohistoricist route. The present history of sickness funds has, I hope, provided reasonable explanations for three events and processes that did happen: the rise of competent sickness funds, their role in the failure of Progressive-Era reforms, and their decline due to technological advances by competing insurance providers.

It should also be apparent that the Progressives and their opponents differed little in the quality of their rhetoric. The failure of Progressives to drum up much popular support for state insurance is clear. Theda Skocpol identified the culprit as the unexciting "rationalist discourse" of the AALL and its allies. By relying on facts and figures, they failed to fire up the masses to the same degree that their opponents' bombast and Red-baiting did.[4]

But the wish was father to the thought. The AALL wanted to be perceived as the rational party, but its campaign rhetoric was hardly any more accurate than that of their opponents. Although they could not have been expected to discern moral hazard or savings patterns that emerged from statistical analysis, Progressives offered misleading estimates of sick days and other data. The inaccuracy of these figures should have been evident to them at the time, because it was to others. When Irving Fisher claimed in the pages of the AALL's journal that state health insurance had lengthened life expectancies of German workers by twelve years, one month later an American actuary cited German life expectancy tables to show that the increase was closer to four years and then cited English tables to show that the increase there was nearly as long but had occurred before the advent of national health insurance. Long afterwards Isaac Rubinow admitted that the Progressives had made "extravagant promises" when they claimed that health insurance would simultaneously increase profits, "almost magically" reduce the incidence of illness, and "almost entirely eliminate the necessity for private charity." Health insurance for nearly all industrial workers, he conceded, would have been much more expensive than workmen's compensation, which itself had proved to be "a heavier burden" than the AALL had supposed. The rhetorical equivalence of the two sides can be seen in the Progressives' rationalization for their exaggerations. According to Rubinow, the AALL needed to match its opponents' dire claims but in the opposite direction.[5] The real shortcoming, then, was not too much rationality in their discourse but too little. Ordinary working people were not persuaded by it.

Progressives dug themselves into a deeper hole by expressing their contempt for the working class. Fisher lamented the need to provide insurance for the "ninety nine workmen out of one hundred" who refused to eliminate "the evils of bad air, bad food, imperfect teeth, wrong posture, improper clothing, constipation, self-drugging, [and] alcoholism" from their lives. Rubinow bitterly explained why "frightened" workers remained uninterested in government insurance despite the experts' best efforts to enlighten them: "The whole scheme was un-American, the American workman did not want any bargains. He wanted a wage sufficiently high to buy his medical aid according to his own choice. He wanted nothing that smacked of charity. . . . But back of all these reasons—some real, some very fanciful—there was a very materialistic, crude, infantile objection to having a deduction made from the weekly pay envelope." He concluded that in the AALL "there was the not unreasonable hope that the working masses would see, and would demand. But the working masses did not see and certainly they did not demand. The opposition did see and it worked intelligently albeit not always honestly."[6] In three sentences Rubinow managed to plant the seed of the historicist explanation by simultaneously patronizing the working classes and transforming the lobbying and speechifying efforts of intellectual elites into political martyrdom. In this case his rhetoric was all too persuasive.

Voluntary employee benefit associations still have legal standing, although their importance is geographically limited to the Pacific Northwest.[7] The same institutional structure once mattered a great deal. As late as 1945 most Americans who had medical insurance were insured through fraternal, union, and employer sickness funds. By 1950, however, they accounted for only about 13 percent of the market for medical insurance, a share that continued to decline over the years. Growth in Blue Cross as well as group insurance spelled their growing irrelevance.[8] Yet their historical importance has been largely overlooked.

The evidence presented in this book refutes two important arguments made by historians. The Progressive reformers who proposed to insert the state into markets for health insurance, and thereby replace its voluntary character with mandatory participation by a wide swath of the working class, were ultimately defeated. Commercial insurers were aggressive in their attacks on government insurance proposals, in particular as led by Metropolitan Life, Prudential, and the Equitable.[9] But it is important to understand why they did so. In the Progressive period the insurers were fighting against government life insurance, not government health insurance. Any desire by commercial insurers to keep the market for group health insurance to themselves was based more on hope than on actual profit. The fatal flaw of the American Association for Labor Legislation's model bill was the inclusion of burial benefits. According to Rubinow, the lack of a death benefit in English law was a grievous failure that the AALL was not about to repeat.[10] Without it, the sleeping giants of commercial insurance were likely to have left well enough alone. Because they knew that group life insurance was manageable, actuarially sound, and profitable, that was the market they wanted to keep.[11]

In analyzing the great struggle between public and private welfare provision, Roy Lubove described the activities of voluntary institutions as doubly tragic.[12] Not only did private initiatives fail to protect the public interest, but they also effectively prevented the state from stepping in and doing so. In regard to health insurance, Lubove was half right for the wrong reasons. He and many later historians posited the basis of the private side's success as the uncanny ability of powerful insurers, physicians, businesses, and unions to circumvent the political process so that the outcome favored them rather than the public interest (however defined). An unappreciated factor as important as political activism was the value of alternative sources of sickness insurance—establishment, union, and fraternal sickness funds. As this book shows, private provision of health insurance was a careful and reasonably well run operation, and as Rubinow observed, workers were already familiar with it. As Benedict Flynn observed in his presidential address to the Casualty Actuarial and Statistical Society in 1920, the consequences of voluntary private insurance were considerable.[13]

Where health insurance was concerned, sickness funds did not really need to engage in underhanded political activities. From all available evidence sickness funds appeared where workers needed them, were operated by workers who understood the basics (if nothing more) of fund management, and until the late 1930s, provided a degree of financial protection equal to or better than that available from commercial insurers or proposed government programs. Progressives failed to show that their proposals were sufficiently better than this existing network so as to justify a large-scale government program.

The sickness funds were imperfect, but with historical perspective and analysis we can see that some of those shortcomings were not quite as grave as they seemed at the time. If sickness funds worked well, then more of them with greater enrollments would have been better. But their failure to enroll more workers than they did was in part a demand-side phenomenon. Young and healthy workers were not interested in paying for sickness benefits they did not see themselves as needing, and older workers were able to save against losses due to ill health. Workers knew what they wanted in a sickness insurance program, and it was simply lower premiums and higher benefit payments. Funds that offered them what they wanted enjoyed higher enrollments.

Lack of medical benefits was a deficit only in retrospect. The fact that only a large minority of workers received medical benefits was not much of a problem until after the Progressive Era, because the limited state of medical knowledge made access to a physician less valuable than it would later become. During the Progressive period, workers understood that the physician's job was to declare them fit to work as soon as possible. Greater access to such diagnoses was not an attractive feature to most workers. Progressives promoted the preventive nature of medical consultations, which encouraged workers to keep a clean house and employers to maintain a safe workplace. The value of such exhortations is impossible to quantify, and it probably paled in comparison to the well-known mission of the doctor to keep the sick fund financially healthy.

Thus the lack of medical benefits, though a minor problem, contained the seed of the sickness funds' downfall. Medical benefits were expensive, and as long as such benefits tended to have little effect on the worker's actual health, failure to offer them would not lead large numbers of workers to shun those funds, as Chapter 5 indicated. That would not be the case for long. During the 1930s it became clear that medicine was developing considerable abilities to heal patients through courses of therapy such as sulfonamides. As a result the demand for medical benefits increased, although it was held back somewhat by declining incomes during the Depression. The ability of the funding agency, whether patient, sick fund, or commercial insurer, to assess net costs of treatment required an understanding of its efficacy that could be obtained only by analysis of large data sets. That played to the strengths of the commercial insurers. In this regard, sickness funds as they existed in the Progressive period could not have continued into the postwar period unchanged, even if commercial insurers had not developed actuarial techniques that enabled their growth.

A further failure of sickness funds occurred during the Great Depression. Absenteeism declined because employers laid off workers who were in poor health, in the hope of increasing the average productivity of the remaining labor force. From the firm's perspective such a decision would have been necessary for business reasons. One can only imagine the calamity facing a worker, sick to begin with, who had generally gone to work to avoid appearing to be a poor producer and who was then fired. He was left with no job, no pay packet, no medical benefits. It would have been grim. The statistics indicate it was not uncommon. Workers recognized this problem and said they would be willing to pay higher premiums to extend their coverage after job loss.

It is important not to compare sickness funds that operated in early twentieth-century America to an idealized health benefit arrangement that could not exist under real-world conditions. Workers who lost their jobs were generally dismissed from their sickness funds right away, and this was true of workers who held certificates in group health insurance policies as well. In a system that makes health insurance coverage contingent on employment, loss of employment entails loss of coverage. Not all workers were burdened by this feature, but the funds of workers who enjoyed portable benefits faced their own problems. Union funds to which members belonged when employed and unemployed came under severe pressure during the Depression. Government health insurance could, of course, continue benefits during unemployment, but even in this instance was subject to a moral hazard. Unemployed workers in Britain were more likely to claim sickness benefits, but whether that was due to greater sickness or to impoverishment in the absence of sickness is not clear.[14]

The ability of sickness funds to deliver a reasonable degree of financial protection and a more limited degree of medical care is the most important point of this book. How were they able to do it? It is convenient to separate sickness insurance systems at the turn of the twentieth century into three categories: universal or near-universal, as in Great Britain and Germany, voluntary with outside funding, as in Denmark, Belgium, and France, and voluntary with internal funding, as in the United States. *Internal funding* refers to fund revenue only from members and employers (and such entertainments as they may have arranged) and *external funding* refers to payments into sickness funds made by the government or socially minded bourgeois who were not full members. The government-operated or -supervised systems of Britain and Germany were expensive relative to worker pay, and they funded an increasing rate of absenteeism. Early in the century, it seems, it was likely that these systems, for all their evident moral hazard problems, enabled sick workers to take necessary time off. But the long-term stability of well-funded sick leave programs is questionable. Their logical outcome could be seen in Sweden around 1990, when the average worker took five weeks of paid sick leave.[15]

The systems of France and Belgium were supported to a large degree by payments from honorary members. These systems were failures. Far from making all of France one "'vast mutual society,'" the French reliance on small state subsidies and large donations from the bourgeoisie made the system appear to be an "organization for legalized begging, subject to the domination of the rich." The honorary members, in particular, took away the specifically friendly aspect of English societies and made them one more means for paternalistic employers to maneuver politically to maintain all their economic and political strengths.[16] The problem with the mutualist movement, then, was more than a lack of actuarial foundation for its beneficial operation. The deeper problem was that its dependence on outsiders rendered it less than a truly mutual enterprise.

The American situation was much closer to that mutual ideal. It is a commonplace to invoke Tocqueville on the ability of Americans to form voluntary groups to deal with collective problems. His views of early nineteenth-century America still inform our understanding of sickness funds three-quarters of a century later. "Americans of all ages, all conditions, all minds constantly unite," he wrote, connecting associations and a more general level of equality. The consequences of "the reciprocal action of men upon one another," which he described metaphorically as making those men more great-hearted, can be seen in the sickness funds. Union funds, which had no sources of external support, maintained their responsibilities in the United States during the depression of the 1890s, whereas in Britain they encountered the moral hazard of increasing sickness benefit payments during high unemployment. Later, these interpersonal bonds accounted for the ability of sickness funds to maintain their existence despite the technological superiority of group insurance.[17] One result was that until the Great Depression, absence rates in the United States did not rise as in Germany and Britain, or fall as in France and Belgium, but remained stable. The American path was a middle way between the high-cost compulsory systems and the failing voluntary systems of Europe. In that sense sickness funds succeeded in privately providing a collective good and obviating a need for government social insurance for a large number of working-class Americans.

* * *

Although historians have justly criticized business-operated welfare programs for their paternalism, they have underemphasized the paternalism inherent in much of the Progressive insurance reform program. Tocqueville would have recognized it. His description of aristocratic perceptions neatly characterized Progressive motivations: "As citizens become weaker and more incapable, it is necessary to render the government more skillful and more active in order that society be able to execute what individuals can no longer do." Since the essence of social insurance was rationality at a level far higher than ordinary citizens could achieve, according to Progressives, only the government could provide such security.[18] But that was not always the case. Evidence presented in this book suggests that voluntary associations could in fact provide such security quite well.

When sickness funds worked, they provided much-needed financial protection to workers in relatively modest circumstances. Their beneficiaries remembered the aid they provided at a time of vulnerability. That loyalty was a contested commodity; all parties wanted workers to offer it to them. The allegiance of the working classes was a prize worth competing for. Bismarck understood this and fought efforts to make workers pay premiums into the German system. "If the worker must pay, the effect on him is lost," he said, because then the worker would put the puzzle together and see that he himself had produced the resources that paid for the benefits. Closer to home, Progressive reformers also understood how security provided by the state would lead to worker loyalty to that state. Jane Addams wrote: "Almost every Sunday in the Italian quarter in which I live various mutual benefit societies march with fife and drum and with a brave showing of banners, celebrating their achievement in having surrounded themselves by at least a thin wall of protection against disaster, upon having set up their mutual good will against the day of misfortune. . . . [O]ne longs to pour into the government of their adopted country all this affection and zeal, this real patriotism. A system of State insurance would be a very simple device and secure a large return."[19] Addams hoped not for workers to consider themselves as American or to form bonds with their new country or its ideals—but, rather, to form bonds with its government. Worker gratitude to the state could be a powerful political force.

Contemporary statements about insurance provision and worker loyalty offer curious parallels. Addams hoped that state insurance would pay for itself ("secure a large return") by increasing worker loyalty to the state, and employers hoped that company-provided insurance would bond the worker to the firm. On the basis of an extensive benefit program, National Cash Register trumpeted that its "employees are proud of their connection to the Company." Overall, "it pays for employers to enlist the sympathy of their employees by looking after their physical and mental comfort." The same metaphor appears: invest in insurance because it pays, not only financially but in terms of loyalty as well. Commercial insurers played on this desire of client companies. Metropolitan Life sold the idea of group insurance by its ability to "create appreciation of the employer's generosity and thoughtfulness, thus winning over to him many a fireside ally back in the home." Samuel Gompers intended that union members look first to their union for help in time of need, not to the employer or the state. The last thing he wanted was for workers in need to believe that some other institution, not their union, would come to their aid. The remarkable thing is not that ailing workers would grant some degree of loyalty to the bringer of aid but that historians would find loyalty to the state acceptable but loyalty to the firm, union, or insurer misguided, manipulative, and especially problematic to the degree that it interfered with the first process.[20]

The failure of Progressive efforts was not due in any fundamental sense to underhanded political campaigns led by physicians, insurers, businesses, and unions. They only magnified tendencies of the day's realities. There simply was little public support for government insurance. The sickness funds that were available did not cover a majority of workers, but they competently covered most of the workers who wanted to obtain such coverage. Many of those who did not join were young enough not to worry too much about their health or old enough to have saved against health-related problems. Progressives promised a system in which benefits would be marginally better but costs considerably higher. That was common knowledge. There may have been a conspiracy of the powerful, but it emphasized what most people had known all along. In the legislatures and the 1918 California referendum, the consistent defeats of government insurance programs reflected this deeper reality.

And so it goes in the present. Use of extreme rhetoric by advocates of government insurance raises red flags among the majority of Americans who have reasonably good insurance coverage. Quadagno's title is an example of this exaggerated rhetoric. Our "One Nation" is "Uninsured" because "The U. S. Has No National Health Insurance." But the nation is not uninsured. To the contrary, about 85 percent of Americans are covered; a lack of government insurance does not imply a lack of insurance. Americans who have reasonably good health insurance recognize that the arguments of government insurance advocates bear little resemblance to reality and so ignore them. As in the Progressive Era, failure to acknowledge the potential shortcomings of government health insurance by its advocates may lead the insured majority to think that they are being asked to sacrifice for a most nebulous purpose.[21]

If the strategies of the promoters of government insurance have managed to whip up support for the status quo, the real misfortune might lay in a genuine public need for government insurance. Whereas in Progressive times only the exceptionally credulous could be bankrupted by medical bills, in our day such debt accounts for an important share of liabilities among the insolvent. Job-lock may well keep workers in less productive and less well-paying positions. And we do have a moral obligation to ensure that members of the low-earning working class can get medical care when they need it. But to create an insurance system that would cover all Americans will entail serious costs, not least of which is the moral hazard question of lengthy queues. If the political debate shifts away from one in which weaknesses of the present health care system and alternatives to it are ignored and toward one in which both costs and benefits are acknowledged and examined in detail, a national health insurance system could become a reality. On the other hand, as long as government insurance advocates use anecdotes to describe a health care system that few outside of universities and think tanks recognize, the present system will soldier on.

Health care provision and financing is so complex that any system will bring with it severe shortcomings. We choose the failures we are willing to live with via the political system. So far our polity has looked on the present health insurance system much as it looked on the sickness funds of the early twentieth century: as not perfect but not obviously worse than the state-led alternative.

APPENDIX A

Data Sources

This appendix reports on bodies of data about workers or sickness funds that were collected during this study.

1. U.S. Commissioner of Labor, *Twenty-third Annual Report*. This survey collected information concerning about twelve hundred benefit funds in the United States, most of which offered sickness insurance benefits. Most information reported on fiscal years 1906 or 1907, and some was from 1905 or 1908. Investigators surveyed 88 national labor union funds, 530 local union funds, 461 establishment funds, and 66 hospital, industrial benefit, and miscellaneous funds. Information reported for each fund included date of founding, number of members, terms of membership, and value of benefits.
2. U.S. Commissioner of Labor, *Twenty-fourth Annual Report*. This survey was compiled by some of the leading experts in the field. It reported in great detail on insurance for workers in case of accident, sickness, and unemployment and in somewhat less detail on old-age pension and invalidity insurance. The following authors produced the chapters about their respective countries: Henry J. Harris, Austria and Germany; E. H. Lewinski-Corwin, Belgium; J. E. Pope, Denmark and Norway; L. D. Clark, Great Britain; I. M. Rubinow, Italy, Russia, and Spain; and H. O. Hansen, Sweden.
3. Kaiserlichen Statistischen Amt, *Statistik der Krankenversicherung der*

Arbeiter im Jahre xxxx. These government reports on social insurance statistics by region show close agreement with the chapter concerning Germany in U. S. Commissioner of Labor, *Twenty-fourth Annual Report*.

4. U.S. Department of the Interior, Census Office, *Report on Insurance Business in the United States*. The census reported on life insurers, including in this category fraternal and other societies that paid benefits in case of sickness. By reporting the value of the benefits for each insurer, it was possible to separate sickness funds from those not paying sickness benefits. "Fraternal beneficiary societies" in Class C were defined as those "based on the lodge system and insuring lives, or paying sick, funeral, strike, or other benefit[s]." Independent beneficiary societies in Class C2 were defined as "independent organizations paying sick, funeral, strike, and kindred benefits" (p. vii). Table 34 reported benefits offered according to society regulations, but not all societies reported the actual dollar value of benefits paid out. Thus, table 35 reported membership in all societies (those offering sickness benefits only, death benefits only, or both) and numbers of sickness claims and the value of benefits paid out. Not every such sickness fund provided a detailed financial statement, so it was not possible to consider how much in premiums and benefits were paid, nor to estimate the number of insured members.
5. Michigan Bureau of Labor and Industrial Statistics, *Thirteenth Annual Report*. This was the first survey in Michigan of union benefit activities. Most investigators were connected with the union about which they reported. This survey described benefit activities of 237 unions throughout Michigan.
6. Connecticut Bureau of Labor Statistics, *Seventh Annual Report*. This project attempted a census of all benefit societies in Connecticut. Most of the work was done by door-to-door canvassing, although the mail response rate was high. It counted 386 benefit societies with 974 branches, insuring 126,613 persons. Since the Connecticut investigators followed in the footsteps of the 1890 Census, they were able to note that "a very large number of societies" (p. 63) had not been contacted by Census marshals, which suggests that the number of 1,259 nonfraternal benefit societies nationally (Chapter 4) could underestimate the true number substantially. The Connecticut inves-

tigation asked about the number of members and the value of benefits, but it did not ask about the number of claims.

7. This book has relied on the digitized versions of surveys conducted in the late nineteenth century by several state-level bureaus of labor statistics. The Historical Labor Statistics Project of the University of California digitized these surveys and has made them available for public use for free through the Eh.net Web site for economic historians. See www.eh.net/databases/labor for both data files and detailed codebooks.

APPENDIX B

Additional Regressions for Chapter 7

The most important statistical results reported in Chapter 7 were consistent across a variety of measures of insurance coverage. Tables B.1 and B.3 in this appendix report additional regression results of these alternative coverage measures, the number of benefit societies to which a worker belonged, and the value of weekly sickness benefits in dollar terms. Methods used to estimate these regressions included Poisson for the second set of regressions and Tobit for the third owing to the large number of zeroes from the uninsured. In the second set of regressions, negative binomial estimates tended to converge slowly and exceed iteration limits. The Poisson regressions produced a ratio of the Pearson chi-squared to degrees of freedom close to one, so the Poisson results were reported. See Kennedy, *Guide*, pp. 263–64, 272, 279–80.

It is possible that savings and wealth were endogenously related to these measures of benefit society membership, for example, if workers who had joined more than one benefit society, or one that granted high levels of benefits, then decided to save less. This problem can be resolved through the use of instrumental variable techniques. To produce instruments for the savings and wealth variables, I estimated first-stage regressions of savings or wealth on the number of weeks of work missed for reasons other than sickness, its square, its cube, and its quartic. The results of the first-stage regressions are reported in tables B.2 and B.4.

Table B.1.

Regressions of health insurance coverage on savings

DEPENDENT VARIABLE AND METHOD	NUMBER OF BENEFIT SOCIETIES TO WHICH RESPONDENT BELONGS; POISSON			VALUE OF SICK BENEFITS PER WEEK; TOBIT		
	A	B	C	A	B	C
Age under 20	−1.19***	−1.23***	−1.11***	−5.26***	−5.33***	−5.50***
	(0.12)	(0.13)	(0.29)	(0.56)	(0.60)	(1.24)
Age 30–39	0.13**	0.16***	0.11	0.88***	1.15***	0.40
	(0.05)	(0.06)	(0.13)	(0.34)	(0.37)	(0.77)
Age over 40	−0.05	0.12*	−0.20	0.03	0.46	−1.51*
	(0.06)	(0.07)	(0.14)	(0.39)	(0.42)	(0.86)
Married	0.19***	0.19***	0.18***	1.04***	1.09***	1.04***
	(0.06)	(0.06)	(0.06)	(0.39)	(0.39)	(0.39)
Family size	0.03**	0.03**	0.03**	0.19**	0.18**	0.21**
	(0.01)	(0.01)	(0.01)	(0.09)	(0.09)	(0.09)
Any sick days	0.03	0.03	−0.02	0.22	0.18	0.16
	(0.05)	(0.05)	(0.05)	(0.33)	(0.33)	(0.34)
Annual earnings	1.07***	1.08***	0.98***	9.37***	9.37***	8.70***
	(0.10)	(0.11)	(0.11)	(0.78)	(0.78)	(0.80)

(continued)

Table B.1.

Regressions of health insurance coverage on savings (*continued*)

DEPENDENT VARIABLE AND METHOD	NUMBER OF BENEFIT SOCIETIES TO WHICH RESPONDENT BELONGS; POISSON			VALUE OF SICK BENEFITS PER WEEK; TOBIT		
	A	B	C	A	B	C
Owns home	0.12**	0.13***	0.12**	1.05***	1.09***	1.07***
	(0.05)	(0.05)	(0.05)	(0.30)	(0.31)	(0.30)
Value of savings/100	−0.03	0.05	0.10	−0.22	0.27	0.54
	(0.02)	(0.03)	(0.06)	(0.14)	(0.23)	(0.35)
Savings*		0.47**	0.06		1.82	−0.15
age under 20		(0.23)	(0.19)		(1.11)	(0.77)
Savings*		−0.07*	−0.01		−0.63**	−0.35
age 30–39		(0.04)	(0.10)		(0.30)	(0.52)
Savings*		−0.14***	−0.20**		−1.01***	−1.18**
age over 40		(0.05)	(0.10)		(0.33)	(0.59)
Goodness of fit	0.88	0.88	0.89	−10,282	−10,268	−10,274

Sources: Carter et al., "Codebook . . . Detroit, 1890"; "Codebook . . . Outside of Detroit, 1890."

Note: Standard errors in parentheses. Model A lacks finance-age interaction variables; Model B includes interaction variables; Model C represents an instrument for savings using weeks of work missed for reasons other than sickness, its square, its cube, and its quartic. Intercepts and dummy variables were included in regressions but not reported here. They included (number of categories including the omitted ones) city of residence (12), occupation (13), number of employees in establishment (5), and country of birth (6). Goodness of fit statistics: for Tobit=log likelihood; for Poisson=Pearson χ_2 /d.f.

*significantly different from zero at the 0.10 level; **significantly different from zero at the 0.05 level; ***significantly different from zero at the 0.01 level

Table B.2.
First-stage Tobit regression to obtain instruments for savings

	PARAMETER ESTIMATE	STANDARD ERROR
Intercept	−1.04***	0.05
Weeks missed for reasons other than sickness	0.013	0.034
Weeks missed, squared	−0.016***	0.006
Weeks missed, cubed	0.00073***	0.00028
Weeks missed, to the fourth power	−0.00001**	0.000004

**significantly different from zero at 0.05 level; ***at 0.01 level.

Table B.3.

Regressions of health insurance coverage on wealth

DEPENDENT VARIABLE AND METHOD	NUMBER OF BENEFIT SOCIETIES TO WHICH RESPONDENT BELONGS; POISSON			VALUE OF SICK BENEFITS PER WEEK; TOBIT		
	A	B	C	A	B	C
Age under 20	−1.19***	−1.20***	−1.12***	−5.28***	−5.18***	−4.53**
	(0.12)	(0.13)	(0.46)	(0.56)	(0.60)	(2.01)
Age 30–39	0.12**	0.16**	−0.20	0.84**	1.33***	−0.17
	(0.05)	(0.07)	(0.22)	(0.34)	(0.44)	(1.29)
Age over 40	0.05	0.13*	0.45*	−0.09	0.56	3.19**
	(0.06)	(0.08)	(0.24)	(0.40)	(0.49)	(1.46)
Married	0.19***	0.17***	0.19***	1.07***	0.90**	1.06***
	(0.06)	(0.06)	(0.06)	(0.39)	(0.40)	(0.39)
Family size	0.03**	0.03**	0.03**	0.21**	0.20**	0.20**
	(0.01)	(0.01)	(0.01)	(0.09)	(0.08)	(0.09)
Any sick days	0.03	0.03	−0.05	0.22	0.23	−0.31
	(0.05)	(0.05)	(0.06)	(0.33)	(0.33)	(0.37)

Annual earnings	1.02***	0.99***	0.89***	8.59***	8.38***	7.77***
	(0.10)	(0.10)	(0.11)	(0.76)	(0.76)	(0.79)
Owns home	0.12**	0.11**	0.11**	0.92***	0.82**	1.04***
	(0.05)	(0.05)	(0.05)	(0.33)	(0.34)	(0.30)
Value of wealth/10C	0.002	0.07	0.47**	0.16	0.82***	3.72***
	(0.02)	(0.04)	(0.21)	(0.13)	(0.30)	(1.24)
Wealth*		0.36	−0.0002		0.84	−1.42
age under 20		(0.58)	(0.66)		(2.89)	(2.85)
Wealth*		−0.05	0.45		−0.68*	1.45
age 30–39		(0.05)	(0.30)		(0.35)	(1.76)
Wealth*		−0.08*	−0.55*		−0.76**	−4.34**
age over 40		(0.05)	(0.32)		(0.32)	(1.96)
Goodness of fit	0.88	0.88	0.88	−10275	−10272	−10269

Sources: Carter et al., "Codebook . . . Detroit, 1890"; "Codebook . . . Outside of Detroit, 1890."

Note: Standard errors in parentheses. Model A lacks wealth-age interactions; Model B includes those interactions; Model C represents an instrument for savings using weeks of work missed for reasons other than sickness, its square, its cube, and its quartic. Intercepts and dummy variables were included in regressions but not reported here. They included (number of categories including the omitted ones) city of residence (12), occupation (13), number of employees in establishment (5), and country of birth (6). Goodness of fit statistics: for Tobit=log likelihood; for Poisson=Pearson χ^2 /d.f.

*significantly different from zero at the 0.10 level; **significantly different from zero at the 0.05 level; ***significantly different from zero at the 0.01 level

Table B.4.

First-stage OLS regression to obtain instruments for wealth

	PARAMETER ESTIMATE	STANDARD ERROR
Intercept	0.84***	0.015
Weeks missed for reasons other than sickness	−0.06***	0.007
Weeks missed squared	0.002***	0.0005
Weeks missed cubed	−0.00002**	0.00001

Note: Adjusted $R^2 = 0.03$.

*significantly different from zero at the 0.10 level; **significantly different from zero at the 0.05 level; ***significantly different from zero at the 0.01 level

NOTES

CHAPTER 1. INDUSTRIAL SICKNESS FUNDS

1. Health Insurance Commission of Pennsylvania, *Report,* p. 119.
2. Industrial Mutual Association and Manufacturers' Association collections, Scharchburg Archives, Kettering University, Flint, Michigan. See the trustees' minute books of the Manufacturers' Association, pp. 88–101, and U.S. Census manuscript schedules for Genesee County, Michigan, 1910.
3. Other vignettes in Health Insurance Commission of Pennsylvania, *Report,* describe the virtual absence of sickness insurance and the unwillingness of funds to pay benefits to the few workers who were covered (e.g., pp. 149, 156). Eastman, *Work-Accidents,* p. 4, describes an injured postal worker who enjoyed superfluous overpayments from his sickness fund while the Post Office continued to pay his wage. A fictional example of an injured, uncovered worker is Jurgis Rudkis in Upton Sinclair's *The Jungle,* chapter 23.
4. Glied, "Employer-Based Health Insurance System," p. 38; Blumenthal, "Employer-Sponsored Health Insurance"; Quadagno, *One Nation.* Anderson, "Health Insurance," offers an early historical view of the Progressive episode.
5. Other terms used in this book include *sick funds, sickness funds, mutual societies,* and *mutual benefit associations.*
6. Rubinow, *Quest,* p. 173; Numbers, *Almost Persuaded,* pp. 25, 76; American Association for Labor Legislation, "Tentative Draft," p. 239. The rhetorical success of the reformers can be seen in the grumbling of their most forceful opponent, Frederick Hoffman, *Facts and Fallacies,* p. 33: "Compulsory sickness insurance [has been] adroitly disguised as 'health' insurance." A recent historical work got it backwards when it claimed that reformers presented their proposals as sickness insurance: Kaufman, *For the Common Good,* p. 145.

7. Commonwealth of Massachusetts, *Report,* p. 24; Forman, "Cost of Industrial Insurance"; Glied, "Employer-Based Health Insurance System."
8. For contemporary references see Lapp, "Health Insurance," 941; Brundage, "Survey," p. 2102; State of Connecticut, *Report,* p. 6; Health Insurance Commission of Pennsylvania, *Report,* p. 125; Byington, *Homestead,* p. 163. For present-day references see Derickson, *Workers' Health,* p. 63; Moss, *Socializing Security,* p. 137 (quoting Miles Dawson's testimony to the Massachusetts commission).
9. More detail about the operations of employer-based funds appears in Chapter 5; for union funds, see Chapter 6.
10. U.S. Bureau of the Census, *Historical Statistics,* ser. D 802. The state labor bureau surveys used later in this book yield similar estimates; see Costa, "Wage and Length," p. 161.
11. Derickson, *Workers' Health,* pp. 69–71; NICB, *Experience,* pp. 59–60, 63–64.
12. For patient-doctor relationships see Keelor, "Sickness Insurance," pp. 130–131. Similar restrictions appeared in commercial health policies: ibid., p. 127; State of Illinois, *Report,* p. 139; Derickson, *Workers' Health,* p. 66; U.S. Commissioner of Labor, *Twenty-third Annual Report,* p. 672.
13. U.S. Commissioner of Labor, *Twenty-third Annual Report,* pp. 202, 389. State of Illinois, *Report,* p. 117. Rubinow, *Quest,* p. 213; Klein, *For All These Rights,* p. 23; Moss, *Socializing Security,* p. 146.
14. For diversity of funds see U.S. Commissioner of Labor, *Twenty-third Annual Report.* See also Chapter 4 below. For fraternals see Beito, *From Mutual Aid to the Welfare State;* Emery and Emery, *Young Man's Benefit.*
15. Rubinow, "Health Insurance," p. 76. Lubove, *Struggle,* pp. 1–24; Hacker, *Divided Welfare State,* pp. 191–201.

    I think it is fair to use *Progressive* as a term to describe the scholars, politicians, and activists who worked to establish compulsory government health insurance. Their work continued earlier, clearly Progressive efforts in industrial safety and health and workmen's compensation. There is no standard term for those who opposed government health insurance, nor was there such a term at that time. I recognize that it is generally bad form to define a group in terms of what it was not, but I can think of no other term to refer to Frederick Hoffman, William Gale Curtis, the Insurance Economics Society, and their allies than "opponents" of the Progressives.
16. Health Insurance Commission of Pennsylvania, *Report,* pp. 121, estimated that claimants received sickness benefits in only about two-thirds of cases. See also pp. 149 and 156 for anecdotes.
17. On labor markets ca. 1900, see Fishback, "Operations"; Rosenbloom, *Looking for Work.* Rubinow, *Quest,* p. 212, emphasized the gross effect of the premium payment deduction to discourage worker support of state insurance.
18. Lapp, "Health Insurance," pp. 943–944 (Lapp dismissed critics as "childlike in their simplicity"); Meeker, "Social Insurance," p. 19.
19. A good present-day example of moral hazard appears in Fuhrmans, "Health Insurers," p. B4. Demsetz, "Information and Efficiency," p. 7. For concern

with malingering, see California Social Insurance Commission, *Report,* pp. 110, 299; State of Connecticut, *Report,* p. 9; State of Illinois, *Report,* pp. 117, 140, 433, 540; Commonwealth of Massachusetts, *Report,* p. 28; Lambert, "Medical Organization," p. 37; Rubinow, "Health Insurance," p. 78; Rubinow, *Quest,* pp. 586–587; Rubinow, "Prevention"; Hoffman, "Some Fallacies," p. 165; Dawson, "Principles," p. 112; Fisher, "Need for Health Insurance," p. 19; Hoffman, *Facts and Fallacies,* pp. 32, 74; Huyck, "Establishment Funds," p. 87; Cheney, "Compulsory Health Insurance," p. 493; Curtis, "Economic Disadvantages," p. 24; Sullivan, "Labor and Sickness Insurance"; Boston Chamber of Commerce, "Non-Contributory Old Age Pensions."

20. Black, "Reluctant Paternalism," p. 126.
21. Cheney, "Compulsory Health Insurance"; Dawson, "Principles of Health Insurance," p. 112. Like *moral hazard,* the term *adverse selection* was commonly used in the early twentieth-century insurance literature. Hacker, *Divided Welfare State,* p. 192; Kaufman, *For the Common Good,* p. 47; Emery and Emery, *Young Man's Benefit,* pp. 65–66; Gottlieb, "Asymmetric Information."
22. Keelor, "Sickness Insurance," p. 131 ("very difficult problem"), copied word for word into State of Illinois, *Report,* p. 434. See also Commonwealth of Massachusetts, *Report,* p. 28; Kalet, "Voluntary Health Insurance," p. 148. Hoffman, "Some Fallacies," p. 206 (espionage); Curtis, "Economic Disadvantages," p. 25 (strikes abroad); Frevert, "Professional Medicine," p. 648. The writer of "Attitude of Medical Society of the State of New York," p. 226, proposed that government regulators of physicians would need "inquisitorial" powers.
23. For adverse selection see Glied, "Employer-Based Health Insurance," p. 41; cf. Klein, *For All These Rights,* p. 14. For "job-lock" see Madrian, "Employment-Based Health Insurance." On Progressive claims, see American Association for Labor Legislation, "Brief," p. 198.
24. For criticism of job-lock see American Association for Labor Legislation, "Brief," p. 198; Hamilton, "Trade Unions." Unions with particularly mobile members found it difficult to determine who had rights to sickness fund coverage: Derickson, *Workers' Health,* p. 67. "Industrial Welfare Work in Flint," 1913 [?], Flint Vehicle Factories Mutual Benefit Association records, Scharchburg Archives, Kettering University, Flint, Michigan; *Cyclopaedia of American Biography,* c.v. J. Dallas Dort. U.S. Commissioner of Labor, *Twenty-third Annual Report,* pp. 673–675.

CHAPTER 2. POLITICAL ECONOMY OF PROGRESSIVE-ERA SICKNESS INSURANCE

1. Older, more general political histories remain engaging and thought-provoking. See especially Wiebe, *Search for Order;* Wiebe, *Businessmen and Reform;* and Hofstadter, *Age of Reform.* For the platform see Buenker and Buenker, *Encyclopedia,* p. 1128–1129. For state reforms see Law, "Origins."
2. The development of workmen's compensation has been carefully documented and analyzed in Fishback and Kantor, *Prelude to the Welfare State,* to

which this discussion is heavily indebted. For the relation between accident insurance and sickness insurance see Ohio Health and Old Age Insurance Commission, *Health,* p. 168; Commons and Altmeyer, "Health Insurance Movement," p. 288, citing Adna F. Weber in New York Bureau of Labor, *Seventeenth Annual Report of the Bureau of Labor Statistics of New York,* 1899, pp. 557–1162. Similar hopes of expanding public pensions are discussed in chapter 8 of Costa, *Evolution.* Goldwater is quoted in American Association for Labor Legislation, "Brief," p. 168. Rupert Blue is quoted in Walker, "Compulsory Health Insurance," p. 290.

3. A rich and fair history of the AALL runs through Moss, *Socializing Security.* See also Skocpol, *Protecting Soldiers,* pp. 176–203; Hacker, *Divided Welfare State,* Chapter 4; and Lubove, *Struggle.* Contemporary perspectives appear in Commons and Altmeyer, "Health Insurance Movement," and brief histories of the movement as a whole that were written in the 1930s appear in Williams, *Purchase of Medical Care,* Chapter 2; Rubinow, *Quest,* Chapter 17; Millis and Montgomery, *Labor's Risks,* pp. 321–323; and Hirsh, "Compulsory Health Insurance." On the phossy jaw campaign see Moss, *Socializing Security,* pp. 80–96. The phenomenon of a regulated industry seeking relief from a larger government entity to stave off regulation by many smaller entities is a recurring theme in historical studies of the Progressive Era. Wiebe, *Businessmen,* p. 202.
4. Moss, *Socializing Security,* pp. 132–157; Commons and Altmeyer, "Health Insurance Movement," pp. 291–292; Rubinow, *Quest,* pp. 207–209 (the quotation is on p. 207); Fisher, "Need," pp. 10–11.
5. American Association for Labor Legislation, "Brief," pp. 211–237; Numbers, *Almost Persuaded,* pp. 25–26; U.S. Bureau of the Census, *Historical Statistics,* series D-781; Hoffman, *Wages,* pp. 29–32; Fisher, "Need," p. 17; Lambert, "Medical Organization," p. 38; Walker, "Compulsory Health Insurance," 294–295.
6. Moss, *Socializing Security,* pp. 141–143. (On p. 233, fn. 55, he discusses discrepancies in the number of legislatures that considered health insurance bills; twelve seems to be the more accurate number but it could have been as high as fifteen.) Commons and Altmeyer, "Health Insurance Movement," p. 293; Hirsh, "Compulsory Health Insurance," p. 106.
7. Numbers, *Almost Persuaded,* p. 91. Hoffman, *Wages,* p. 169, notes that results of the Utica petition campaign may show that workers responded under duress. Hoffman considers New York health insurance politics in great detail in *Wages.* Viseltear, "Compulsory Health Insurance." Some historians have suggested that the California referendum was not the best measure of popular support because it would have attracted disproportionately those with the strongest opinions about the issue (Hacker, *Divided Welfare State,* p. 392); however, Costa, in "Demand," noted that fewer than three-fourths of the 714,525 who cast ballots that day voted either way on the health insurance issue, far fewer than the number who voted for a gubernatorial candidate or a constitutional amendment concerning prohibition.

8. Moss, *Socializing Security,* pp. 31, 141–142, 147; Numbers, *Almost Persuaded,* p. 60; Klein, *For All These Rights,* p. 34 ("educate"); Hacker, "Historical Logic," p. 110 ("an organization"); Kaufman, *For the Common Good,* p. 145 ("unusually well-educated"); Skocpol, *Protecting Soldiers,* p. 185. See also Lubove, *Struggle,* pp. 83–86. Compare to Hofstadter's thumbnail sketch in *Age of Reform,* p. 261: "Bad people had pressure groups; the Man of Good Will had only his civic organizations." Compare these distinctions to historiographical discussion in Fox, "Decline of Historicism." Years later, Rubinow, "Public and Private Interests," p. 186, acknowledged Progressive exaggerations, as described in Chapter 11.
9. Kaufman, *For the Common Good,* p. 148; Quadagno, *One Nation,* pp. 201–213; Starr, "*Social Transformation,*" p. 1019. See also Gordon, *Dead on Arrival;* Hacker, *Divided Welfare State;* Lubove, *Struggle.* All describe the outcomes of Progressive-Era health insurance reform attempts as failures or lost opportunities and existing insurance as inadequate. Barbara Nachtrieb Armstrong, an attorney and economist who was a prominent supporter of the California insurance referendum in 1918, later wrote *Insuring the Essentials* in support of New Deal–Era social insurance programs; see especially pp. 370–375.
10. Starr, *Social Transformation,* pp. 240–243; Quadagno, *One Nation,* p. 19; Hacker, *Divided Welfare State,* p. 191, 193. In another example, Hacker, *Divided Welfare State,* pp. 193, 201, mistimed the emergence of and thereby misunderstood the source of private insurance, asserting that it "emerged from the rubble" of Progressive defeats "as a private alternative" to government insurance. The present book documents the widespread availability of private insurance before those debates, which helps explain those defeats.
11. W. Andrew Achenbaum, "Isaac Max Rubinow," *American National Biography* ("immediate classic"); Numbers, *Almost Persuaded,* p. 18; Rubinow, "Sickness Insurance," p. 166; Rubinow, "Health Insurance," pp. 70–76; Rubinow, "Public and Private Interests," p. 185; Rubinow, *Quest for Security,* p. 208. Eastman had some praise for sickness funds. Compare *Work-Accidents,* pp. 161–163 versus pp. 202–204; Dawson, "Principles," p. 117, noted that "democratically managed" benefit societies could be trusted to limit costs appropriately.
12. F. J. Sypher, "Frederick Ludwig Hoffman," *American National Biography;* Numbers, *Almost Persuaded,* p. 18; Hoffman, "Scientific Racism." Hoffman, "Systems," pp. 215–216 ("innumerable failures"). Moss, *Socializing Security,* p. 148 ("Bible of the opposition"). Hoffman, *Facts and Fallacies,* pp. 76, 88. Compare Byington, *Homestead,* 163, on state regulation. Starr, *Social Transformation,* p. 252, described Hoffman as "a respected actuary."
13. Meeker, "Social Insurance"; Rubinow, "Sickness Insurance," p. 166; California Social Insurance Commission, *Report,* p. 110; Rubinow, *Social Insurance,* p. 223; State of Connecticut, *Report,* p. 7; Dawson, "Principles," pp. 116–117.
14. Hoffman, *Facts and Fallacies,* pp. 71–76.
15. Derickson, *Health Security;* U.S. Bureau of the Census, *Historical Statistics,* Series D-233, 567, 603 (farm laborers who were family members were not

counted); Hoffman, *Wages,* pp. 29–32. Rubinow included nonfamily farm laborers and domestics in the wage-earning population: *Social Insurance,* p. 29.

16. American Association for Labor Legislation, "Brief," pp. 212–213; Dawson, "Principles," p. 112; Cheney, "Compulsory"; Fisher, "Need," p. 15; Meeker, "Social Insurance."
17. Gompers, "Labor vs. Its Barnacles," pp. 270–271; Gompers, "Not Even Compulsory Benevolence Will Do"; Rubinow, *Quest,* p. 212; Hoffman, *Facts and Fallacies,* pp. 71–73.
18. Rubinow, "Public and Private Interests," p. 186.
19. Hoffman, "Systems," p. 218; State of Illinois, *Report,* p. 109; North, "Life Insurance."
20. Rubinow, *Quest,* pp. 553–555; Klein, *For All These Rights,* p. 14; Hoffman, *Facts and Fallacies,* p. 5.
21. State of Connecticut, *Report,* pp. 9–10; Moss, *Socializing Security,* pp. 156, 183.
22. American Association for Labor Legislation, "Brief," pp. 213–215; Dawson, "Principles," p. 116; Lott, "Fallacies," p. 42; Meeker, "Social Insurance."
23. Dawson, "Principles," p. 114; Fisher, "Need," pp. 15–16; State of Illinois, *Report;* Ohio Health and Old Age Insurance Commission, *Health;* Lapp, "Health Insurance," p. 942; Forman, "Cost of Industrial Insurance"; NICB, *Industrial Group Insurance;* Moss, *Socializing Security,* p. 138. Life insurance was popular; a Chicago survey described in State of Illinois, *Report* (p. 228), found that four in five workers were so insured. About a third of insured native-born whites and about two-thirds of insured black heads of households had industrial policies. Many industrial sickness policies provided for home nursing care: Health Insurance Commission of Pennsylvania, *Report,* p. 48. The cost of door-to-door collection makes industrial insurance resemble modern microfinance in poor countries, which operates in similar fashion for a similar type of customer, the working poor; a vivid description appears in Bellman, "Entrepreneur Gets Big Banks."
24. Rubinow, "Social Insurance," p. 170; Commonwealth of Massachusetts, *Report,* pp. 31–32; State of Connecticut, *Report,* p. 14; Hoffman, "Some Facts and Fallacies," p. 204.
25. Health Insurance Commission of Pennsylvania, *Report,* pp. 33–34; Fisher, "Need," pp. 16–17; California Social Insurance Commission, *Report,* p. 122.
26. American Association for Labor Legislation, "Brief," pp. 230–236; Walker, "Compulsory Health Insurance," p. 294; Hoffman, "Facts and Fallacies," p. 34; State of Illinois, *Report,* p. 546; Mokyr, *Gifts of Athena,* pp. 195–196. McKeown, *Modern Rise,* and in the American case, McKinlay and McKinlay, "Questionable Contribution," famously argued against a link between medical therapeutics and declines in mortality.
27. Fox, *Health Policies,* pp. 3–21, 37–52; Hoffman, "Facts and Fallacies," pp. 33–34; Dawson in U.S. Department of Labor, *Proceedings,* p. 546; Rubinow, *Quest,* pp. 208–209, 212–214.
28. Rubinow, *Standards,* pp. 241–245; Numbers, *Almost Persuaded,* pp. 37–38,

82–83; Dawson in U.S. Department of Labor, "Proceedings," p. 546. The November 1915 draft of the standard bill omitted discussion of physician choice by the insured (State of Connecticut, *Report,* pp. 51–60). By June 1916 the next draft called for a degree of free choice except for "insured persons in prescribed areas" who saw "district medical officers" (American Association for Labor Legislation, "Tentative Draft," p. 248). This later draft, however, still left open the question of how medical services were to be organized (ibid., pp. 244–246).

29. State of Connecticut, *Report,* pp. 84–85, 95–96; Numbers, *Almost Persuaded;* California Social Insurance Commission, *Report,* p. 122; Lambert, "Medical Organization," pp. 46–47; Rubinow, *Quest,* p. 209; State of Illinois, *Report,* pp. 433–435; Commonwealth of Massachusetts, *Report,* pp. 27–28; Curtis, "Economic Disadvantages," pp. 217–218; American Association for Labor Legislation, "Tentative Draft," p. 244. See also Lewinski-Corwin, "Medical Aspects."

30. These four were identified as early as Rubinow's account in *Quest for Security,* pp. 211–214. Other opponents included Christian Scientists (Ohio Health and Old Age Insurance Commission, *Health,* p. 311; Moss, *Socializing Security,* p. 149; Rubinow, *Quest,* p. 185; Babcock, "Mystery and Menace," p. 230) and fraternal benefit societies (Kaufman, *For the Common Good,* p. 149).

31. Numbers, *Almost Persuaded,* pp. 27–36, 113, estimated that physician incomes rose by 41 percent during the period 1916–1919; the CPI rose 59 percent in those years (*Historical Statistics,* p. 164). Ohio Health and Old Age Insurance Commission, *Health,* pp. 162–164; Dawson in U.S. Department of Labor, *Proceedings,* p. 546; Rubinow, *Quest,* pp. 208–209; Starr, *Social Transformation,* pp. 246–249; Quadagno, *One Nation,* p. 6.

32. Gompers is quoted concerning the living wage in Derickson, *Health Security,* p. 13.

33. Derickson, "'Take Health From the List of Luxuries,'" pp. 173–178; Hoffman, *Wages,* 115–136.

34. Numbers, *Almost Persuaded,* pp. 25–26; American Association for Labor Legislation, "Brief," p. 223; Commons and Altmeyer, "Health Insurance Movement," pp. 297–299. For welfare capitalism see Brandes, *American Welfare Capitalism;* Moriguchi, "Did American Welfare Capitalists Breach Their Implicit Contracts?"

35. For the NCF and its affiliates see Hoffman, *Wages,* p. 94–97. For the prospect that only some states would enact insurance laws see Commons and Altmeyer, "Health Insurance Movement," p. 304. "Chair warmers" was a phrase used by a New York lumber mill owner quoted by Hoffman in *Wages,* p. 35.

36. Klein, *For All These Rights,* pp. 27–34; Hoffman, *Wages,* pp. 106–111; Rubinow, "Public and Private," pp. 185–186. See Rodgers, *Atlantic Crossings,* pp. 259–260, on insurers aiming to hold their ground prospectively.

37. Dryden is quoted in State of Illinois, *Report,* pp. 429–30. This quotation also appears in American Association for Labor Legislation, "Brief," p. 201, and

Starr, *Social Transformation,* p. 242. Regarding the Equitable see Klein, *For All These Rights,* p. 26. As late as 1927 an actuary could write, "Health insurance has been universally unprofitable to the commercial accident and health companies." See Sommer, "Health Insurance Hazards," p. 181. For the death benefit see Moss, *Socializing Security,* p. 146; Rubinow, *Quest,* p. 213.

38. For the quotations see Gordon, *Dead on Arrival,* pp. 261, 268. That which is gratuitously asserted can be gratuitously denied. William Gale Curtis of the Insurance Economics Society claimed in 1918 that "the working people are against health insurance" in Ohio Health and Old Age Insurance Commission, *Health,* p. 439. Hoffman, *Wages,* pp. 14–22; Klein, *For All These Rights,* p. 14; Tone, *Business,* pp. 59, 79–80.
39. Lubove, *Struggle,* p. 83; Starr, *Social Transformation,* p. 3; Hacker, *Divided Welfare State*; Quadagno, *One Nation*; Hoffman, *Wages*; Klein, *For All These Rights*; Gordon, *Dead on Arrival.*
40. See Lapp, "Health Insurance," p. 942. Fisher and Sydenstricker are quoted in Derickson, *Health Security,* p. 15. Warren and Sydenstricker, *Health Insurance,* p. 51. Echoing Rubinow's review in the December 1916 *American Economic Review,* Numbers called this pamphlet "one of the earliest and most influential American studies of health insurance." *Almost Persuaded,* p. 57. American Association for Labor Legislation, "Brief," pp. 180–185, 194–206. See also Henderson, *Industrial Insurance,* pp. 80–81. Activists were not the only critics of the sickness funds; commercial insurers saw them as amateurish and unable to cope with malingering and fraud. James, *Metropolitan Life,* p. 253. On ineptitude see Hoffman, *Wages,* p. 22.
41. Klein, *For All These Rights,* p. 14; Quadagno, *One Nation,* p. 19. Lubove, *Struggle,* p. 2. See also Gordon, *Dead on Arrival,* pp. 47–57.
42. Demsetz, "Information," p. 1 (Demsetz was debating Kenneth Arrow about health insurance); Levine, *Poverty and Society,* p. 179; Kaufman, *For the Common Good,* p. 157 (agreeing with Levine); Hacker, *Divided Welfare State,* pp. 191–196; Skocpol, *Protecting Soldiers,* pp. 253–254. On contemporary claims of lack of public interest in compulsory insurance, see Hoffman, *Facts and Fallacies,* p. 87; Ohio Health and Old Age Insurance Commission, *Health* p. 439.
43. Skocpol, *Protecting Soldiers,* pp. 281–284, citing Royal Meeker and Henry Seager. Meeker was a proponent of government insurance who nonetheless acknowledged that widespread corruption was an obstacle to further government action. See also State of Illinois, *Report,* p. 166; Koch, "Industrial Accident and Health Insurance," p. 142; Gompers, "Labor vs. Its Barnacles," p. 269.
44. Beito, *From Mutual Aid to the Welfare State;* Emery and Emery, *Young Man's Benefit;* Whaples and Buffum, "Fraternalism"; Dobbin, "Origins."
45. Skocpol, *Protecting Soldiers.*

CHAPTER 3. PROGRESSIVE IDEALS

1. Regarding Britain and Germany see State of Connecticut, *Report,* p. 7; Lambert, "Medical Organization," p. 49; Rubinow, "Health Insurance," p. 76; Numbers, *Almost Persuaded,* p. 25; Moss, *Socializing Security,* pp. 138–139; Walker, "Compulsory Health Insurance," p. 294. For Progressives' hope of replicating such funds see Dawson, "Principles," p. 116. For declining mortality in Germany see Fisher, "Need," p. 17; Rubinow, "Sickness Insurance," p. 168; "Attitude of Medical Society of the State of New York"; Hoffman, *Facts and Fallacies,* pp. 42, 51–52. Research has found that expansion of European health insurance coverage was associated with more rapid declines in mortality rates: Winegarden and Murray, "Contributions." On Fisher's exaggeration, see Chapter 11.
2. The literature about European social insurance in general, and sickness insurance in particular, is enormous. General works include Baldwin, *Politics;* Mitchell, *Divided Path;* Rodgers, *Atlantic Crossings;* Köhler et al., *Evolution;* Levine, *Poverty and Society.* Older but useful works include U.S. Commissioner of Labor, *Twenty-fourth Annual Report;* Frankel and Dawson, *Workingmen's Insurance.*
3. Further literature concerning France includes Mitchell, "Function and Malfunction"; Dreyfus, "Mutual Benefit Societies"; Dutton, *Origins;* Herzlich, "Evolution." On Belgium see Schepers, "Belgian Medical Profession."
4. Gibbon, *Medical Benefit,* pp. 10–12. More recent work concerning Scandinavian health insurance includes Henrekson and Persson, "Effects of Sick Leave."
5. Other works about Germany include Frevert, "Professional Medicine," and Spree, *Health and Social Class;* for a more recent work see Khoudour-Castéras, "Welfare State."
6. For the two-thirds figure see Riley, *Sick, Not Dead,* pp. 28–30. For the tax see Harris, *Origins,* p. 163. See more generally Fox, *Health Policies.*
7. One obvious discrepancy appears in the German data, in which the total amount of sick pay divided by the number of sick days converted to only twenty-nine cents, whereas German workers earned about the equivalent of a dollar per day. The problem is that the statutory minimum for sick pay in the German system was 50 percent. The gap could be due to high rates of sickness in low-paying jobs. Regarding opponents see Curtis, "Economic Disadvantages," p. 23.
8. American Association for Labor Legislation, "Brief," pp. 203, 205, 219–220; Rubinow, *Social Insurance,* p. 285.
9. The American figure refers only to workers with medical benefits.
10. Ohio Health and Old Age Insurance Commission, *Health,* p. 167; on sickness absence rates, see table 4.1 in this book.
11. American Association for Labor Legislation, "Brief," p. 229; Lubove, *Struggle,* pp. 75–76.
12. For the United States see U.S. Commissioner of Labor, *Twenty-third Annual*

Report, table XI; Emmet, "Operation." For other countries see U.S. Commissioner of Labor, *Twenty-fourth Annual Report,* pp. 279, 486, 619, 781, 1230. Danish funds broke out transportation costs and counted them under physician expenditures. American Association for Labor Legislation, "Brief," p. 213.

13. Regarding trivial complaints see Gibbon, *Medical Benefit,* p. 64. For Denmark see U.S. Commissioner of Labor, *Twenty-fourth Annual Report,* p. 617. Ito, "Health Insurance."
14. Hoffman, *Facts and Fallacies,* p. 31; State of Connecticut, *Report,* p. 11.
15. Ohio Health and Old Age Insurance Commission, *Health,* p. 172 ("actual duration"). For evidence that actual duration of sickness was not constant see Goldmann and Grotjahn, *Benefits,* p. 61.
16. For the quotation see Rubinow, "Prevention," p. 367. To be precise, the number of days missed per worker-year in German compulsory funds increased from 5.37 in 1888 to 7.12 in 1903. The growing share of funds that offered more than thirteen weeks' benefits could account for (two days' duration × 38% of members making claims × 5% increase in funds) / 1.75-day increase = 2% of the increase in days missed per workers. Elsewhere ("Worker Absenteeism," p. 191) I estimate that increasing sick pay explained 26 percent of the overall increase in absenteeism. In addition, the share of funds offering more than twenty-six weeks' worth of benefits fell by one-half between 1885 and 1903: Murray, "Social Insurance Claims," pp. 242–243; U.S. Commissioner of Labor, *Twenty-fourth Annual Report,* pp. 1242, 1267. It is interesting to speculate whether Rubinow knew about the actuarial argument. He had written much of the *Twenty-fourth Annual Report,* in which the Leipzig actuaries' results appeared. Although his primary responsibility concerned other chapters, he had consulted closely enough with the author of the section about Germany that he claimed "first-hand knowledge" (Rubinow, *Social Insurance,* p. v) of its contents. If so, it suggests that Progressives as well as their opponents could be criticized for misrepresentation.
17. Mitchell, *Divided Path,* p. 246.
18. Few workers exercised their right to be reexamined. For example, in Königsberg in 1909, 15 of 2,635 second examinations were performed at the worker's request. Gibbon, *Medical Benefit,* pp. 111–118.
19. Lewinski-Corwin, "Medical Aspects," p. 340. Rubinow, *Quest,* p. 209; Numbers, *Almost Persuaded,* pp. 37–38; Hoffman, *Wages,* pp. 68–70. American Association for Labor Legislation, "Tentative Draft," pp. 244, 248.
20. On theory and evidence of the adverse selection "death spiral" see Thomasson, "Early Evidence." Concerning Austrian funds see U.S. Commissioner of Labor, *Twenty-fourth Annual Report,* pp. 233–234. For the quotation see Frankel and Dawson, *Workingmen's Insurance,* p. 208. See also Mitchell, "Function and Malfunction," p. 174.
21. U.S. Commissioner of Labor, *Twenty-fourth Annual Report,* pp. 1259–1263; the concluding quotation is from p. 1263, emphasis added. The same pattern of older membership can be seen in the voluntary association funds in Austria from 1891 to 1895, relative to all Austrian males: ibid., p. 362.

22. On examinations see Frankel and Dawson, *Workingmen's Insurance*, p. 208; Mitchell, "Function and Malfunction," p. 174. On preexisting conditions see U.S. Commissioner of Labor, *Twenty-fourth Annual Report*, pp. 594, 611, 1199.
23. Schepers, "Belgian Medical Profession"; Verbruggen, "Mutualist Movement," p. 425.
24. U.S. Commissioner of Labor, *Twenty-fourth Annual Report*, pp. 814, 1227; Zeldin, *France*, p. 299; Dreyfus, "Mutual Benefit Societies." Mitchell, "Function and Malfunction," pp. 174–179; Saint-Jours, "France," p. 121.
25. Mitchell, *Divided Path*, pp. 141, 243–246, 284. U.S. Commissioner of Labor, *Twenty-fourth Annual Report*, p. 620; Schepers, "Belgian Medical Profession"; Gibbon, *Medical Benefit*, p. 40; Herzlich, "Evolution of Relations," p. 245; Frankel and Dawson, *Workingmen's Insurance*, p. 208; Mitchell, "Function and Malfunction," 176.
26. Gibbon, *Medical Benefit*, pp. 31–32, 54, 112; Frevert, "Professional Medicine," p. 647; Mitchell, *Divided Path*, p. 141.
27. Bertillon, "Mortality and Morbidity," p. 561.
28. These terms are adapted from an idealized data set of longitudinal observations of the same group of individuals over time, and the parallel is not exact. For example, "frequency" represents not the number of claims made by an individual but the share of the group that claimed benefits. This statistic would not be able to detect whether individuals within that group of claimants made several claims each. Given the available data, however, the division of all days missed into "frequency" and duration allows further insight into the structure of claims that would be available otherwise.
29. Bynum, *Science*, pp. 132–137.
30. American Association for Labor Legislation, "Brief," p. 214–215; cf. Frevert, "Professional Medicine," p. 647.
31. Hoffman, *Facts and Fallacies*, p. 30.
32. Dawson, "Principles," p. 112.
33. A very few American funds enrolled honorary members. These seem to have been limited to men who helped with women's benefit societies. Connecticut Bureau of Labor Statistics, *Seventh Annual Report*, p. 1347.

CHAPTER 4. THE RISE OF SICKNESS FUNDS

1. This anecdote is drawn from Huyck, "Establishment Funds" (p. 86 for "simple," p. 89 for "worth to our company"). See also Reynolds, *Hudson-Mohawk*, pp. 397–402; Wiebe, *Businessmen*, pp. 210–212; Frankel and Dawson, *Workingmen's Insurance*.
2. Black, "Reluctant Paternalism," p. 130 ("justification"). Read is quoted in Health Insurance Commission of Pennsylvania, *Report*, p. 102.
3. Health Insurance Commission of Pennsylvania, *Report*, pp. 102–103; State of Connecticut, *Report*, p. 8; Commonwealth of Massachusetts, *Report*, pp. 33–34. Tone, *Business*, p. 64 (see p. 80 for "worker's health"). U.S. Department

of Labor, "Welfare Work," p. 13; NICB, *Experience,* p. 124; Dunne, *Observations,* p. 142.

4. Klein, *For All These Rights,* p. 17; Gordon, *Dead on Arrival,* p. 46; Tone, *Business,* p. 59; Hoffman, *Wages,* p. 15; Brandes, *American Welfare Capitalism,* pp. 92–97.
5. Moore employees are quoted in Tone, *Business,* p. 216. Health Insurance Commission of Pennsylvania, *Report,* pp. 102–103. The New York hospital manager is quoted in American Association for Labor Legislation, "Brief," p. 167. See also Chandler, "Sickness Benefit Funds," p. 73.
6. Warren and Sydenstricker, "Health Insurance," p. 62; Health Insurance Commission of Pennsylvania, *Report,* p. 102. Frederick Hoffman countered by branding compulsory health insurance poor relief plus a new tax to pay for it: *Facts and Fallacies,* pp. 5, 91.
7. Connecticut Bureau of Labor Statistics, *Seventh Annual Report,* p. 1313; State of Illinois, *Report,* pp. 110, 532; Commonwealth of Massachusetts, *Report,* p. 18; Derickson, *Workers' Health,* p. 61; Fisher, "Need," p. 22. Potter is quoted in Black, "Reluctant Paternalism," p. 120. NICB, "Experience," pp. 5, 15–17, 137–138.
8. Brundage, "Survey of the Work," p. 2102. NICB, *Experience,* pp. 15–17, 136–138; the quotation concerning Colorado is on p. 138. U.S. Department of the Interior, *Report on Insurance;* U.S. Commissioner of Labor, *Twenty-third Annual Report.*
9. California Social Insurance Commission, *Report,* p. 297; see also Johansson, "Health Transition." For further discussion of definitions of sickness see Murray, "Social Insurance Claims."
10. California Social Insurance Commission, *Report,* p. 297.
11. U.S. Department of Health and Human Services, "Summary Health Statistics," Vital and Health Statistics, ser. 10.
12. Commission on Industrial Relations, *Final Report,* p. 202. California Social Insurance Commission, *Report,* p. 121; Lapp, "Insurance of Thrift"; Bradford, "Industrial Unemployment," p. 32; Lapp, "Health Insurance," p. 939. Even some opponents of government insurance used the figure: Curtis, "Economic Disadvantages." Other opponents charged the commission with guesswork: Hoffman, *Facts and Fallacies,* p. 88. Rubinow, "Sickness Insurance," p. 164, claimed that the rate was ten days per year and in *Social Insurance,* p. 222, gave a high-end estimate of fourteen days, but again, with no supporting evidence.
13. Murray, "Worker Absenteeism," p. 180; Meeker, "Improving Health"; Keelor, "Sickness Insurance," pp. 127–130; State of Connecticut, *Report,* pp. 40–41; Hoffman, *Facts and Fallacies,* pp. 7–10; Bynum, *Science.*
14. Commons et al., *History of Labour,* 1:82–85, 124–125; Munts, *Bargaining for Health,* pp. 3–5.
15. Terris, "Early System."
16. Munts, *Bargaining for Health,* pp. 3–5; Kennedy, *Beneficiary Features,* p. 73; Commons et al., *History of Labour,* 2:314.

17. Keelor, "Sickness Insurance," pp. 120–122.
18. Koch, "Industrial Accident," pp. 135–142. The unattributed quotation in State of Illinois, *Report*, p. 520, could well have come from Koch; see also Klein, *For All These Rights*, pp. 16–52, which considers group health as well as group life insurance.
19. U.S. Commissioner of Labor, *Twenty-third Annual Report*, pp. 387–603.
20. Many early twentieth-century investigators complained about the lack of systematic information about insurance coverage. See California Social Insurance Commission, *Report*, p. 297; Koch, "Industrial Insurance," p. 135; Health Insurance Commission of Pennsylvania, *Report*, p. 43; Rubinow, "Sickness Insurance," p. 165; New York Factory Investigating Committee, *Fourth Report*, p. 1666; Meeker, "Social Insurance," p. 24. U.S. Department of the Interior, *Report on Insurance*. Rubinow, *Social Insurance*, pp. 282–283.
21. U.S. Department of the Interior, *Report on Insurance;* Beito, *From Mutual Aid to the Welfare State*, p. 113.
22. Regarding sickness funds, Lubove claimed that "little was accomplished before the 1890's," but he apparently was unaware of this document: *Struggle*, p. 10. On lack of medical benefits see Warren and Sydenstricker, "Health Insurance," p. 52; State of Illinois, *Report*, p. 117 (on labor union funds); Health Insurance Commission of Pennsylvania, *Report*, p. 34; Ohio Health and Old Age Insurance Commission, *Health*, p. 156. Historians have concurred: Hacker, *Divided Welfare State*, p. 192 (on "medical insurance").
23. Lubove, *Struggle*, p. 12.
24. California Social Insurance Commission, *Report*, p. 84; Skocpol, *Protecting Soldiers*, p. 208. Lubove, *Struggle*, pp. 16–18. U.S. Commissioner of Labor, *Twenty-Third Annual Report*, pp. 23–267. The number of members of the national unions with benefit programs was not reported.
25. For example, Whaples and Buffum, "Fraternalism," examined benefit society membership among Michigan furniture workers in 1889.
26. The results of these surveys have been digitized by the Historical Labor Statistics Project of the University of California and are available at www.eh.net/databases/labor.

    Three surveys reported three responses—"yes," "no," and "no response"—to the question of benefit society membership. The figure shows average membership rates in each of two ways for those surveys. The solid blocks for California and Kansas workers assume that workers who did not answer the question did not have insurance; the open blocks ignore the nonresponses. Thus in the case of the greatest discrepancy for California in 1892, 1,041 respondents said they belonged to a benefit society, 1,542 said they did not, and 1,002 did not answer the question. The open block shows 1,041/(1,041 + 1,542) = 40.3 percent, and the solid block shows 1,041/(1,041 + 1,542 + 1,002) = 29.0 percent.
27. Cummings, *Report;* State of Connecticut, *Seventh Annual Report*, p. 595.

28. Cummings, *Report,* p. 482; Bemis, "Benefit Features," p. 397; Lee et al., *Population Redistribution,* p. 610.
29. Sydenstricker, "Existing Agencies," p. 469; Rubinow, *Social Insurance,* pp. 223, 286, 292; Lapp, "Health Insurance," p. 942.
30. Lubove, *Struggle,* pp. 74–75; Numbers, *Almost Persuaded,* p. 6; Starr, *Social Transformation,* p. 242; California Social Insurance Commission, *Report,* p. 88; State of Illinois, *Report,* p. 146; Ohio Old Age and Health Insurance Commission, *Health,* pp. 120–121; Health Insurance Commission of Pennsylvania, *Report,* pp. 34, 158.
31. Rubinow, "Social Insurance," p. 165; Fisher, "Need," p. 13; Rubinow, *Social Insurance,* pp. 281–296.
32. Health Insurance Commission of Pennsylvania, *Report,* p. 158. An informal survey of thirty-six large sickness funds in New York City that excluded the "thousands of petty health insurance funds" estimated that those funds alone enrolled 170,000 workers as of June 1914: Kalet, "Voluntary Health Insurance."
33. Rubinow, *Quest,* pp. 551–552; Starr, *Social Transformation,* pp. 239–241; Gress et al., "Social Transformation," p. 685. Even in those days Progressives thought that private funds laid the groundwork for public insurance: Rubinow, *Social Insurance,* p. 281.
34. Rubinow (*Quest,* pp. 207–208) admitted later that one reason for the AALL's optimism regarding public support for government insurance was that so many people were already familiar with health insurance from private sources. U.S. Bureau of the Census, *Historical Statistics,* ser. A-7; Gress et al., "Social Transformation," p. 683; Starr, *Social Transformation,* p. 240.

CHAPTER 5. HOW ESTABLISHMENT FUNDS WORKED

1. U.S. Commissioner of Labor, *Twenty-third Annual Report.*
2. Klein, *For All These Rights,* p. 17; Gordon, *Dead on Arrival,* p. 46. For "coercive" see Tone, *Business,* p. 59. Hoffman, *Wages,* p. 15; Brandes, *American Welfare Capitalism,* pp. 92–97.
3. U.S. Commissioner of Labor, *Twenty-third Annual Report,* p. 394; Emmet, "Operation," p. 19. NICB, *Experience,* p. 18, also noted laws against compulsion in Michigan, New York, Ohio, New Jersey, Connecticut, and Oregon. American Association for Labor Legislation, "Brief," p. 197–198. One legal scholar recommended compulsion for railroad workers: McKinney, *Treatise,* pp. 333–337. See also U.S. Commissioner of Labor, *Twenty-third Annual Report,* pp. 749–787, and in particular pp. 758 and 791 (Indiana), 779 (Michigan), 780–781 (New Jersey), and 781–782 (Ohio).
4. Eastman, *Work-Accidents,* pp. 202–203; Black, "Reluctant Paternalism," p. 129; NICB, *Experience* (for the Indiana quotation see p. 19; for Chicago and New York see p. 21). Compare Thomasson, "Early Evidence." Chandler, "Sickness Benefit Funds," p. 81; Hoffman, *Wages,* pp. 92, 101. For more on

contemporary views of malingering, see Ohio Health and Old Age Insurance Commission, *Health,* pp. 171–173.

5. On productivity see Tone, *Business,* p. 64; U.S. Department of Labor, "Welfare Work," p. 13; NICB, *Experience,* p. 124. On detesting charity see Chandler, "Sickness Benefit Funds," p. 73. On mobility see Fishback, "Operations"; Fishback, *Soft Coal.*
6. One well-informed researcher, Boris Emmet, claimed that company officials and employees alike were equally incompetent at the insurance business: Ohio Health and Old Age Insurance Commission, *Health,* p. 442. American Association for Labor Legislation, "Brief," p. 197 ("in some cases"). For worker management as the odd arrangement see U.S. Commissioner of Labor, *Twenty-third Annual Report,* p. 394. NICB, *Experience,* pp. 98–104.
7. Warren and Sydenstricker, "Health Insurance," p. 56.
8. American Association for Labor Legislation, "Brief," p. 229; Rubinow, *Social Insurance,* pp. 10–12, 284–286, 297.
9. U.S. Commissioner of Labor, *Twenty-third Annual Report,* p. 399; Emmet, "Operations," p. 20; Sydenstricker, "Existing Agencies," p. 456. On in-kind donations see NICB, *Experience,* pp. 96–97.
10. U.S. Commissioner of Labor, *Twenty-third Annual Report,* pp. 554–559; Derickson, *Workers' Health,* pp. 69–70. Derickson notes (p. 65) that unions that used entertainments to fund benefit operations hoped to bring in money from nonmembers. Byington, *Homestead,* p. 163. Beito, *From Mutual Aid to the Welfare State,* pp. 11, 27–31, 59–62.
11. NICB, *Experience,* pp. 4, 87–90, 144–146. Compare Tone, *Business,* p. 59; Klein, *For All These Rights,* p. 17.
12. For the view of membership restrictions as objectionable, see Sydenstricker, "Existing Agencies," pp. 453, 471; Henderson, *Industrial Insurance,* p. 80; Hoffman, *Wages,* pp. 10, 15; Gordon, *Dead on Arrival,* p. 46. On preexisting conditions see NICB, *Experience,* p. 122. U.S. Commissioner of Labor, *Twenty-third Annual Report,* p. 395; compare the recommended limit in France of forty years (pp. 52–53, above.)
13. Hoffman, *Wages,* p. 15, 138–150 (on the moral hazard of pregnancy). Lee et al., *Population Redistribution,* p. 609. U.S. Commissioner of Labor, *Twenty-third Annual Report,* pp. 429–439, 522–537 (see p. 732 for the Women Clerks' Benefits Association quotation). As late as 1960 an actuary could write, "Most insurers agree that expenses of normal childbirth cannot be efficiently covered by insurance" (Angle, "Premium Rates," p. 383.)
14. Hoffman, *Wages,* p. 16. Connecticut Bureau of Labor Statistics, *Seventh Annual Report,* pp. 118–119.U.S. Commissioner of Labor, *Twenty-third Annual Report,* p. 396. NICB, *Experience,* p. 26.
15. Henderson, *Industrial Insurance,* pp. 80, 210. See also Rubinow, *Social Insurance,* p. 223.
16. U.S. Commissioner of Labor, *Twenty-third Annual Report,* p. 393. Emmet,

"Operations," p. 221. Ohio Health and Old Age Insurance Commission, *Health,* p. 157. Cunningham and Cunningham, *The Blues,* p. 5.

17. Lubove, *Struggle,* p. 20. Riley, *Sick, Not Dead,* pp. 118, 147–150. Emery, "Risky Business?"; Emery and Emery, *Young Man's Benefit,* pp. 64–85.
18. U.S. Commissioner of Labor, *Twenty-third Annual Report,* pp. 413–416. Numbers reported a two-week waiting period for fraternals: *Almost Persuaded,* p. 6. Emery and Emery, *Young Man's Benefit,* p. 56, report that many Canadian fraternals paid after a one-week waiting period.
19. Morris, "Group Life Insurance," p. 152; NICB, *Experience,* pp. 44–49, 59.
20. U.S. Commissioner of Labor, *Twenty-third Annual Report,* pp. 398–399; NICB, *Experience,* pp. 71–74.
21. U.S. Commissioner of Labor, *Twenty-third Annual Report,* p. 399; NICB, *Experience,* p. 71.
22. U.S. Commissioner of Labor, *Twenty-third Annual Report,* pp. 399, 406, 448–487.
23. Beito, *From Mutual Aid to the Welfare State,* pp. 109–129. The statistics are found in Starr, *Social Transformation,* pp. 206–209; Numbers, *Almost Persuaded,* pp. 39–42; on English contract practice, see Riley, *Sick, Not Dead,* pp. 45–74.
24. For the Progressive argument see Warren and Sydenstricker, "Health Insurance," p. 52. U.S. Commissioner of Labor, *Twenty-third Annual Report,* pp. 488–507; Emmet, "Operations"; NICB, *Experience,* p. 117.
25. Starr, *Social Transformation,* pp. 134–140, 156–157; Bynum, *Science,* pp. 132–137, 173–175. Song and Nguyen, "Effect of Hernias."
26. Warner, *Therapeutic Perspective;* Bynum, *Science.* Henderson is quoted in Bynum, "Nature's Helping Hand," p. 21. Lewis Thomas's memoirs of life as a medical student emphasized physicians' frustration at the lack of efficacious therapies as late as the 1930s: "[W]e didn't know much that was really useful" (*Youngest Science,* pp. 26–35; the quotation is on p. 28). This viewpoint changed dramatically with the introduction of sulfonamides later in the 1930s. Shorter, "Primary Care," p. 136.
27. Incentives facing a lodge physician, who received a capitation payment of a couple of dollars or so for every member of a fraternal society, differed. Like fund physicians, a lodge physician was contractually obligated to see enrolled patients when they believed they might be sick, but unlike fund physicians he needed to keep lodge members happy in order to get his contract renewed. Beito, *From Mutual Aid to the Welfare State,* pp. 109–129. Many fraternals offered medical benefits, which often provided the only way members of the lower working class could afford to see a physician. Kalet, "Voluntary Health Insurance," found that twelve of fourteen New York City fraternals, which all together covered more than one hundred thousand members, included these benefits. Starr, *Social Transformation,* pp. 200–209. Sydenstricker, "Existing Agencies," pp. 435–436, 459, 471–473. Chandler, "Sickness Benefit Funds," p. 75; American Association for Labor Legislation, "Brief," pp. 198–199.

28. For simplicity, the formula to convert logit coefficients to changes in probability was $\delta P/\delta X = \beta^*(P^*(1-P))$ where $P = P(Y = 1)$, Y being the dependent variable and X the independent variable of interest. See Allison, *Logistic Regression,* p. 30.

    The significance of the probationary period coefficients suggests that it was intended to screen out bad health risks; the longer it took to join the fund, the more likely that membership included medical benefits.
29. If premiums cost about 10 percent more than the expected value of benefits, that figure would be consistent with estimates of administrative costs of funds at around 10 percent or so of income; see Chapter 3.
30. Warren and Sydenstricker, "Health Insurance," p. 52; see also Rubinow, *Social Insurance,* p. 7; American Association for Labor Legislation, "Brief," p. 229. U.S. Commissioner of Labor, *Twenty-fourth Annual Report,* pp. 1237–1239.
31. Commons and Altmeyer, "Health Insurance," p. 296. Warren and Sydenstricker, "Health Insurance," p. 54. Numbers, *Almost Persuaded,* p. 26.
32. Tone, *Business,* p. 59. NICB, *Experience,* pp. 77–82 (for "operat[ing] a collection agency" see p. 79). U.S. Commissioner of Labor, *Twenty-third Annual Report,* p. 406.
33. Compare Fishback, "Operations" and *Soft Coal* on the effects of such market forces in other areas of worker life.
34. NICB, *Experience,* pp. 40–41, 87.
35. Compare the similar case of housing in company towns offered by bituminous coal mining firms in Fishback, *Soft Coal,* pp. 152–166. NICB, *Experience,* pp. 39–44; the quotation is on p. 39. Tone, *Business,* pp. 200–225.
36. U.S. Commissioner of Labor, *Twenty-third Annual Report,* pp. 522–537. Sydenstricker, "Existing Agencies," p. 453.
37. This interpretation is consistent with the results shown in Chapter 3 for European voluntary funds as well as the results shown in Chapter 8 for duration of illnesses.
38. This is roughly consistent with Starr's interpretation in *Social Transformation,* pp. 202–203.

CHAPTER 6. HOW LABOR UNION FUNDS WORKED

1. Derickson, " 'Take Health from the List of Luxuries.' "
2. Derickson, *Workers' Health,* especially pp. 57–85, is an admirable exception that documents the struggles and achievements of the Western miners' sickness funds. He notes the lack of interest on the part of historians in union sick funds on p. xi. Lubove, *Struggle,* p. 16. Gordon, *Dead on Arrival,* p. 54 ("actuarial dilemmas"); Skocpol, *Protecting Soldiers,* p. 208. For the idea that union funds were financially unstable, see State of Illinois, *Report,* p. 109; Robbins, "Trade Union Benefits."
3. Gompers, *Labor,* p. 149. Fink, "Rejection of Voluntarism"; Hoffman, *Wages,* p. 118.

4. Green, "Trade Union Sick Funds," p. 91. Newman is quoted in Derickson, "'Take Health from the List of Luxuries,'" p. 176; Hoffman, *Wages,* p. 118.
5. Derickson, *Workers' Health,* p. 64. Lynch, "Trade Union Sickness Insurance," p. 82. Ott is quoted in Ohio Health and Old Age Insurance Commission, *Health,* pp. 422–423.
6. U.S. Commissioner of Labor, *Twenty-third Annual Report,* pp. 184–189. Hoffman, *Wages,* pp. 125–126; Hamilton, "Trade Unions," p. 123.
7. Munts, *Bargaining for Health,* pp. 3–5; Derickson, *Workers' Health,* p. 64.
8. Kennedy, *Beneficiary Features,* p. 72. Lynch, "Trade Union," p. 86. U.S. Commissioner of Labor, *Twenty-third Annual Report,* p. 203. Kalet, "Voluntary Health Insurance." Ohio Health and Old Age Insurance Commission, *Health,* pp. 120–121; California Social Insurance Commission, *Report,* pp. 96–100; State of Illinois, *Report,* pp. 115–116. Rubinow, *Social Insurance,* p. 292, estimated union coverage at nearly a half-million workers. The American Association for Labor Legislation "Brief," pp. 184–185 proposed that slightly more than one-half million workers were covered through nationals and internationals in 1914–1915, with an unspecified number of workers eligible for benefits through their locals. For historians' views of limited union fund coverage, see Hoffman, *Wages,* pp. 14–15; Gordon, *Dead on Arrival,* pp. 52–54.
9. Kennedy, *Beneficiary Features,* pp. 17–18.
10. Lynch, "Trade Union," pp. 87–88.
11. U.S. Commissioner of Labor, *Twenty-third Annual Report,* pp. 201–211. On the iron molders see Kennedy, *Beneficiary Features,* p. 82.
12. Robinson, *Amalgamated Association,* p. 80.
13. Lubove, *Struggle,* pp. 73–74. Skemp is quoted in Hoffman, *Wages,* p. 125. U.S. Commissioner of Labor, *Twenty-third Annual Report,* p. 410.
14. Skemp is quoted in Hoffman, *Wages,* p. 125. U.S. Commissioner of Labor, *Twenty-third Annual Report,* pp. 141–143, 208–209. NICB, *Experience,* p. 110.
15. Robinson, *Amalgamated Association,* p. 84.
16. Details are in Carter et al., "Codebook and User's Manual: A Survey of 6,051 Male Railway Employees in Michigan, 1893."
17. Michigan, *Thirteenth Annual Report,* p. 232–233.
18. According to Hoffman, *Wages,* p. 102, workers used sickness and strike benefits as substitutes, though this does not seem to have occurred in Michigan. She also wrote that they used unemployment and sickness benefits as substitutes, which might have been the case.
19. U.S. Commissioner of Labor, *Twenty-third Annual Report,* pp. 234–267. On criticism of benefit levels see Rosner and Markowitz, "Struggle over Employee Benefits," p. 54; Lubove, *Struggle,* p. 17; Rubinow, *Social Insurance,* p. 285.
20. Kalet, "Voluntary Health Insurance." Sydenstricker, "Existing Agencies," p. 465.
21. On the Carpenters and Joiners see U.S. Commissioner of Labor, *Twenty-third Annual Report,* pp. 67–69; Bemis, "Benefit Features," p. 365; Kennedy, *Bene-*

ficiary Features, p. 73. On comparability of union and fraternal sickness insurance more generally, see Kaufman, *For the Common Good,* p. 106. On the Tunnel and Subway Constructors see Hoffman, *Wages,* p. 125.

22. Hoffman, *Facts and Fallacies,* p. 32; see also State of Connecticut, *Report,* p. 11. Murray, "Worker Absenteeism," p. 187, found this relationship among voluntary funds only. A detailed study of this topic in the United Kingdom in the 1920s and 1930s is Whitehead, "Counting the Cost."
23. Ashton, "Relation," p. 398. Riley, *Sick, Not Dead,* pp. 142–143.
24. Ohio Health and Old Age Insurance Commission, *Health,* p. 442. State of Illinois, *Report,* p. 117; cf. p. 166.
25. Kennedy, *Beneficiary Features;* Bemis, "Benefit Features."
26. Bemis, "Benefit Features," p. 386; see also Kennedy, *Beneficiary Features;* U.S. Commissioner of Labor, *Twenty-third Annual Report,* pp. 182–184; Emmet, "Operations."
27. Rosner and Markowitz, "Struggle over Employee Benefits," p. 54.
28. Bemis, "Benefit Features," pp. 391, 395. Lynch, "Trade Union," p. 89.
29. NICB, *Experience,* pp. 45, 59, 75–77. Emery, "Risky Business?"
30. California Social Insurance Commission, *Report,* p. 84; State of Illinois, *Report,* pp. 115 (for "few could not pay" see p. 166).
31. Kennedy, *Beneficiary Features,* p. 81.
32. Tone, *Business,* p. 80. Green is quoted in Derickson, " 'Take Health from the List of Luxuries,' " p. 177.
33. Lynch, "Trade Union," p. 90. Bemis, "Benefit Features," p. 397. Munts, *Bargaining,* p. 5. Lubove, *Struggle,* p. 16.

CHAPTER 7. WORKERS' DECISIONS TO SAVE OR BUY INSURANCE

1. Williamson, "Evolution."
2. Broadberry, "How Did the United States and Germany Overtake Britain?" Atack, Bateman, and Margo, "Skill Intensity."
3. On migration see Ferrie, *Yankeys Now.* On labor exchanges see Rosenbloom, *Looking for Work,* pp. 46–79. On rates of job leaving see Brissenden and Frankel, "Mobility of Labor."
4. Jacoby and Sharma, "Employment Duration," pp. 173–174. James and Thomas, "A Golden Age?"
5. Fisher, "Need for Health Insurance," p. 21. On independence see Lapp, "Health Insurance." Hoffman, *Facts and Fallacies,* p. 6. The quotation is from State of Illinois, *Report,* p. 165. For a similar view see Health Insurance Commission of Pennsylvania, *Report,* p. 125. Note also I. M. Rubinow's assessment of such claims in Chapter 11 below.
6. Commission on Industrial Relations, *Final Report,* pp. 202–207. Warren and Sydenstricker, "Health Insurance," p. 36. As Chapter 4 noted, most estimates at this time found that on average a worker lost six to seven workdays per year.

7. Ohio Health and Old Age Insurance Commission, *Health,* pp. 55–57. American Association for Labor Legislation, "Brief," p. 155. For the figure of $800 million see Rubinow, *Social Insurance,* 212–214.
8. U.S. Bureau of the Census, *Historical Statistics,* sers. D 778, E 135. Rubinow, *Social Insurance,* pp. 28–41.
9. For the idea that medical expenses were large and unexpected, see Hoffman, *Wages,* p. 8; Numbers, *Almost Persuaded,* p. 10; Sydenstricker, "Existing Agencies," pp. 471–472; NICB, *Experience,* p. 106. For the figure of $26.78 see U.S. Commissioner of Labor, *Eighteenth Annual Report,* pp. 505, 509. New York Factory Investigating Committee, *Fourth Report,* p. 1666. Chapin, *Standard of Living,* p. 70. Ohio Health and Old Age Insurance Commission, *Health,* pp. 114–117.
10. Lambert, "Medical Organization," p. 28. Cheney, "Compulsory Health Insurance," pp. 493–494; Keynes, *General Theory,* pp. 210–213, 367–368; Rubinow, *Social Insurance,* pp. 9, 30–41. See also Health Insurance Commission of Pennsylvania, *Report,* p. 126. Lapp, "Insurance of Thrift," p. 32.
11. Ohio Health and Old Age Insurance Commission, *Health,* pp. 62–63; Health Insurance Commission of Pennsylvania, *Report,* pp. 112–113. See also Lapp, "Health Insurance," on the prevalence of chattel loans to pay sickness expenses.
12. See Commission on Industrial Relations, *Final Report,* p. 203; American Association for Labor Legislation, "Brief for Health Insurance," pp. 176–180 (for the article see p. 176); Ohio Health and Old Age Insurance Commission, *Health,* p. 58; Health Insurance Commission of Pennsylvania, *Report,* p. 126; Lapp, "Insurance of Thrift." On historians see Hoffman, *Wages,* p. 7; Lubove, *Struggle,* pp. 36–37 (summarizing Rubinow); Moss, *Socializing Security,* p. 137. From the period immediately following the Progressive defeats, see also Williams, *Purchase of Medical Care,* p. 37.
13. On the efficiency of turn-of-the-century labor markets, see Fishback, "Operations."
14. Hubbard et al., "Precautionary Saving"; see also Gruber and Yelowitz, "Public Health Insurance." For a contrary view, see Starr-McCluer, "Health Insurance."
15. Kantor and Fishback, "Precautionary Saving." Their data source was the 1917–1919 U.S. Bureau of Labor Statistics Cost of Living Survey, which did not directly ask about savings. Palumbo, "Estimating."
16. Palumbo, "Estimating," p. 75. Whaples and Buffum, "Fraternalism." Emery and Emery, *Young Man's Benefit,* pp. 102–116.
17. Levin, "Demand for Health Insurance," pp. 362, 365.
18. The samples are described more fully in Carter et al., "Codebook and User's Manual . . . Industries of Detroit, 1890" and "Codebook and User's Manual . . . Outside of Detroit, 1890." See also Appendix A.
19. Note that the California labor survey examined in Chapter 8 did ask specifically about the number of days missed due to sickness but failed to ask about savings. See Carter et al., "Codebook and User's Manual . . . California,

1892." Likewise, surveys of Kansas workers that included questions about lost work time asked whether workers had saved anything but did not ask the amount. The Michigan surveys were the only digitized state labor bureau surveys that could address the question of health insurance and savings.

20. Whaples and Buffum, "Fraternalism"; Palumbo, "Effects." On the complex relation between health and wealth or income, see Smith, "Healthy Bodies"; Ruhm, "Good Times"; and Lee, "Wealth Accumulation."
21. Levin, "Demand for Health Insurance."
22. I thank Herb Emery for suggesting that wealth effects, as well as savings, should be investigated.
23. Details of this sample can be found in Carter et al., "Codebook and User's Manual . . . Furniture Industry of Michigan, 1889." Jacoby and Sharma, "Employment Duration," pp. 173–174. James and Thomas, "Golden Age?"
24. U.S. Commissioner of Labor, *Twenty-third Annual Report,* p. 417.
25. Examining savings behavior as a function of age, job tenure, and benefit society membership would ordinarily call for regression analysis. Yet this chapter has established that benefit society membership was a function of savings, which indicates that there would be identification problems in conducting a regression analysis. In order to avoid them, I am falling back on simple cross-tabulations.

CHAPTER 8. WORKERS' DECISIONS TO WORK OR STAY HOME SICK

1. Plato *Republic,* bk. 3, 406c–407a.
2. This paragraph summarizes arguments made in American Association for Labor Legislation, "Brief," Rubinow, *Social Insurance,* and Warren and Sydenstricker, "Health Insurance."
3. A broad view of influences on sickness absence appears in Johansson, "Health Transition."
4. Ohio Health and Old Age Insurance Commission, *Health,* p. 160. See also Chapter 4 above. Rubinow, "Labor Insurance," p. 371. Present-day tests for the moral hazard of short-term sick benefits such as those examined here have been inconclusive. Allen, "Empirical Model," and Vistnes, "Gender Differences," found no relation between paid sick leave and absenteeism; Gilleskie, "Dynamic Stochastic Model," and Henrekson and Persson, "Effects of Sick Leave," found a strong relation between sick benefits and absence.
5. Health Insurance Commission of Pennsylvania, *Report,* p. 114.
6. State of Illinois, *Report,* p. 540; Boston Chamber of Commerce, "Non-Contributory Old Age Pensions." Hoffman, *Wages,* pp. 101–104. Rubinow, *Social Insurance,* p. 497.
7. Rubinow, *Social Insurance,* p. 496. Ohio Health and Old Age Insurance Commission, *Health,* p. 438. Lambert, "Medical Organization," p. 37
8. Ohio Health and Old Age Insurance Commission, *Health,* p. 81 (for the three examples of funds see p. 172). Warren and Sydenstricker, "Health In-

surance," pp. 27–33. Compare the quotation from Bertillon in Chapter 3, page 56, above.

9. Warren and Sydenstricker, "Health Insurance," p. 61. Ohio Health and Old Age Insurance Commission, *Health,* p. 171 (Hexter is quoted on p. 422). The New York executive is quoted in Hoffman, *Wages,* p. 104. Progressives had earlier denied the existence of compensating wage differentials for workers in risky jobs, an important point in debates about workmen's compensation: Moss, *Socializing Security,* pp. 62–63, 121–122. Fishback and Kantor present evidence of such differentials in " 'Square Deal,' " as do Kim and Fishback in "Institutional Change."
10. On malingering see Rubinow, *Social Insurance,* pp. 495–496; Warren and Sydenstricker, "Health Insurance," p. 61. American Association for Labor Legislation, "Brief," p. 220. NICB, *Experience,* p. 144. Recall Mr. Dooley's suggestion that the sick worker looked forward to absence from work even with no promise of sick pay (p. 67, above). Dunne, *Observations,* p. 142.
11. Derickson, *Workers' Health,* pp. 69–70: NICB, *Experience,* pp. 131–134, 136–144; the reference to detectives is on p. 133.
12. Dawson, "Principles," p. 112, proposed that the upward trend in German absenteeism was due not to moral hazard, strictly speaking, but to workers' following doctor's orders to take longer periods of rest. As noted below, this will not explain the American situation. The New York reformer is quoted in Kalet, "Voluntary Health Insurance," p. 148. Dunne, *Mr. Dooley Says,* p. 92.
13. NICB, *Experience,* pp. 119–120, 131–132.
14. Ohio Health and Old Age Insurance Commission, *Health,* pp. 161–162. NICB, *Experience,* p. 12. The quotation about union funds is in Sydenstricker, "Existing Agencies," p. 465.
15. Ohio Health and Old Age Insurance Commission, *Health,* pp. 118–119.
16. The quotation from Robert Hunter, *Poverty* (1904), appears in Derickson, *Health Security,* p. 4. Compare similar statements by union officials in Hoffman, *Wages,* p. 118. NICB, *Experience,* p. 135. Ohio Health and Old Age Insurance Commission, *Health,* p. 432.
17. On the New York City manufacturer see Henderson, *Industrial Insurance,* p. 209. U.S. Department of Labor, "Welfare Work," p. 13. NICB, *Experience,* pp. 136–144.
18. NICB, *Experience,* pp. 136–144.
19. See Carter et al. "Codebook and User's Manual . . . California, 1892"; Codebook and User's Manual . . . Detroit, 1890"; Codebook and User's Manual . . . Outside of Detroit, 1890"; "Codebook and User's Manual . . . Michigan, 1889." The data files they used are available at www.eh.net/databases/labor. The Michigan and California surveys are the best available for considering the relation between benefits and absenteeism. Some Kansas and Maine surveys asked about benefit society membership but not about benefit values; results from a Missouri survey that asked about benefit values were similar to those of the Michigan and California surveys but came from a small sample.
20. U.S. Commissioner of Labor, *Twenty-third Annual Report.*

21. Another potential source of absenteeism data, company personnel records, may not be very accurate. A contemporary observer claimed that firm-level absenteeism estimates were biased by the tendency of workers simply to walk off the job without giving notice. The first few days after a worker had in fact quit in this fashion were recorded as absences. Frankel, "Labor Absenteeism," p. 487. See also James and Thomas, "A Golden Age?" on short-term employment at this time, and Fishback, "Operations," and Rosenbloom, *Looking for Work,* on Progressive-Era labor markets generally.
22. There is no obvious explanation for the greater frequency of absence in each age group among Californians. Part of it may be due to differences in the questions asked in each survey. The California survey asked about absence due to sickness as part of a triplet in which the respondent was asked about "days lost by cause" including sickness, lack of work, and other. The Michigan workers were asked about "causes for loss of time" and allowed to respond in open-ended fashion. See citations in note 19 above.
23. The Aldrich Committee estimated in 1892 that the minimum annual income a working family needed to ensure a basic standard of living was $500. Chapin, *Standard of Living,* pp. 5, 246.
24. The source of the negative and significant earnings coefficient is unclear. Because furniture workers reported an odd variety of time periods over which they were paid, monthly earnings for them were computed by dividing annual earnings by twelve, whereas for the agricultural implement and iron workers, monthly earnings equaled their regular weekly wage multiplied by a factor of 4.33. The negative coefficient might have been due to better-paid workers' being less likely to absent themselves, indicating an income effect, or to greater absence resulting in more days without pay, which would have reduced earnings directly.
25. Whaples and Buffum, "Fraternalism," p. 112, found no significant relation between incidence of sickness and insurance purchases in the furniture worker sample.
26. The composition of the sample and the universe it was drawn from have been the subjects of scholarly debate, which should not affect the results derived here. The major questions involved the highly transient nature of the California workforce, which created problems for the generalization of job tenure estimates from hazard regression models. See Carter and Savoca, "Labor Mobility," and Jacoby and Sharma, "Employment Duration," both of which consider the California sample. The quotation is from Carter et al., "Codebook and User's Manual . . . California, 1892," p. 4. Costa, "Wage and Length of the Work Day." The Michigan surveys did not ask about hours per workday.
27. Men were about 10 percent less likely to report any absence than were women, consistent with present-day results reported in Vistnes, "Gender Differences."
28. On the Progressive claim see Hoffman, *Wages,* p. 8.
29. Availability of medical benefits was defined as eligibility for the following:

"doctor" (n=14), "doctor and medicines" (n=162), "doctor and burial expenses" (n=1), "expenses" (n=2), or "free hospital" (n=6).

30. U.S. Commissioner of Labor, *Twenty-third Annual Report,* p. 440, table 2, and p. 488, table 4. This survey did not report wage information, so replacement rates could not be estimated.
31. U.S. Commissioner of Labor, *Twenty-third Annual Report,* pp. 271–383. Starr, *Social Transformation,* pp. 201–202. See also Kim and Fishback, "Institutional Change"; Black, "Reluctant Paternalism."
32. NICB, *Experience,* p. 11.
33. Ibid., p. 142.
34. Murray, "Social Insurance Claims"; Gilleskie, "Dynamic Stochastic Model." Hoffman, *Wages,* p. 118; NICB, *Experience,* pp. 119–120.
35. Chapter 7 above; Thomasson, "Early Evidence." See also Gottlieb, "Asymmetric Information." In regressions not reported in this book, exclusion of the trial period variable in establishment funds (but not railroad funds) resulted in a voluntary membership parameter twice as large and far more significant. Apparently, trial periods counteracted selection problems induced by voluntary membership.
36. The types of historical sources included digitized state surveys that reported on work missed specifically due to sickness, data from a large sickness insurance society that paid benefits from the first day of sickness, the Metropolitan Life Insurance Company sickness surveys, and the survey by the Committee on the Cost of Medical Care. None attempted to collect a representative sample; all aimed to study the white working class. Rubinow, *Social Insurance,* p. 222. Regarding work time lost to a variety of causes see Rosenbloom, "Male Labor Supply."

    Costa, "Wage," used 309 workdays per year as a standard; earlier in the nineteenth century this figure was subject to seasonal variation, especially in manufacturing. See Atack et al., "Part Year Operation."

    Ohio Health and Old Age Insurance Commission, *Health,* p. 447 (testimony of H. G. Barr of National Cash Register, Dayton); a detailed analysis of NCR's benefit programs is found in Tone, *Business.* Ansley Salz reported to the federal Conference on Social Insurance that the 255 employees at his tannery missed, on average, 6.8 days per year due to illness, U.S. Department of Labor, "Proceedings," pp. 546–547. An estimate of 2.1 percent of workdays missed for the Hood Rubber Co. (1919–1921) in Massachusetts appears in Quinby, "Study." The physician Alexander Lambert, a supporter of the AALL, proposed that under government insurance the list of eligible patients whom a panel physician would be expected to serve should be limited to one thousand, which would provide a manageable average of twenty to thirty patients a day; that implied a rate of sickness of 2–3 percent: "Medical Organization," p. 40. Hoffman, "Fallacies," guessed a maximum of 3 percent and probably closer to 2 percent.
37. NICB, *Present Status,* pp. 12, 64; NICB, *Experience,* p. 117; Dobbin, "Origins of Private Social Insurance." See also Chapter 10.

38. When H. W. Kuhn made such a comparison for the Ohio commission, he considered the following differences. State insurance would include higher-risk workers, older workers, and more women and in financial terms would be administered "in a more liberal manner." He did not include any incentive effects of higher and more widespread sickness benefits. Ohio Health and Old Age Insurance Commission, *Health,* p. 81.
39. American Association for Labor Legislation, "Tentative Draft," pp. 247–249. Numbers, *Almost Persuaded.*

CHAPTER 9. INSURED WORKERS' HEALTH IN THE GREAT DEPRESSION

1. Brundage, "Sickness"; Gafafer and Fraser, "Frequency"; and Gafafer, "Sickness Absenteeism." Dublin et al., "Industrial Morbidity Statistics." An index to the series appears in *Public Health Reports* of 23 November 1951, p. 1552.
2. On Progressive-Era views regarding health and unemployment, see Ohio Health and Old Age Insurance Commission, *Health,* pp. 441–442; State of Illinois, *Report,* pp. 117, 166; Hoffman, *Facts and Fallacies,* p. 32; State of Connecticut, *Report,* p. 11; Hoffman, *Wages,* p. 102. On means testing see Sydenstricker and Perrott, "How Unemployment Affects Illness."
3. Brundage, "Sickness"; Gafafer and Fraser, "Frequency."
4. Collins and Lehmann, "Excess Deaths."
5. Compare Margo's similar findings in "Microeconomics" and Lebergott, " 'Wage Rigidity.' "
6. Diehl, "Physical Condition."
7. Ibid., p. 1617.
8. NICB, *Health Insurance Plans,* vol. A, p. 21.
9. Collins, "Cases and Days," p. 19. The actual percentages were 35.5 percent among the employed and 35.9 percent among the unemployed. Echoing earlier complaints, the same researcher also noted in regard to the committee's data collection efforts: "As compared with mortality, the paucity of sickness records is almost unbelievable." Collins, "Causes of Illness."
10. Perrott and Collins, "Relation of Sickness to Income."
11. U.S. Public Health Service, "National Health Survey." Hailman, "Prevalence of Disabling Illness," p. 28.
12. The failure of experiments in providing coverage to former employees centered on monitoring difficulties when they claimed benefits. For criticism of nonportability see American Association for Labor Legislation, "Brief," p. 198. On willingness to pay see NICB, *Experience,* p. 144. Ashton, "Relation"; Whiteside, "Counting the Cost."
13. Higgs, "Wartime Prosperity."
14. Sloan, *My Years,* p. 382.
15. Gafafer, "Absenteeism." In particular, the increase in absenteeism from 1938 onward does not support Ruhm's claim in "Good Times," p. 638, that "dramatic reductions in joblessness at the end of the great depression were ac-

companied by spuriously correlated improvements in health due to better nutrition and increased availability of antibiotics." No evidence reported in figure 9.1 or table 9.1 is consistent with improving health at the end of the Depression.

16. On the Social Security surveys see Sanders and Federman, "Prevalence of Disability," p. 8. On National Health Survey comparisons see Hailman, "Prevalence of Disabling Illness," pp. 9, 38.
17. On the struggle of the union funds see Robbins, "Trade Union Benefits"; Rosenthal, "Union-Management Welfare." Moriguchi, "Did American Welfare Capitalists Breach Their Implicit Contracts?" See also Dobbin, "Origins."

CHAPTER 10. ACTUARIAL SCIENCE AND THE DECLINE OF SICKNESS FUNDS

1. State of Illinois, *Report*, p. 140. See also Chapter 2, note 37 and references there.
2. NICB, *Health Insurance Plans*, vol. A, p. 22.
3. Klein, *For All These Rights*, pp. 16, 19; for economic historians' views of the Armstrong commission's work, see North, "Life Insurance"; Ransom and Sutch, "Tontine Insurance."
4. Yates, *Structuring the Information Age*, pp. 48–49. See also Morris, "Group Life," p. 154.
5. Mowbray, "Age, Occupation, and Residence." Hart, "Recent Developments," p. 298; Sommer, "Health Insurance," p. 181; Crane, "Commercial Accident," p. 310.
6. Keelor, "Sickness Insurance," pp. 123–124.
7. Craig, "Group Health," pp. 79–80.
8. For the quotations see King, "Accident and Health Insurance," pp. 52–53. See also James D. Craig's comments on the King paper on p. 59; Craig, "Group Health," p. 84.
9. Craig, "Group Health." For the quotation see Cammack, "Premiums and Reserves," p. 279. The Manchester Unity tables corresponded to job categories: A = agricultural; B = outdoor building trades; C = railway service; D = seafaring, fishing, and so on; E = quarry workers; F = metal, chemical, and glass works; G = mining occupations; H = all other occupations, rural; J = all other occupations, urban. See Rusher, "Statistics of Industrial Morbidity," p. 54.
10. The sickness surveys conducted by Metropolitan Life in 1915–1917 were deemed useful as descriptive devices but insufficiently detailed for use in actuarial calculations. See Mowbray, "Age, Occupation, and Residence," pp. 215–216. Dawson, "Sickness and Accident Disability Tables." Cammack, "Premiums and Reserves," p. 269.
11. Klein, *For All These Rights*, pp. 24–25.
12. For the first four quotations see Koch, "Industrial Accident and Health Insurance," pp. 138–139; State of Illinois, *Report*, pp. 140, 406.

13. Cammack, "Premiums and Reserves," p. 279; Koch, "Industrial Accident and Health Insurance," pp. 137–138. On increased premiums see Keffer, "Group Sickness and Accident Insurance," p. 17.
14. NICB, *Present Status,* p. 20. Sayers et al., "General Aspects," p. 1572. James, *Metropolitan Life,* p. 264.
15. Messenger, "Rate of Sickness." Keffer described the tables and the Aetna data in "Group Sickness and Accident Insurance"; Bassford described the Metropolitan Life tables in the discussion that followed Keffer's article on p. 264. Fitzhugh, "Recent Morbidity," pp. 355, 365. The quotation is from Craig, "Actuarial Basis," p. 54.
16. NICB, *Present Status,* p. 21; similar figures appeared in a contemporary survey by the National Conference on Mutual Benefit Associations and the Public Health Service: Brundage, "Survey," pp. 2102–2103. See also NICB, *Industrial Group Insurance,* pp. 31–34. NICB, *Effect,* p. 4.
17. U.S. Department of Labor, "Health and Recreation Activities," p. 69; Graham, "Group Insurance," pp. 41–42. See also Marshall, "Dubious Position," for a contemporary perspective. A classic article about this phenomenon in the present is Parsons, "Decline."
18. Emmet, "Operation," p. 21; NICB, *Present Status,* p. 95.
19. Smith, "Group Disability." Programs similar to those set up under the Mailler-Condon Law appeared in Rhode Island (1942), California (1946), and New Jersey (1948). Schwartz, "New York Statutory Disability Benefits Law," pp. 61–62. For a citation to the compilation see Miller and Courant, "Some Observations," p. 355. Firms contributing data included Aetna (1931–1935), Connecticut General (1935), General American (1935), Metropolitan (1931–1935), Prudential (1935), and Travelers (1931–1935); see Fitzhugh, "Recent Morbidity," p. 357. Keffer, "Group Sickness and Accident Insurance." Reinard Keelor's speculations, mentioned above (p. 222), were based on about ten thousand life years: "Sickness Insurance," p. 125.
20. Fitzhugh, "Recent Morbidity." James, *Metropolitan Life,* p. 264, reported declining premiums in the 1920s.
21. For group health characteristics see Craig, "Group Health," pp. 81–87. For establishment fund characteristics see Emmet, "Operation," pp. 18–19, and NICB, *Experience,* p. 110. Another survey of sickness funds conducted independently found a median benefit rate of between nine and eleven dollars per week but did not report on dues: Brundage, "Survey," p. 2105. For the 1931 figures see NICB, *Present Status,* pp. 70, 89, and Sayers et al., "General Aspects," pp. 1578. Unfortunately, this article reported dues, premiums, and benefit payment patterns in a way that did not enable further comparison of benefit associations and group insurance (pp. 1577–1579).
22. Rubinow, *Social Insurance,* pp. 273–275; Hoffman, *Wages,* pp. 137–150.
23. NICB, *Health Insurance Plans,* volumes A and B.
24. Dobbin, "Origins"; Graham, "Group Insurance."
25. U.S. Department of Labor, "Health and Recreation Activities," pp. 14–15. Rosenthal, "Union-Management Welfare Plans."

26. Follmann, "Development of Group Health Insurance," pp. 64–65.
27. NICB, *Industrial Group Insurance,* p. 33. NICB, *Health Insurance Plans,* volume A, p. 21.
28. U.S. Commissioner of Labor, *Twenty-third Annual Report,* p. 389; Emmet, "Operations," p. 17; U.S. Department of Labor, "Health and Recreation," p. 59; Otey, "Cash Benefits," p. 32.

CHAPTER 11. SUCCESSION IN THE FOREST OF HEALTH CARE REFORM

1. The classic description is Cowles, "Ecological Relations."
2. Fox, "Decline of Historicism," pp. 601, 609–610. Fox criticized the historicists for writing "a stirring tale of heroes and villains, the few against the many, and morality vs. greed." On the topic more broadly, see Popper, *Poverty of Historicism.*
3. Klein, *For All These Rights*; Gordon, *Dead on Arrival*; Hacker, *Divided Welfare State*; Kaufman, *For the Common Good*; Quadagno, *One Nation*; Derickson, *Health Security*; Hoffman, *Wages.*
4. Skocpol, *Protecting Soldiers,* p. 281.
5. Fisher, "Need," p. 17; Craig, "Address," pp. 135–137. Rubinow, "Public and Private Interests," pp. 185–186.
6. Fisher, "Need," p. 18. Rubinow, *Quest,* pp. 212–214.
7. Panszczyk, *1997 U.S. Master Employee Benefits Guide,* pp. 399–416.
8. Follman, "Development," p. 65. On the growth of Blue Cross, see Cunningham and Cunningham, *The Blues,* and Thomasson, "From Sickness."
9. On the commercial insurers see Klein, *For All These Rights,* pp. 16–39.
10. On the death benefit see Rubinow, *Quest,* pp. 212–213; Moss, *Socializing Security,* p. 146.
11. Likewise, commercial insurers saw fraternals as competitors in the life insurance market. Witt, "Toward a New History," p. 824.
12. Lubove, *Struggle,* 1–4.
13. Rubinow, *Quest,* p. 208. Flynn, "Effect of the War."
14. On idealization see Demsetz, "Information and Efficiency." Cawley and Simon, "Health Insurance Coverage," consider coverage and employment in the present. On moral hazard see Robbins, "Trade Union Benefits." For the British case see Whiteside, "Counting the Cost."
15. Henrekson and Persson, "Effects on Sick Leave," p. 90.
16. Zeldin, *France,* pp. 296–307, esp. p. 298. The quotation from Paul Deschanel is on p. 296.
17. Tocqueville, *Democracy,* vol. 2, pt. 2, p. 489. On union funds see Chapter 4 above. On interpersonal bonds see NICB, *Present Status,* p. 23.
18. Tocqueville, *Democracy,* vol. 2, pt. 2, p. 491. Lubove, *Struggle,* pp. 1–24; Rubinow, *Social Insurance,* pp. 232–234, 248–249, 281–283.
19. NICB, *Experience,* pp. 144–146. See also Starr, *Social Transformation,* pp. 235–237. For the Bismarck quotation see Rodgers, *Atlantic Crossings,* p. 223. For

the Addams quotation see Henderson, *Industrial Insurance,* pp. 82–83, quoting her *Newer Ideals of Peace,* p. 91.

20. For the NCR quotation see Tone, *Business,* p. 68. For the Metropolitan Life strategy see Klein, *For All These Rights,* p. 37. Parallels concerning worker allegiance to private or public patrons appear also in Alston and Ferrie, *Southern Paternalism,* especially pp. 87–88. More generally, see Hirschman, *Exit,* especially chap. 7.
21. Derickson, *Health Security,* p. x, described present arrangements as "a tragedy of human sacrifice"; see also Klein, *For All These Rights,* p. 1; Quadagno, *One Nation,* pp. 201–213. The extreme rhetoric is reminiscent of that used by physicians as the Progressive debates entered their endgame. Numbers (*Almost Persuaded,* p. 97) noted that as their victory became more certain their language became more strident, a phenomenon he called "death by hysteria." He left Rubinow's later acknowledgment of the AALL's exaggerations unmentioned.

BIBLIOGRAPHY

Allen, Steven G. "An Empirical Model of Work Attendance." *Review of Economics and Statistics* 63 (1981): 77–87.

Allison, Paul D. *Logistic Regression Using the SAS System: Theory and Application.* Cary, N.C.: SAS Institute.

Alston, Lee J., and Joseph P. Ferrie. *Southern Paternalism and the American Welfare State: Economics, Politics, and Institutions in the South, 1865–1965.* New York: Cambridge University Press, 1999.

American Association for Labor Legislation. "Brief for Health Insurance." *American Labor Legislation Review* 6 (1916): 155–236.

———. "Tentative Draft of an Act." *American Labor Legislation Review* 6 (1916): 239–268.

Anderson, Odin W. "Health Insurance in the United States, 1910–1920." *Journal of the History of Medicine and Allied Sciences* 5 (1950): 363–396.

Angle, John C. "Premium Rates." In Edwin J. Faulkner, *Health Insurance,* pp. 364–405. New York: McGraw-Hill, 1960.

Armstrong, Barbara Nachtrieb. *Insuring the Essentials: Minimum Wage Plus Social Insurance—A Living Wage Program.* New York: Macmillan, 1932.

Ashton, T. S. "The Relation Between Unemployment and Sickness." *Economic Journal* 26 (1916): 396–400.

Atack, Jeremy, Fred Bateman, and Robert A. Margo. "Part-Year Operation in Nineteenth-Century American Manufacturing: Evidence from the 1870 and 1880 Censuses." *Journal of Economic History* 62 (2002): 792–809.

———. "Skill Intensity and Rising Wage Dispersion in Nineteenth-Century American Manufacturing." *Journal of Economic History* 64 (2004): 172–192.

"Attitude of Medical Society of the State of New York Toward Compulsory Health Insurance." *Monthly Labor Review* 10 (January 1920):255–258. In Julia E.

Johnsen, comp., *Selected Articles on Social Insurance,* comp. Julia E. Johnson, pp. 223–227. New York: Wilson, 1922.

Babcock C. D. "Mystery and the Menace of Compulsory Health Insurance in the United States." *Economic World* n.s. 17:489–490, 5 April 1919. In *Selected Articles on Social Insurance,* comp. Julia E. Johnson, pp. 229–230. New York: Wilson, 1922.

Baldwin, Peter. *The Politics of Social Solidarity: Class Bases of the European Welfare State, 1875–1975.* New York: Cambridge University Press, 1990.

Bassford, H. R. "Written Discussion." *Transactions of the Actuarial Society of America* 28 (1927): 264–275.

Beito, David T. *From Mutual Aid to the Welfare State: Fraternal Societies and Social Services, 1890–1967.* Chapel Hill: University of North Carolina Press, 2000.

Bellman, Eric. "Entrepreneur Gets Big Banks to Back Very Small Loans." *Wall Street Journal,* 15 May 2006, p. A1.

Bemis, Edward W. "Benefit Features of American Trade Unions." *Bulletin of the Department of Labor* 22 (May 1899): 361–400.

Bertillon, J. "Morbidity and Mortality According to Occupation." *Journal of the Royal Statistical Society* 55 (1892): 559–600.

Bhandari, Shailesh. "Employment-Based Health Insurance 1997: Household Economic Studies." In U.S. Department of Commerce, Bureau of the Census, *Current Population Reports,* P70–81 (December 2002): 1–16.

Black, Paul V. "Reluctant Paternalism: Employee Relief Activities of the Chicago, Burlington, & Quincy Railroad in the 19th Century." *Business and Economic History* 6 (1977): 120–134.

Blumenthal, David. "Employer-Sponsored Health Insurance in the United States: Origins and Implications." *New England Journal of Medicine* 355 (6 July 2006): 82–88.

Boston Chamber of Commerce. "Non-Contributory Old Age Pensions and Health Insurance." Boston: Boston Chamber of Commerce, 1917.

Bradford, Ernest Smith. "Industrial Unemployment: A Statistical Study of Its Extent and Causes." *Bulletin of the U. S. Bureau of Labor Statistics,* no. 310. Washington, D.C.: GPO, 1922.

Brandes, Stuart D. *American Welfare Capitalism.* Chicago: University of Chicago Press, 1976.

Brissenden, Paul F., and Emil Frankel. "Mobility of Labor in American Industry." *Monthly Labor Review* 10 (June 1920): 1342–1362.

Broadberry, Stephen N. "How Did the United States and Germany Overtake Britain? A Sectoral Analysis of Comparative Productivity Levels, 1870–1990." *Journal of Economic History* 58 (1998): 375–407.

Brundage, Dean K. "Sickness Among Industrial Employees." *Public Health Reports* 45, no. 3 (January 17, 1930): 107–116.

———. "A Survey of the Work of Employees' Mutual Benefit Associations." *Public Health Reports* 46, no. 36 (September 4, 1931): 2102–2119.

Byington, Margaret F. *Homestead: The Households of a Mill Town.* New York: Russell Sage Foundation, 1910.

Bynum, W. F. "Nature's Helping Hand." *Science* 414 (2001): 21.

———. *Science and the Practice of Medicine in the Nineteenth Century.* New York: Cambridge University Press, 1994.

California Social Insurance Commission. *Report of the Social Insurance Commission of the State of California, January 25, 1917.* Sacramento: California State Printing Office, 1917.

Cammack, E. E. "Premiums and Reserves for Non-Cancellable Accident and Health Policies." *Proceedings of the Casualty Actuarial Society* 7 (1921): 267–301.

Carter, Susan B., Roger L. Ransom, Richard Sutch, Samuel H. Williamson, and Hongcheng Zhao. "Codebook and User's Manual: A Survey of 6,051 Male Railway Employees in Michigan, 1893; Reported in the Eleventh Annual Report of the Michigan Bureau of Labor and Industrial Statistics." Berkeley: Institute of Business and Economic Research, 1993.

Carter, Susan B., Roger L. Ransom, Richard Sutch, and Hongcheng Zhao. "Codebook and User's Manual: A Survey of 3,494 Wage-Earners in California, 1892." Historical Labor Statistics Project, University of California, Berkeley, 1993. Available at www.eh.net/databases/labor.

———. "Codebook and User's Manual: A Survey of 3,920 Male Workers in the Agricultural Implement and Iron Industries of Detroit, 1890; Reported in the Eighth Annual Report of the Michigan Bureau of Labor and Industrial Statistics." Berkeley: Institute of Business and Economic Research, 1993. Available at www.eh.net/databases/labor.

———. "Codebook and User's Manual: A Survey of 4,918 Male Workers in the Agricultural Implement and Iron Industries in Michigan Outside of Detroit, 1890; Reported in the Eighth Annual Report of the Michigan Bureau of Labor and Industrial Statistics." Berkeley: Institute of Business and Economic Research, 1993. Available at www.eh.net/databases/labor.

———. "Codebook and User's Manual: A Survey of 5,419 Workers in the Furniture Industry of Michigan, 1889; Reported in the Seventh Annual Report of the Michigan Bureau of Labor and Industrial Statistics." Berkeley: Institute of Business and Economic Research, 1993. Available at www.eh.net/databases/labor.

Carter, Susan B., and Elizabeth Savoca. "Labor Mobility and Lengthy Jobs in Nineteenth-Century America." *Journal of Economic History* 50 (1990): 1–16.

Cawley, John, and Kosali I. Simon. "Health Insurance Coverage and the Macroeconomy." *Journal of Health Economics* 24 (2005): 299–315.

Chandler, W. L. "Sickness Benefit Funds Among Industrial Workers." *American Labor Legislation Review* 4 (1914): 73–81.

Chapin, Robert Coit. *The Standard of Living Among Workingmen's Families in New York City.* New York: Charities Publication Committee, 1909.

Cheney, Howell. "Compulsory Health Insurance." *North American Review* 209 (1919): 490–498.

Collins, Selwyn D. "Cases and Days of Illness Among Males and Females with Special Reference to Confinement to Bed: Based on 9,000 Families Visited Periodically for 12 Months, 1928–1931." *Public Health Reports* 55, no. 2 (12 January 1940): 47–93.

———. "Causes of Illness in 9,000 Families, Based on Nationwide Periodic Canvasses, 1928–1931." *Public Health Reports* 48, no. 12 (March 24, 1933): 283–308.

———. "Economic Status and Health." Public Health Bulletin 165 (1927).

Collins, Selwyn D., and Josephine Lehmann. "Excess Deaths from Influenza and Pneumonia and from Important Chronic Diseases During Epidemic Periods, 1918–1951." Public Health Monograph no. 10 (1952).

Commission on Industrial Relations. *Final Report of the Commission on Industrial Relations.* Washington, D.C.: Barnard & Muller, 1915.

Commons, John R., and A. J. Altmeyer. "The Health Insurance Movement in the United States." In Ohio Health and Old Age Insurance Commission, *Health, Health Insurance, Old Age Pensions: Report, Recommendations, Dissenting Opinions,* pp. 287–311. Columbus: Heer, 1919.

Commons, John R., David J. Saposs, Helen L. Sumner, E. B. Mittelman, H. E. Hoagland, John B. Andrews, and Selig Perlman. *History of Labour in the United States.* New York: Macmillan, 1926.

Commonwealth of Massachusetts. *Report of the Special Commission on Social Insurance.* Boston: Wright & Potter, 1917.

Connecticut Bureau of Labor Statistics. *Seventh Annual Report of the Bureau of Labor Statistics of the State of Connecticut for the Year Ending November 30, 1891.* Hartford: Fowler & Miller, 1892.

Costa, Dora L. "Demand for Private and State Provided Health Insurance in the 1910s: Evidence from California." Photocopy, MIT, 1996.

———. *The Evolution of Retirement: An American Economic History, 1880–1990.* Chicago: University of Chicago Press, 1998.

———. "The Wage and the Length of the Work Day: From the 1890s to 1991." *Journal of Labor Economics* 18 (2000): 156–181.

Cowles, Henry Chandler. "The Ecological Relations of the Vegetation on the Sand Dunes of Lake Michigan." *Botanical Gazette* 27 (1899): 95–117, 167–202, 281–308, 361–391.

Craig, James D. "Address of the President." *Proceedings of the Casualty Actuarial Society* 3 (1917): 129–139.

———. "Actuarial Basis for Premiums and Reserves in Personal Accident and Health Insurance." *Proceedings of the Casualty Actuarial Society* 17 (1930): 51–73.

———. "Group Health Insurance." *Proceedings of the Casualty Actuarial Society* 7 (1920): 78–103.

Crane, Howard G. "Commercial Accident and Health Insurance from the Standpoint of the Reinsurance Company." *Proceedings of the Casualty Actuarial Society* 21 (1934): 303–312.

Cummings, Edward. "Report of Connecticut Labor Bureau." *Quarterly Journal of Economics* 7 (1893): 480–487.

Cunningham III, Robert and Robert M. Cunningham Jr. *The Blues: A History of the Blue Cross and Blue Shield System.* DeKalb: Northern Illinois University Press, 1997.

Curtis, William Gale. "Economic Disadvantages of Compulsory Health Insurance." *Modern City* 1 (May 1917): 23–25.

Dawson, Miles M. "Principles of Health Insurance." *American Labor Legislation Review* 7 (1917) 111–118.

———. "Sickness and Accident Disability Tables." *Transactions of the Actuarial Society of America* 17 (1916): 274–280.

Demsetz, Harold. "Information and Efficiency: Another Viewpoint." *Journal of Law and Economics* 12 (1969): 1–22.

Derickson, Alan. *Health Security for All: Dreams of Universal Health Care in America*. Baltimore: Johns Hopkins University Press, 2005.

———. " 'Take Health from the List of Luxuries': Labor and the Right to Health Care, 1915–1949." *Labor History* 41 (2000): 171–187.

———. *Workers' Health, Workers' Democracy: The Western Miners' Struggle, 1891–1925*. Ithaca: Cornell University Press, 1988.

Diehl, Harold S. "Physical Condition and Unemployment." *Public Health Reports* (November 15, 1935): 1610–1618.

Dobbin, Frank. "The Origins of Private Social Insurance: Public Policy and Fringe Benefits in America, 1920–1950." *American Journal of Sociology* 97 (1992): 1416–1450.

Dreyfus, M. "Mutual Benefit Societies in France: A Complex Endeavour." In *Social Security Mutualism: The Comparative History of Mutual Benefit Societies*, ed. M. van der Linden, pp. 209–224. Bern: Peter Lang, 1996.

Dublin, Louis I., Carl B. Auel, William A. Hathaway, George F. Tucker, and B. S. Warren. "Industrial Morbidity Statistics." *Public Health Reports* 33 (August 30, 1918): 1429–1434.

Dunne, Finley Peter. *Mr. Dooley Says*. New York: Charles Scribner's Sons, 1910.

———. *Observations by Mr. Dooley*. New York: Russell, 1902.

Dutton, Paul V. *Origins of the French Welfare State: The Struggle for Social Reform in France, 1914–1947*. New York: Cambridge University Press, 2002.

Eastman, Crystal. *Work-Accidents and the Law*. New York: Charities Publication Committee, 1910.

Elman, Cheryl, and George Myers, "Age and Sex Differentials in Morbidity at the Start of an Epidemiological Transition: Returns from the 1880 U.S. Census." *Social Science and Medicine* 45 (1997): 943–956.

Emery, George, and J. C. Herbert Emery. *A Young Man's Benefit: The Independent Order of Odd Fellows and Sickness Insurance in the United States and Canada, 1860–1929*. Montreal: McGill–Queen's University Press, 1999.

Emery, J. C. Herbert. "Risky Business? Nonactuarial Pricing Practices and the Financial Viability of Fraternal Sickness Insurers." *Explorations in Economic History* 33 (1996): 195–226.

Emmet, Boris. "Disability Among Wage Earners." *Monthly Labor Review* 9 (1919): 20–39.

———. "Operation of Establishment and Trade-Union Disability Funds." *Monthly Review of the Bureau of Labor Statistics* 5 (1917): 217–236.

Feinstein, Charles. "New Estimates of Average Earnings in the United Kingdom, 1880–1913." *Economic History Review* 43 (1990): 595–632.

Ferrie, Joseph P. *Yankeys Now: Immigrants in the Antebellum U.S., 1840–1860*. New York: Oxford University Press, 1999.

Fink, Gary M. "The Rejection of Voluntarism." *Industrial and Labor Relations Review* 26 (1973): 805–819.

Fishback, Price V. "Operations of 'Unfettered' Labor Markets: Exit and Voice in American Labor Markets at the Turn of the Century." *Journal of Economic Literature* 36 (1998): 722–765.

———. *Soft Coal, Hard Choices: The Economic Welfare of Bituminous Coal Miners, 1890–1930*. New York: Oxford University Press, 1992.

Fishback, Price V., and Shawn E. Kantor. *Prelude to the Welfare State: The Origins of Workers' Compensation*. Chicago: University of Chicago Press, 2000.

———. " 'Square Deal' or Raw Deal? Market Compensation for Workplace Disamenities, 1884–1903." *Journal of Economic History* 52 (1992): 826–848.

Fisher, Irving. "The Need for Health Insurance." *American Labor Legislation Review* 7 (1917): 9–23.

Fitzhugh, Gilbert W. "Recent Morbidity Upon Lives Insured Under Group Accident and Health Policies and Premiums Based Thereon." *Transactions of the Actuarial Society of America* 38 (1937): 354–383.

Flynn, B. D. "Effect of the War Upon the Development of Social Insurance in this Country." *Proceedings of the Casualty Actuarial Society* 6 (1920): 169–176.

Follman, J. F. "Development and Significance of Group Health Insurance." In *Group Insurance Handbook*, ed. Robert D. Eilers and Robert M. Crowe, pp. 57–84. Homewood, Ill.: Irwin, 1965.

Forman, S. E. "Cost of Industrial Insurance in the District of Columbia." *Bulletin of the Bureau of Labor* 13 (1906): 781–822.

Fox, Daniel M. "The Decline of Historicism: The Case of Compulsory Health Insurance in the United States." *Bulletin of the History of Medicine* 57 (1983): 596–610.

———. *Health Policies, Health Politics: The British and American Experience, 1911–1965*. Princeton: Princeton University Press, 1986.

Frankel, Emil. "Labor Absenteeism." *Journal of Political Economy* 29 (1921): 487–499.

Frankel, Lee K. "Comment." in U.S. Department of Labor, "Proceedings," pp. 641–644.

Frankel, Lee K., and Miles M. Dawson with the co-operation of Louis I. Dublin. *Workingmen's Insurance in Europe*. New York: Charities Publication Committee, 1911.

Frevert, Ute. "Professional Medicine and the Working Classes in Imperial Germany." *Journal of Contemporary History* 20 (1985): 637–658.

Fuhrmans, Vanessa. "Health Insurers' New Target." *Wall Street Journal*, 31 May 2005, pp. B1, B4.

Gafafer, William M. "Sickness Absenteeism Among Male and Female Industrial

Workers During 1945, with a Note on the Respiratory Epidemic of 1945–46." *Public Health Reports* (November 8, 1946): 1620–1630.

Gafafer, William M., and Elisabeth S. Frasier. "Frequency of Disabling Illness Among Industrial Employees During 1932–1937 and the First Quarter of 1938." *Public Health Reports* (September 2, 1938): 1562–1571.

Gibbon, I. G. *Medical Benefit: A Study of the Experience of Germany and Denmark.* New York: Dutton, 1913.

Gilleskie, Donna B. "A Dynamic Stochastic Model of Medical Care Use and Work Absence." *Econometrica* 66 (1998): 1–45.

Glied, Sherry A. "The Employer-Based Health Insurance System: Mistake or Cornerstone?" In *Policy Challenges in Modern Health Care,* ed. David Mechanic, Lynn B. Rogut, David C. Colby, and James R. Knickman, pp. 37–52. New Brunswick: Rutgers University Press, 2005.

Goldmann, Franz, and Alfred Grotjahn, *Benefits of the German Sickness Insurance System from the Point of View of Social Hygiene.* Geneva: International Labour Office, 1928.

Gompers, Samuel. *Labor and the Employer.* New York: Dutton, 1920.

———. "Labor vs. Its Barnacles." *American Federationist* 13 (April 1916): 268–274.

———. "Not Even Compulsory Benevolence Will Do." National Civic Federation Annual Meeting Addresses, pp. 5–10, January 22, 1917. In *Selected Articles on Social Insurance,* comp. Julia E. Johnsen, pp. 209–212. New York: Wilson, 1922.

Gordon, Colin. *Dead on Arrival: The Politics of Health Care in Twentieth-Century America.* Princeton: Princeton University Press, 2003.

Gottlieb, Daniel. "Asymmetric Information in Late 19th Century Cooperative Insurance Societies." *Explorations in Economic History* 44 (2007): 270–292.

Graham, William J., "Group Insurance." *Annals of the American Academy of Political and Social Science* 161 (1932): 40–45.

Green, William. "Trade Union Sick Funds and Compulsory Health Insurance." *American Labor Legislation Review* 7 (1917): 91–95.

Gress, Stefan, Stefan Gildemeister, and Jürgen Wasem. "The Social Transformation of American Medicine: A Comparative View from Germany." *Journal of Health Politics, Policy, and Law* 29 (2004): 681–699.

Gruber, Jonathan, and Aaron Yelowitz. "Public Health Insurance and Private Savings." *Journal of Political Economy* 107 (1999): 1249–1274.

Hacker, Jacob S. *The Divided Welfare State: The Battle Over Public and Private Social Benefits in the United States.* New York: Cambridge University Press, 2002.

. "The Historical Logic of National Health Insurance: Structure and Sequence in the Development of British, Canadian, and U.S. Medical Policy." *Studies in American Political Development* 12 (1998): 57–130.

Hailman, David E. "The Prevalence of Disabling Illness Among Male and Female Workers and Housewives." *Public Health Bulletin* no. 260 (1941).

Hamilton, Grant. "Trade Unions and Social Insurance." *American Federationist* 24 (1917): 122–125.

Harris, Bernard. *The Origins of the British Welfare State: Social Welfare in England and Wales, 1800–1945*. London: Palgrave Macmillan, 2003.

Hart, Ward Van Buren. "Recent Developments in Commercial Accident and Health Insurance." *Proceedings of the Casualty Actuarial Society* 21 (1934): 291–312.

Health Insurance Commission of Pennsylvania. *Report of the Health Insurance Commission of Pennsylvania, January 1919*. Harrisburg: Kuhn, 1919.

Henderson, Charles Richmond. *Industrial Insurance in the United States*. 2d ed. Chicago: University of Chicago Press, 1911.

Henrekson, Magnus, and Mats Persson. "The Effects on Sick Leave of Changes in the Sickness Insurance System." *Journal of Labor Economics* 22 (2004): 87–113.

Herzlich, C. "Evolution of Relations Between French Physicians and the State, 1880–1980." *Sociology of Health and Illness* 4 (1982): 241–253.

Higgs, Robert. "Wartime Prosperity? A Reassessment of the United States Economy in the 1940s." *Journal of Economic History* 52 (1992): 41–60.

Hirschman, Albert O. *Exit, Voice, and Loyalty: Responses to Decline in Firms, Organizations, and States*. Cambridge: Harvard University Press, 1970.

Hirsh, Joseph. "The Compulsory Health Insurance Movement in the United States." *Social Forces* 18 (1939): 102–114.

Hoffman, Beatrix. "Scientific Racism, Insurance, and Opposition to the Welfare State: Frederick L. Hoffman's Transatlantic Journey." *Journal of the Gilded Age and Progressive Era* (2003): 150–190.

———. *The Wages of Sickness: The Politics of Health Insurance in Progressive America*. Chapel Hill: University of North Carolina Press, 2001.

Hoffman, Frederick L. *Facts and Fallacies of Compulsory Health Insurance*. Newark, N.J.: Prudential, 1917.

———. "Some Fallacies of the Arguments for the Introduction of Social Insurance into the United States." *Economic World* n.s. 13 (February 3, 1917): 165–166.

———. "Systems of Wage-Earners' Insurance." *American Labor Legislation Review* 3 (1913): 213–228.

Hofstadter, Richard. *The Age of Reform: From Bryan to F. D. R*. New York: Vintage, 1955.

Hubbard, R. Glenn, Jonathan Skinner, and Stephen P. Zeldes. "Precautionary Saving and Social Insurance." *Journal of Political Economy* 103 (1995): 360–399.

Huyck, Edmund N. "Establishment Funds and Universal Health Insurance." *American Labor Legislation Review* 7 (1917): 85–90.

Ito, H. "Health Insurance and Medical Services in Sweden and Denmark, 1850–1950." In *The Shaping of the Swedish Health System*, ed. A. J. Heidenheimer and N. Elvander, pp. 44–67. New York: St. Martin's, 1980.

Jacoby, Sanford, and Sunil Sharma. "Employment Duration and Industrial Labor Mobility in the United States, 1880–1980." *Journal of Economic History* 52 (1992): 161 179.

James, John. and Mark Thomas. "A Golden Age? Unemployment and the American Labor Market, 1880–1910." *Journal of Economic History* 63 (2003): 959–994.

James, Marquis. *The Metropolitan Life: A Study in Business Growth.* New York: Viking, 1947.

Johansson, S. Ryan. "The Health Transition: The Cultural Inflation of Morbidity During the Decline of Mortality." *Health Transition Review* 1 (1991): 39–65.

Johnson, Rossiter, ed. *Cyclopaedia of American Biography: The Twentieth Century Biographical Dictionary of Notable Americans.* Boston: Biographical Society, 1904.

Kaiserlichen Statistischen Amt, *Statistik der Krankenversicherung der Arbeiter im Jahre xxxx,* Statistik des Deutschen Reichs, rev. ed. Vol. 38, 1889; vol. 90, 1897; vol. 96, 1898; vol. 121, 1900; vol. 170, 1904; vol. 229, 1908.

Kalet, Anna. "Voluntary Health Insurance in New York City." *American Labor Legislation Review* 6 (1916): 142–154.

Kantor, Shawn Everett, and Price V. Fishback. "Precautionary Saving, Insurance, and the Origins of Workers' Compensation." *Journal of Political Economy* 104 (1996): 419–442.

Kaufman, Jason. *For the Common Good? American Civic Life and the Golden Age of Fraternity.* New York: Oxford University Press, 2002.

Keelor, Reinard S. "Sickness Insurance." In *The Business of Insurance: A Textbook and Reference Work Covering All Lines of Insurance,* ed. Howard P. Dunham, 2:120–134. New York: Ronald Press, 1912.

Keffer, Ralph. "Group Sickness and Accident Insurance." *Transactions of the Actuarial Society of America* 26 (1927): 5–34.

Kennedy, James B. *Beneficiary Features of American Trade Unions.* Baltimore: Johns Hopkins Press, 1908.

Kennedy, Peter. *A Guide to Econometrics,* 5th ed. Cambridge: MIT Press, 2003.

Khoudour-Castéras, David. "Welfare State and Labor Mobility: The Impact of Bismarck's Social Legislation on German Emigration Before World War I." Photocopy, University of California, Berkeley, 2006.

Kim, Seung-Wook, and Price V. Fishback. "Institutional Change, Compensating Differentials, and Accident Risk in American Railroading, 1892–1945." *Journal of Economic History* 53 (1993): 796–823.

King, Walter I. "Accident and Health Insurance from an Actuarial Viewpoint." *Proceedings of the Casualty Actuarial Society* 2 (1916): 49–60 (includes comments).

Klein, Jennifer. *For All These Rights: Business, Labor, and the Shaping of America's Public Private Welfare State.* Princeton: Princeton University Press, 2003.

Koch, Reinhold R. "Industrial Accident and Health Insurance." In *The Business of Insurance: A Textbook and Reference Work Covering All Lines of Insurance,* ed. Howard P. Dunham, 2:135–142. New York: Ronald Press, 1912.

Köhler, Peter A., Hans Friedrich Zacher, and Martin Partington, eds. *The Evolution of Social Insurance, 1881–1981: Studies of Germany, France, Great Britain, Austria, and Switzerland.* London: Frances Pinter for the Max-Planck-Institut, 1982.

Lambert, Alexander. "Medical Organization Under Health Insurance." *American Labor Legislation Review* 7 (1917): 36–50.

Lapp, John A. "Health Insurance." *Monthly Labor Review* 9 (September 1919): 938–944.

———. "Insurance of Thrift." *Annals of the American Academy* (January 1920) 87: 21–26.

Law, Marc T. "The Origins of State Pure Food Regulation." *Journal of Economic History* 63 (2003): 1103–1130.

Lebergott, Stanley. " 'Wage Rigidity' in the Depression: Concept or Phrase?" Photocopy, Wesleyan University, 1989.

Lee, Chulhee. "Wealth Accumulation and Health of Union Army Veterans, 1860–1870." *Journal of Economic History* 65 (2004): 352–385.

Lee, Everett S., Ann Ratner Miller, Carol P. Brainerd, and Richard A. Easterlin, under the direction of Simon Kuznets and Dorothy Swaine Thomas. *Population Redistribution and Economic Growth, 1870–1950:* vol. 1, *Methodological Considerations and Reference Tables.* Philadelphia: American Philosophical Society, 1957.

Levin, Laurence. "Demand for Health Insurance and Precautionary Motives for Saving Among the Elderly." *Journal of Public Economics* 57 (1995): 337–367.

Levine, Daniel. *Poverty and Society: The Growth of the American Welfare State in International Comparison.* New Brunswick: Rutgers University Press, 1988.

Lewinski-Corwin, E. H. "Medical Aspects of Health Insurance Administration." *Monthly Labor Review* 9 (September 1919): 946–949.

Lott, Edson S. "Fallacies of Compulsory Social Insurance." Address to American Association for the Advancement of Science, December 18, 1916. In *Selected Articles on Social Insurance,* comp. Julia E. Johnsen, pp. 37–42. New York: Wilson, 1922.

Lubove, Roy. *The Struggle for Social Security, 1900–1930.* 2d ed. Pittsburgh: University of Pittsburgh Press, 1986.

Lynch, James M. "Trade Union Sickness Insurance." *American Labor Legislation Review* 4 (1914): 82–91.

Madrian, Brigitte. "Employment-Based Health Insurance and Job Mobility: Is There Evidence of Job Lock?" *Quarterly Journal of Economics* 109 (1994): 27–54.

Margo, Robert A. "The Microeconomics of Depression Unemployment." *Journal of Economic History* 51 (1991): 333–341.

Marshall, Edward W. "The Dubious Position of the Disability Income Provision in Life Insurance Contracts." *Annals of the American Academy of Political and Social Science* 161 (1932): 46–51.

McKeown, Thomas. *The Modern Rise of Population.* London: Edward Arnold, 1976.

McKinlay, John B., and Sonja M. McKinlay. "The Questionable Contribution of Medical Measures to the Decline of Mortality in the United States in the Twentieth Century." *Milbank Memorial Fund Quarterly* 55 (1977): 405–428.

McKinney, William M. *A Treatise on the Law of Fellow-Servants . . . Embracing Employees' Insurance Societies.* Northport, N.Y.: Thompson, 1890.

Meeker, Edward. "The Improving Health of the United States, 1850–1915." *Explorations in Economic History* 9 (1972): 353–373.

Meeker, Royal. "Social Insurance in the United States." Proceedings, National Conference of Social Work 1917. In *Selected Articles on Social Insurance,* comp. Julia E. Johnsen, pp. 17–26. New York: Wilson, 1922.

Messenger, Hiram J. "The Rate of Sickness." *Transactions of the Actuarial Society of America* 10 (1909): 371–382.

Michigan Bureau of Labor and Industrial Statistics. *Thirteenth Annual Report of the Bureau of Labor and Industrial Statistics.* Lansing: Smith, 1896.

Miller, John H., and Simon Courant. "Some Observations on the Nature of the Risk of Disability, Its Measurement and Control." *Transactions of the Society of Actuaries* 24 (1972): 349–369.

Millis, Harry A., and Royal E. Montgomery. *Labor's Risks and Social Insurance.* New York: McGraw-Hill, 1938.

Mitchell, Allan. *The Divided Path: The German Influence on Social Reform in France After 1870.* Chapel Hill: University of North Carolina Press, 1991.

———. "The Function and Malfunction of Mutual Aid Societies in Nineteenth-Century France." In *Medicine and Charity Before the Welfare State,* ed. Jonathan Barry and Colin Jones, pp. 172–189. London: Routledge, 1991.

Mitchell, Brian R. *European Historical Statistics, 1750–1970.* New York: Columbia University Press, 1978.

Mokyr, Joel. *The Gifts of Athena: Historical Origins of the Knowledge Economy.* Princeton: Princeton University Press, 2002.

Moriguchi, Chiaki. "Did American Welfare Capitalists Breach Their Implicit Contracts? Preliminary Findings From Company-Level Data, 1920–1940." *Industrial and Labor Relations Review* 59 (2005): 51–81.

Morris, Edward B. "Group Life Insurance and Its Possible Development." *Proceedings of the Casualty Actuarial Society* 3 (1917): 149–174.

Moss, David. *Socializing Security: Progressive-Era Economists and the Origins of American Social Policy.* Cambridge: Harvard University Press, 1996.

Mowbray, Albert H. "Age, Occupation, and Residence as Variants of the Rate of Sickness." *Proceedings of the Casualty Actuarial Society* 3 (1916): 213–228.

Munts, Raymond. *Bargaining for Health: Labor Unions, Health Insurance, and Medical Care.* Madison: University of Wisconsin Press, 1967.

Murray, John E. "Social Insurance Claims as Morbidity Data: Sickness or Absence?" *Social History of Medicine* 16 (2003): 225–245.

———. "Worker Absenteeism Under Voluntary and Compulsory Sickness Insurance: Continental Europe, 1885–1908." *Research in Economic History* 23 (2005): 177–205.

National Industrial Conference Board. *Effect of the Depression on Industrial Relations Programs.* New York: National Industrial Conference Board, 1934.

New York Bureau of Labor. *Seventeenth Annual Report of the Bureau of Labor Statistics of New York.* Albany: Weed, Parsons, 1899.

New York Factory Investigating Committee. *Fourth Report of the Factory Investigating Committee, 1915.* Albany: Lyon, 1915.

———. *Experience with Mutual Benefit Associations in the United States.* Research Report no. 65. New York: National Industrial Conference Board, 1923.

———. *Health Insurance Plans,* vol. A: *Mutual Benefit Associations.* Studies in Personnel Policy 9. New York: National Industrial Conference Board, 1938.

———. *Health Insurance Plans,* vol. B: *Group Health Insurance Plans.* Studies in Personnel Policy 10. New York: National Industrial Conference Board, 1939.

———. *Industrial Group Insurance.* New York: National Industrial Conference Board, 1927.

———. *The Present Status of Mutual Benefit Associations.* New York: National Industrial Conference Board, 1931.

North, Douglass C. "Life Insurance and Investment Banking at the Time of the Armstrong Investigation of 1905–1906." *Journal of Economic History* 14 (1954): 209–228.

Numbers, Ronald L. *Almost Persuaded: American Physicians and Compulsory Health Insurance, 1912–1920.* Baltimore: Johns Hopkins University Press, 1978.

Ohio Health and Old Age Insurance Commission. *Health, Health Insurance, Old Age Pensions: Report, Recommendations, Dissenting Opinions.* Columbus: Heer, 1919.

Otey, Elizabeth L. "Cash Benefits Under Voluntary Disability Insurance." *Social Security Bulletin* 2 (1939): 27–33.

Palumbo, Michael G. "Estimating the Effects of Earnings Uncertainty on Families' Savings and Insurance Decisions." *Southern Economic Journal* 67 (2000): 64–86.

Panszczyk, Linda. *1997 U.S. Master Employee Benefits Guide.* Chicago: CCH, 1997.

Parsons, Donald O. "The Decline in Male Labor Force Participation." *Journal of Political Economy* 88 (1980): 117–134.

Perrott, G. St. J., and Selwyn D. Collins. "Relation of Sickness to Income and Income Change in 10 Surveyed Communities." *Public Health Reports* 50 (May 3, 1935): 595–622.

Popper, Karl R. *The Poverty of Historicism.* New York: Harper Torchbooks, 1964.

Quadagno, Jill. *One Nation, Uninsured: Why the U.S. Has No National Health Insurance.* New York: Oxford University Press, 2005.

Quinby, Robert S. "A Study of Industrial Absenteeism." *Monthly Labor Review* 13 (1921): 713–721.

Ransom, Roger L., and Richard Sutch. "Tontine Insurance and the Armstrong Investigation: A Case of Stifled Innovation, 1868–1905." *Journal of Economic History* 47 (1987): 379–390.

Reynolds, Cuyler, ed. *Hudson-Mohawk Genealogical and Family Memoirs,* vol. 1. New York: Lewis Historical Publishing, 1911.

Riley, James C. *Sick, Not Dead: The Health of British Workingmen During the Mortality Decline.* Baltimore: Johns Hopkins University Press, 1997.

Robbins, Rainard B. "Trade Union Benefits and Our Social Insurance Problems." *Proceedings of the Casualty Actuarial Society* 16 (1930): 14–21.

Robinson, Jesse S. *The Amalgamated Association of Iron, Steel, and Tin Workers.* Baltimore: Johns Hopkins Press, 1920.

Rodgers, Daniel T. *Atlantic Crossings: Social Politics in a Progressive Age.* Cambridge: Harvard University Press, 1998.

Rosenbloom, Joshua L. *Looking for Work, Searching for Workers: American Labor Markets During Industrialization*. New York: Cambridge University Press, 2002.

Rosenthal, Robert J. "Union-Management Welfare Plans." *Quarterly Journal of Economics* 62 (1947): 64–94.

Rosner, David, and Gerald Markowitz. "The Struggle Over Employee Benefits: The Role of Labor in Influencing Modern Health Policy." *Milbank Quarterly* 81 (2003): 45–73.

Rubinow, I. M. "Health Insurance Through Local Mutual Funds." *American Labor Legislation Review* 7 (1917): 69–90.

———. "Labor Insurance." *Journal of Political Economy* 12 (1904): 362–381.

———. "Prevention vs. Insurance?" *New Republic* 15 (1918): 364–367.

———. "Public and Private Interests in Social Insurance." *American Labor Legislation Review* 21 (1931): 181–191.

———. *The Quest for Security*. New York: Henry Holt, 1934.

———. *Social Insurance with Special Reference to American Conditions*. New York: Henry Holt, 1913.

Ruhm, Christopher J. "Good Times Make You Sick." *Journal of Health Economics* 22 (2003): 637–658.

Rusher, Edward A. "The Statistics of Industrial Morbidity in Great Britain: A Retrospect and a Scheme for Development." *Journal of the Royal Statistical Society* 85 (1922): 27–86.

Saint-Jours, Yves. "France." In *The Evolution of Social Insurance, 1881–1981: Studies of Germany, France, Great Britain, Austria, and Switzerland*, ed. Peter A. Köhler, Hans Friedrich Zacher, and Martin Partington, pp. 93–149. London: Frances Pinter for the Max-Planck-Institut, 1982.

Sanders, Barkev S., and David Federman. "The Prevalence of Disability Recorded Through Four Monthly Sample Surveys." *Social Security Bulletin* 6 (August 1943): 5–11.

Sayers, R. R., Gertrud Kroeger, and W. M. Gafafer. "General Aspects and Functions of the Sick Benefit Organization." *Public Health Reports* 52 (November 5, 1937): 1563–1580.

Schepers, Rita. "The Belgian Medical Profession and the Sickness Funds." *Sociology of Illness and Health* 15 (1993) 375–392.

Schwartz, Max J. "New York Statutory Disability Benefits Law, Coverage, Rates, and Rating Plans." *Proceedings of the Casualty Actuarial Society* 68 (1950): 57–73.

Shorter, Edward. "Primary Care." In *The Cambridge Illustrated History of Medicine*, ed. Roy Porter, pp. 118–153. New York: Cambridge University Press, 1996.

Skocpol, Theda. *Protecting Soldiers and Mothers: The Political Origins of Social Policy in the United States*. Cambridge: Harvard University Press, 1992.

Sloan, Alfred P., Jr. *My Years with General Motors*. New York: Doubleday, 1990.

Smith, J. Henry. "Group Disability Income Benefits." In *Group Insurance Handbook*, ed. Robert D. Eilers and Robert M. Crowe, pp. 373–391. Homewood, Ill.: Irwin, 1965.

Smith, James P. "Healthy Bodies and Thick Wallets: The Dual Relation Between

Health and Economic Status." *Journal of Economic Perspectives* 13 (1999): 145–166.

Sommer, Armand. "Health Insurance Hazards Reflected in Occupational Health Loss Ratios." *Proceedings of the Casualty Actuarial Society* 13, no. 28 (1927): 181–187.

Song, Chen, and Louis L. Nguyen. "The Effect of Hernias on the Labor Force Participation of Union Army Veterans." In *Health and Labor Force Participation Over the Life Cycle: Evidence from the Past,* ed. Dora L. Costa, pp. 253–310. Chicago: University of Chicago Press, 2003.

Spree, Reinhold. *Health and Social Class in Imperial Germany: A Social History of Mortality, Morbidity, and Inequality.* Oxford: Berg, 1988.

Starr, Paul. *The Social Transformation of American Medicine: The Rise of a Sovereign Profession and the Making of a Vast Industry.* New York: Basic, 1982.

———. "*Social Transformation* Twenty Years On." *Journal of Health Politics, Policy, and Law* 29 (2004): 1005–1019.

Starr-McCluer, Martha. "Health Insurance and Precautionary Savings." *American Economic Review* 86 (1996): 285–295.

State of Connecticut. *Report of the Commission of Public Welfare Under the Authority of Chapter 163 of the Public Acts of 1917, and House Joint Resolution 104 of the 1917 Session of the General Assembly.* Hartford: State of Connecticut, 1919.

State of Illinois. *Report of the Health Insurance Commission of the State of Illinois, May 1, 1919.* Springfield: State of Illinois, 1919.

Sullivan, James. "Labor and Sickness Insurance." Address to the National Civic Federation, 30 January 1920. In *Selected Articles on Social Insurance,* comp. Julia E. Johnsen, pp. 203–204. New York: Wilson, 1922.

Sydenstricker, Edgar. "Existing Agencies for Health Insurance in the United States." In U.S. Department of Labor, "Proceedings of the Conference on Social Insurance." *Bulletin of the U.S. Bureau of Labor Statistics* 212 (1917): 430–475.

Sydenstricker, Edgar, and Dean K. Brundage. "Industrial Establishment Disability Records as a Source of Morbidity Statistics." *Quarterly Publications of the American Statistical Association* 17 (1921): 584–598.

Sydenstricker, Edgar, and G. St. John Perrott. "How Unemployment Affects Illness and Hospital Care." *Modern Hospital* 42 (1934): 41–44.

Terris, Milton. "An Early System of Compulsory Health Insurance in the United States, 1798–1884." *Bulletin of the History of Medicine* 15 (1944): 433–444.

Thomas, Lewis. *The Youngest Science: Notes of a Medicine Watcher.* New York: Viking, 1983.

Thomasson, Melissa A. "From Sickness to Health: The Twentieth-Century Development of U.S. Health Insurance." *Explorations in Economic History* 39 (2002): 233–253.

———. "Early Evidence of an Adverse Selection Death Spiral? The Case of Blue Cross and Blue Shield." *Explorations in Economic History* 41 (2004): 313–328.

Tocqueville, Alexis de. *Democracy in America.* Trans. and ed. Harvey C. Mansfield and Delba Winthrop. Chicago: University of Chicago Press, 2000.

Tone, Andrea. *The Business of Benevolence: Industrial Paternalism in Progressive America.* Ithaca: Cornell University Press, 1997.

U.S. Bureau of the Census. *Historical Statistics of the United States: Colonial Times to 1970,* bicentennial ed. Washington, D.C.: GPO, 1975.

U.S. Commissioner of Labor. *Eighteenth Annual Report of Commissioner of Labor: Cost of Living and Retail Prices of Food.* Washington, D.C.: GPO, 1904.

———. *Twenty-fourth Annual Report of the Commissioner of Labor: Workmen's Insurance and Compensation Systems in Europe.* 2 vols. Washington: U.S. Department of Labor and Commerce, 1911.

———. *Twenty-third Annual Report of the Commissioner of Labor, 1908: Workmen's Insurance and Benefit Funds in the United States.* Washington, D.C.: GPO, 1909.

U. S. Department of Health and Human Services, National Center for Health Statistics, "Summary Health Statistics for U.S. Adults: National Health Interview Survey, 2004." Vital and Health Statistics, ser. 10, no. 228. Washington, D.C.: GPO, 2006.

U.S. Department of Labor. "Health and Recreational Activities in Industrial Establishments, 1926." *Bulletin of the U.S. Bureau of Labor Statistics* 458 (1928).

———. "Proceedings of the Conference on Social Insurance." *Bulletin of the U.S. Bureau of Labor Statistics* 212 (1917).

———. "Welfare Work for Employees in Industrial Establishments in the United States." *Bulletin of the U.S. Bureau of Labor Statistics* 250 (1919).

U.S. Department of the Interior, Census Office. *Report on Insurance Business in the United States at the Eleventh Census: 1890;* pt. 2, "Life Insurance." Washington, D.C.: GPO, 1895.

U.S. Public Health Service. "The National Health Survey, 1935–36: Part I. Scope and Method; Part II. Annotated Bibliography, 1936–50." Public Health Bibliography Series 5 (1951).

Verbruggen, Paule. "The Mutualist Movement in Belgium." In *Social Security Mutualism: The Comparative History of Mutual Benefit Societies,* ed. M. van der Linden, pp. 419–429. Bern: Peter Lang, 1996.

Viseltear, Arthur J. "Compulsory Health Insurance in California, 1915–1918." *Journal of the History of Medicine and Allied Sciences* 24 (1969): 151–182.

Vistnes, Jessica Primoff. "Gender Differences in Days Lost Due to Illness." *Industrial and Labor Relations Review* 50 (1997): 304–323.

Walker, Forrest A. "Compulsory Health Insurance: 'The Next Great Step in Social Legislation.'" *Journal of American History* 56 (1969): 290–304.

Warner, John Harley. *The Therapeutic Perspective: Medical Practice, Knowledge, and Identity in America, 1820–1885.* Cambridge: Harvard University Press, 1986.

Warren, B. S., and Edgar Sydenstricker. "Health Insurance: Its Relation to the Public Health." *Public Health Bulletin* 76 (1916).

———. "Statistics of Disability: A Compilation of Some of the Data Available in the United States." *Public Health Reports* 31, no. 16 (April 21, 1916): 989–999.

Whaples, Robert, and David Buffum. "Fraternalism, Paternalism, the Family, and the Market: Insurance a Century Ago." *Social Science History* 15 (1991): 97–122.

Whiteside, Noel. "Counting the Cost: Sickness and Disability Among Working People in an Era of Industrial Recession, 1920–39." *Economic History Review* 40 (1987): 228–246.

Wiebe, Robert H. *Businessmen and Reform: A Study of the Progressive Movement.* Cambridge: Harvard University Press, 1962.

———. *The Search for Order, 1877–1920.* New York: Hill & Wang, 1967.

Williams, Pierce, assisted by Isabel C. Chamberlain. *The Purchase of Medical Care Through Fixed Periodic Payment.* New York: National Bureau of Economic Research, 1932.

Williamson, Jeffrey G. "The Evolution of Global Labor Markets Since 1830: Background Evidence and Hypotheses." *Explorations in Economic History* 32, no. 2 (1995): 141–196.

Winegarden, C. R., and John E. Murray. "The Contributions of Early Health Insurance Programs to Mortality Declines in Pre–World War I Europe: Evidence from Fixed-Effects Models." *Explorations in Economic History* 35 (1998): 431–446.

Witt, John Fabian. "Toward a New History of American Accident Law: Classical Tort Law and the Cooperative First-Party Insurance Movement." *Harvard Law Review* 114 (2001): 690–841.

Woolsey, Theodore D. "Estimates of Disabling Illness Prevalence in the United States Based on the February 1949 Current Population Survey." *Public Health Reports* 65 (February 1950): 163–184.

Yates, JoAnne. *Structuring the Information Age: Life Insurance and Technology in the Twentieth Century.* Baltimore: Johns Hopkins University Press, 2005.

Zacher, [Georg], ed. *Die Arbeiter-Versicherung im Auslande.* Berlin: Verlag der Arbeiter-Versorgung, 1902–1906.

Zeldin, Theodore. *France, 1848–1945: Politics and Anger.* New York, Oxford University Press, 1979.

INDEX